CREATOR, ARE YOU LISTENING?

Jewish Literature and Culture
Series Editor, Alvin H. Rosenfeld

CREATOR, ARE YOU LISTENING?

Israeli Poets on God and Prayer

David C. Jacobson

Indiana University Press / *Bloomington and Indianapolis*

This book is a publication of

Indiana University Press
601 North Morton Street
Bloomington, IN 47404-3797 USA

http://iupress.indiana.edu

Telephone orders 800-842-6796
Fax orders 812-855-7931
Orders by e-mail iuporder@indiana.edu

The paper used in this publication meets the minimum requirements of American
National Standard for Information Sciences—Permanence of Paper for Printed
Library Materials, ANSI Z39.48-1984.

Manufactured in the United States of America

Library of Congress Cataloging-in-Publication Data

Jacobson, David C., date
Creator, are you listening? : Israeli poets on God and prayer / David C. Jacobson.
p. cm. — (Jewish literature and culture)
Text in English; poems in Hebrew with English translation.
Includes bibliographical references and index.
ISBN-13: 978-0-253-34818-0 (cloth : alk. paper) 1. Israeli poetry—History and
criticism. 2. God in literature. 3. Prayer in literature. 4. Israeli poetry—Translations
into English. I. Title.
PJ5024.J325 2007
892.4'1608382—dc22

2006018274

1 2 3 4 5   12 11 10 09 08 07

For Shelly

CONTENTS

ACKNOWLEDGMENTS

I BEGAN RESEARCH on this book as a recipient of a Cross Currents Research Colloquium Fellowship. This fellowship brings together scholars, in a variety of disciplines, who are exploring the religious dimensions of human existence. During several weeks in the summer of 2000, we were based at Columbia University, Union Theological Seminary, and Jewish Theological Seminary, and we had access to the libraries of those and other institutions in New York City. My research during that summer, primarily at the library of Jewish Theological Seminary, yielded important material for this study. In addition, the stimulating experiences of the weekly sessions in which we shared our research and informal interactions among the participants created an excellent atmosphere in which I was able to define the parameters of this project and begin to conceptualize the methodological approaches I would take. Following that summer, I was fortunate to have a semester sabbatical leave from Brown, during which I embarked on the writing of the book. I also benefited from opportunities I had to undertake research at the Jewish National Library on the Givat Ram campus of the Hebrew University in Jerusalem and at the Hebrew University library on the Mount Scopus campus. I am grateful for research funds provided by the Program in Judaic Studies, the Faculty Travel Grants Program, and the Office of the Vice President for Research at Brown University, which supported research trips to Israel and other expenses related to this project.

I learned much from interviews generously granted to me by three of the poets included in this study: Admiel Kosman, Rivka Miriam, and Hava Pinhas-Cohen. I gained many additional insights from observations made by colleagues at the Brown Program in Judaic Studies Faculty Seminar, to whom I presented portions of this study. In addition, my understanding of the poems I analyze in this book was deepened as a result of teaching this material to students in my "God and Poetry" seminar course at Brown and to adult audiences in the Providence Jewish community.

I am delighted for the opportunity to have Indiana University Press as the publisher of this book. I am profoundly grateful to Janet Rabinowitch, Director, Lee Ann Sandweiss, Sponsoring Editor, and Alvin Rosenfeld, Editor of the Jewish Literature and Culture Series, for their support.

Two years before I began working on this project, I met the woman who is now my wife, Shelly Greene. My dedication of this book to her is an expression of love and appreciation for her support, with the hope that we will continue to grow together as individuals and as a couple in the coming years. The dedication, however, goes beyond an expression of love and appreciation. The truth is that I am not sure this book would have ever been written without her inspiration. For some two decades, I had toyed with the idea of writing a book about religious themes in modern Hebrew poetry, but my own ambivalence about matters of faith proved to be an insurmountable barrier to the fulfillment of that idea. Early in our relationship, Shelly and I began to discuss religion, and the insights she shared with me made it possible for me to begin to explore this topic in a fresh and creative way, and to see this project to its completion.

Originally, I considered the focus of this book to be on the ways that Israeli poets write about God. During the period when I was writing the book, my father, Clarence Jacobson, passed away at the age of ninety-one. My year-long daily commitment to reciting Kaddish in his memory at synagogue services awakened in me a deeper appreciation for the experience of prayer than I had ever had before. In the course of that year, therefore, I began to pay greater attention to the ways that the poets in this study write about the experience of prayer along with their explorations of theological issues. I would like to think that my father, who was personally dedicated to daily prayer, would be pleased to know that in the process of my expression of filial respect during the year of mourning following his death, I found new ways to appreciate the power of prayer and religious faith.

Acknowledgment is made for permission to include the following material:

ACUM, Ltd. for permission to reprint the original Hebrew versions of the poems by Admiel Kosman, Rivka Miriam, Zelda Mishkovsky, Hava Pinhas-Cohen, and Asher Reich included in this book and for permission to publish my translations of their poetry. Copyright is held by each of the authors and by ACUM, Ltd., Ramat Gan, Israel.

Schocken Publishing House, Ltd. for permission to reprint the original Hebrew versions of the poems by Yehudah Amichai included in this book. Copyright is held by Schocken Publishing House, Ltd., Tel Aviv, Israel.

Hana Amichai for permission to publish my translations of the poetry of Yehuda Amichai.

A NOTE ON TRANSLATION

ALL POETRY TRANSLATIONS in this anthology are mine. The art of translation involves the search for a proper balance between conveying the literal meaning of the original and producing a text that is readable as poetry. All translators of poetry from Hebrew to English forgo, to some extent, the literal meaning of the Hebrew text in order to transform the Hebrew poem into a text in English that is in as aesthetically pleasing a poetic style as possible. In my translations, I chose to focus more than some translators do on preserving the literal meaning of the original in as accurate a manner as possible given the inherent linguistic differences between Hebrew and English. I adopted this approach because this work is not merely an anthology in which the poetic texts are meant to stand on their own. Each poem is accompanied by an analysis which focuses on the nuances of the Hebrew and, in particular, on the wealth of allusions to classical Jewish texts that pervade this poetry. The further I would have departed from the original Hebrew, the more difficult it would have been for me to convey the kind of analytical points I wished to make.

When my translations depart from the literal meaning of the Hebrew, it is generally in order to choose words and expressions that make more sense in English than would more literally equivalent words or expressions, or to produce an aesthetically pleasing metrical flow. Occasionally, for syntactical reasons, the position of lines had to be changed. I also took some liberties with the punctuation, when I thought such changes would convey the meaning of the poem more precisely.

Often in these poems Hebrew expressions familiar from classical Jewish sources signal to the reader that the being to which the speaker refers is God. Because these expressions do not always refer as clearly to God in English translation, I chose to adopt the well-established English convention of capitalizing the first letter of all pronouns that refer to God, even though Hebrew has no capital letters. For the sake of consistency, I adhered to this convention in my commentaries on the poems as well.

Although one finds a wide range of contemporary conceptions of God in this poetry, when these poets refer to the traditional God of Israel, they follow the tradition of referring to God with masculine word forms, and in my translations and interpretations I preserved that tradition. Another gender-related issue is the question of how to translate *adam*, the Hebrew term that refers to Adam, the first man created in Genesis, but that also can mean "Man," which, in less gender-sensitive periods in the past, referred in English to both male and female members of humanity as a whole. In my interpretive comments, I have avoided the use of "Man" to refer to humanity. However, in order to convey the original sense of the term *adam* and to preserve the metrical flow, I did sometimes translate *adam* as "Man."

It is my hope that the translation of each poem is literal enough to support my interpretation of that poem and to serve as an aid to those attempting to read the Hebrew original, while at the same time providing a pleasurable reading experience to those referring only to the English version. In the notes, I cite sources for alternative translations that I have located, for readers who wish to compare them with my translations. All other translations from Hebrew are mine, unless otherwise indicated.

CREATOR, ARE YOU LISTENING?

The Religious Dimension of Israeli Poetry

T HE PURPOSE OF THIS BOOK is to challenge the conventional wisdom that Hebrew poetry by contemporary Israeli writers is essentially secular in nature. Because Hebrew poetry published since the nineteenth century has been so intertwined with the spread of secularism in Jewish culture, there has been a persistent reluctance on the part of many readers to acknowledge the pervasiveness of religious themes in modern Hebrew poetry in general, and in Israeli poetry in particular.[1] The truth is, however, that a considerable number of Hebrew poets writing in the Diaspora and in the Land of Israel over the past one hundred years in which modern Hebrew poetry has reached its highest levels of aesthetic achievement have explored the theological dilemmas of modern Jews and suggested new ways to write about God.

These Hebrew poets inherited a distinguished literary tradition from the biblical period through the Middle Ages of writing about God in Hebrew, which, according to the Jewish tradition, is the language of divine revelation. Although many had a problematic relationship with traditional Jewish faith and the observance of Jewish law, these poets could not escape the impulse to search for God's presence in their lives. They knew that the primary barrier to religious faith was the tendency of religious language to lose its vitality and relevance over time, so they persisted in reworking the language of the psalms, the traditional prayer book, and medieval sacred poetry to develop an idiom that reflected both their sense of the absence of God and their search for the possibility of discerning God's presence.[2]

The fact that this body of poetry is in Hebrew places it in a unique position to come to terms with secular challenges to religious faith. André Neher notes an important difference between the secularization process that European Christians underwent from the Renaissance to the modern period and that which European Jews underwent from the eighteenth to the twentieth century. For European Christians, he writes, "the conflict between the sacred and the profane implied a rivalry between the secular languages and the holy tongue — in this case, Latin — and the progress of secularisation was reflected in the abandonment of Latin for the national languages."[3] In contrast, observes Neher, for those Jews who were committed to the development of Hebrew as the language of national renaissance, "the secularisation [took] place within the sacred tongue itself [Hebrew]."[4] It is this choice to make use of the Hebrew language to express the move toward secularism that has kept Hebrew writers connected to the very sacred culture against which they have sought to rebel. "Chosen to be the instrument . . . of a profane and secular conquest of the world by the Jewish spirit," writes Neher, "the Hebrew language at the same time prevented that spirit from becoming entirely secular, since the tongue in which it expressed itself remained, despite everything, sacred in its origins and in its close association with the liturgical and scholarly Hebrew which was still in use in the synagogue."[5] Neher insists that even in contemporary Israel, in which Hebrew serves as the vernacular of its Jewish citizens, the secular has not succeeded in defeating the sacred. Both dimensions continue to be engaged in a creative tension, because, as he puts it, "Jewish culture contains an ineradicable theological element which will not allow it to disregard the absolute."[6]

Writing at the end of the first decade of Israel's existence, Eli Schweid expressed surprise at the fact that younger Israeli writers, particularly those who write lyrical poetry, evoke God in their literary works. "Young Hebrew poets," he wrote, "whose worldview and lifestyle have no connection to religion, turn to God as if forgetting their worldview, and bother him with prayer, supplication, and blessing. . . ."[7] The problem is, observed Schweid, that when they evoke God, the writers "do not attempt at all to explain to themselves and to the reader to what they are referring."[8] While these poets may not express any explicit identification with traditional Jewish theological concepts, they are, according to Schweid, engaged in the universal longing for some form of religious experience: "The actual prayer gesture and the actual words of prayer are not fictitious, the need to pray is real and it is liable to create in the heart of the poet an actual feeling of 'standing before,' although this feeling still does not constitute standing before something real, and certainly not standing before God."[9]

Ariel Hirschfeld has observed that God continued to play an important role in later Israeli poetry: "[T]he impression that the divine presence, both as a private presence that draws on the power of the inner world of the poet and as a presence that bears with it something of the traditional religious contexts of God, was cut out of the secular world of Hebrew poetry of the [nineteen-]sixties, seventies, and eighties, is a mistaken impression."[10] In response to the recent insistence by a literary scholar that modern poetry is mainly secular in nature, Hirschfeld wrote: "The matter of religion has not only not been outside of the thematics of Hebrew literature . . . but also not at its margins. It is among the most central, if not *the* central matter. Faith, its contents, its struggles, the presence of God, the ways of contacting Him, and the forms of His revelation in the world, in the life of the individual and the community, religious experience, mystical and non-mystical, the love of God, are all matters of concern in the greatest parts of the writings of [the major twentieth-century Hebrew writers]."[11] Indeed, argues Hirschfeld, "the most serious writing about [Jewish religious experience] during the past one hundred years, took place precisely and mainly in Hebrew litera-ture, in the context of what it is customary to label 'secular.'"[12]

Although he is a member of a secular kibbutz, Zvi Luz has played a leading role in the exploration of religious themes in modern Hebrew poetry. One could argue that he is the most prolific writer on this topic in contemporary literary criticism. In numerous monographs on modern Hebrew poets, Luz has explored specific examples of poetic conceptions of God in their work. In a recent essay on images of God in twentieth-century Hebrew poetry, Luz declares that "'the God problem,' which is apparently the primary problem of our Jewishness in the modern period, still 'flickers' (as [the Hebrew poet] Bialik would say) in the depths of the majority of our cultural expressions. As it flickers it becomes ignited in a most interesting and representative manner in modern Hebrew poetry, es-pecially in the course of the twentieth century."[13] In this body of poetry, he ar-gues, the "high tensions between faith and heresy [are exposed], clarifying the difficulties and revealing 'answers,' if answers are even still possible."[14] To those who would argue that only conventionally pious statements could be of religious value, he retorts, "In my opinion, it is better to listen to the [theological] difficul-ties of true poets than to the official positions of 'ordained' rabbis, whose obliga-tion to 'teaching' in the traditional manner obscures their creative originality."[15]

As noted above, throughout most of the twentieth-century Hebrew poetry on religious themes was written primarily by authors with a problematic relation-ship with traditional faith and observance. The best known exceptions to this rule were the religiously observant poets Yosef Zvi Rimon (1889–1958) and one of the poets in this study, Zelda Mishkovsky (1914–1984). Toward the end of the twentieth century, however, significant numbers of believing, religiously obser-vant writers began to publish poetry on religious themes.[16] As the poet and liter-ary scholar Hamutal Bar-Yosef observes, this new trend has unequivocally estab-lished religiosity as one of the central elements of Israeli poetry in recent decades. She goes so far as to say that as the result of the emergence of this liter-ary movement, "it is now impossible to say that secularity is the central quality of Hebrew literature in our time. Alongside secular Israeli literature stands today a literature that puts forth spiritually varied additional possibilities."[17] Two poets included in this study, Hava Pinhas-Cohen (1955–) and Admiel Kosman (1957–) are often cited as leading figures in this movement, although, as we will see, they are not as conventionally religious in their private lives as many of the other poets who have contributed to it.

The religious dimension of modern Hebrew poetry has been featured in four anthologies of Hebrew poetry on religious themes, one published over fifty years ago, and the others more recently. In selecting which poems to include and in their introductory comments, the editors of these anthologies make important contributions to our understanding of the nature of religiosity in modern Hebrew poetry. In 1945, the publishing house of the Orthodox yeshiva Mosad Harav Kook published an anthology, *Beran yahad: yalqut shirei tefillah attiqim gam hadashim* (Singing Together: A Collection of Prayer Poems Both Ancient and Modern), edited by A. M. Habermann. The poems included in this anthology range from the early *payyetanim* (liturgical poets) of the Land of Israel to Hebrew poets of the first decades of the twentieth century. The more recent poets include both observant and non-observant Jews. In Habermann's introduction, he makes clear his belief that, in some sense, the modern poems included in the anthology have contributed to the continuation of the tradition of Hebrew liturgical poetry, even if, as he notes, the intention of the modern poets has not been to create "public prayer in the synagogue."[18] This notion of the modern poet as *payyetan* caused Habermann to limit his selection of poems. "And as for the modern poets," he writes, "I only included poems that had in them some aspect of prayer and [religious] petitionary longing."[19] In this anthology, the poets' works are presented in chronological order, but there is no table of contents. The only listing of the poets is in an index at the end of the book, which presents the poets in an integrated manner arranged alphabetically according to the last name of the poet, thereby reinforcing the notion of an equal religious significance shared by ancient and modern poets.

The three more recently published anthologies reflect an unprecedented intensification of interest in Israel in the religious dimension of Hebrew poetry toward the end of the twentieth century, which corresponds with the emergence in Israel of greater numbers of religiously observant poets discussed above.[20] The first of these anthologies, *Va'ani tefillati: shirat hatefillah shel meshorerim benei zemanenu* (Behold My Prayer: Prayer Poetry of Contemporary Poets, 1991), edited by Hillel Weiss, covers twentieth-century Hebrew poetry of Europe and Israel. Unlike Habermann, Weiss does not seek to equate modern religious poetry with traditional liturgical poetry by including both in the same anthology. Nevertheless, he does signal to the reader that he sees a connection between these modern poems and traditional expressions of faith by referring to them in the subtitle of the anthology as "prayer poetry" (*shirat hatefillah*) and by including throughout the anthology quotes from traditional Jewish sources that relate intertextually with the poems. Weiss explains that he "tried to trace the phenomena of the spirit and the dialogue between a nation and its God in the field of prayer during the past one hundred years, since the period of the [Jewish] national revival. I did this by including different types of prayer poems that constituted a voice for the generation and for the individual. This book attempts to reconnect them to sacred expressions and thereby to signal the possibility of healing to an extent the ruptures that developed in the House of Israel since the days of the 'Haskalah [Enlightenment].'"[21]

Weiss allowed himself greater latitude than did Habermann in his selection of poetry. He notes near the beginning of his introduction, "Perhaps the inclusion of some of the poems will arouse wonder and perhaps also complaints in some circles."[22] As examples of possibly objectionable poems, he cites a poem by Yonatan Ratosh, known for his radical anti-traditional "Canaanite" ideology, and another poem by the contemporary Israeli poet Be'eri Hazak that would appear to be heretical in nature. In Ratosh's poem, Weiss argues, elements of the Jewish tradition are much more central than references to the poet's anti-traditional worldview, while the central question in Hazak's poem—Where is God?—is actually found throughout traditional texts, including the Torah and Psalms. Despite the relatively broader principle of selection employed by Weiss, as a traditionally observant Jew he still puts greater religious value on poetry written by observant Jews than that written by nonobservant Jews. "In this collection," writes Weiss, "are included prayer poems by religious [i.e., traditionally observant] people, but there is no intention here to turn into religious poetry the poetry of those who are not like that [i.e., religiously observant]. Perhaps certain sparks of faith flicker in a poet, but that does not turn him into a religious person who sees in Jewish law and faith [and] in the worship of God . . . the core of his existence."[23]

The second anthology to appear in the 1990s, *Elohim Elohim* (God God, 1992), edited by Amir Or and Irit Sela, was published as an issue of *Helicon Poetry Quarterly*, a periodical devoted to the publication of contemporary poetry. The title has a playful tone to it that signals a less religiously conservative approach than those of Habermann and Weiss. While the other anthologies bear titles that come from traditional sources, the term *Elohim Elohim* is an invention of the editors. In his introduction, co-editor Amir Or is clearly intent on pushing the definition of religiosity beyond the bounds of traditional Jewish conceptions. He draws his understanding of the nature of religious poetry less from traditional Jewish texts and more from the history of Western literature since antiquity. He notes that unlike today when we consider poetry and religion to belong to different realms, in antiquity all poetry was connected to the religious worldview that permeated Western humanity. "Even if today it will not occur to people to identify poetry with religion," he writes, "relations between the poetic and religious domains have always existed."[24]

This continues to be true today from Or's point of view. "[P]oetry that deals with the human experience of the sublime or the holy includes not only poetry that is explicitly religious or poetry that turns directly to God; but rather it includes to no smaller degree poetry that struggles in its search for a way beyond the individual ego. Such poetry connects extremely isolated points of view to a focused religious perspective, whether it is that of an individual or it is created in a cultural context. Here poetry expresses moods that range from the longing to break through the enclosed ego to an abundance of experiences of the metapersonal."[25] Clearly, there is an attempt here to expand the definition of religiosity beyond the traditional language of faith in order to make it accessible to secular readers who, it is suggested, can relate their own longing for the metapersonal to the poetry included in the anthology. Central to this approach is the notion that there is a kind of generic religious experience beyond specific cultural elements in which individuals transcend themselves. Such religious experience, according to Or, can even include what appears to be heretical or radically secular:

> A perspective of protest or denial is liable to express a deep religious feeling, and even atheistic thought systems express themselves on more than one occasion bearing the same emotive weight and armed with the same symbolic and metaphorical religious jargon. Whether we speak of a doctrine of secular redemption (communism, fascism, pacifism, etc.) or an individualistic method to arrive at a trance that would transcend the ego (aesthetics, love, sex, insanity)—it is difficult to miss the religious ethos and pathos.[26]

True to the universalistic orientation of its editors, the anthology includes religiously observant and nonobservant contemporary Israeli Jewish poets with a wide range of theological perspectives who write in Hebrew, as well as Hebrew translations of works by poets from a variety of cultural backgrounds who write in Arabic, English, French, Polish, Tamil, Serbo-Croatian, and Finnish.

The third anthology, *Shirah ḥadashah* (A New Song, 1997), edited by Miron Isaacson and Admiel Kosman, was published as an issue of the literary journal *Apirion*. As in *Elohim Elohim*, the range of poetry is quite broad and the selection of Israeli poetry is contemporary. Both editors are well known for their own poems on religious themes. Their purpose in producing this anthology, as Admiel Kosman puts it, is to collect "the best of the poems of those writers [including themselves] whose poetry has an affinity for religion."[27] In his preface, Isaacson writes, "It is important for us to emphasize in this anthology the intensifying closeness between questions of faith and Jewish identity [on the one hand] and poetry [on the other]. This closeness is expressed in a variety of ways, sometimes by the use of language from sources of other periods of history, sometimes by the emphasis on elements of thought."[28] Of particular importance to Isaacson is the role that the Jewish tradition can play in enriching Israeli poetry and the way that such an enriched Hebrew poetry can contribute to the viability of Israeli culture.[29]

A full consideration of Israeli poets who have explored the nature of religious experience is far beyond the scope of any one book-length study. I have chosen to focus on the works of six Israeli writers whose poetry has been published during a period that stretches from the late 1950s to the beginning of the twenty-first century: Zelda Mishkovsky (1914–1984), Yehuda Amichai (1924–2000), Asher Reich (1937–), Rivka Miriam (1952–), Hava Pinhas-Cohen (1955–), and Admiel Kosman (1957–). Whenever one seeks to understand a literary phenomenon by focusing on a limited selection of writers, inevitably the question arises, why were these and not other poets chosen? My initial response to this question is to confess that, in part, I chose these poets because I found myself personally drawn to their poetry. Beyond my subjective point of view, however, I do believe that the poets included in this study constitute a good basis on which to engage my fellow scholars and lovers of Hebrew poetry in a consideration of the religious dimension of Israeli poetry. I purposely chose to consider three men and three women, not merely to conform to current notions of political correctness, but because I am convinced that gender differences (whether of a biological or cultural origin) influence religious perspectives to some degree, and so it is important to consider poetry by both male and female writers.

The most significant justification for my selection is that each of these poets has had a direct personal involvement with the world of traditional Judaism as well as with modern Western culture. It is their position as mediators between the world of traditional faith and that of modern skepticism that allows us to gain important insights into the challenges of renewing the language of faith in recent decades. Zelda Mishkovsky was raised in a traditional Jewish home that was open to the influence of modern Western culture, and she remained religiously observant her entire life. Yehuda Amichai and Asher Reich were brought up in traditional Jewish homes (Amichai in a modern Orthodox Zionist home and Reich in an Ultra-Orthodox home), and while both ceased to fully observe the tradition in which they were raised, much of their poetry has continued to be informed by the language of traditional Jewish faith. Rivka Miriam's father was a yeshiva-trained Holocaust survivor who had lost his faith as a youth, yet he imbued her with a love of Jewish tradition and made sure that she received a traditional Jewish education. While she does not formally identify with any religious Jewish community in Israel, she has maintained an active interest in the study of traditional Jewish texts, and her ways of writing about God reflect her ongoing immersion in Jewish study. Hava Pinhas-Cohen was raised in a politically leftist secular home, but became religiously observant and began studying traditional Jewish texts as a young adult. Admiel Kosman was raised in a modern Orthodox home, studied in a yeshiva, and has taught Talmud at an Orthodox Zionist institution of higher learning, Bar Ilan University. Nevertheless, his own theological thinking is quite iconoclastic.

These poets adopt a variety of approaches to God. They address God directly, convey experiences of sensing God's presence or lamenting His absence, and reflect on the nature of God. Some poems partake of a degree of prayerful piety in which the speaker conveys a sense of intimacy with God as either petitioner or celebrator of God's praises. Other poems are burdened by agonizing doubts about God's existence in a world that is so plagued by moral chaos. In some poems, the speaker expresses anger or even mocks God for His failure to help humanity in times of trouble. A number of poems explore the nature of prayer itself.

Poetry and Theology

Poets have always played a central role in creating language that conveys the nature of religious experience. Moreover, whatever theological language is created by one generation of poets is inevitably transformed by a later generation of poets dissatisfied with how the understanding of divinity has been expressed in the past. The contribution of poets to the renewal of the language of religious faith was well understood by nineteenth-century European Romantics, who looked to artists in general to provide the most viable responses to criticisms of religious belief. As J. Hillis Miller writes, "romanticism . . . define[d] the artist as the creator or discoverer of hitherto unapprehended symbols, symbols which establish a new relationship across the gap between man and God. The artist is the man who goes out into the empty space between man and God and takes the enormous risk of attempting to create in that vacancy a new fabric of connections between man and the divine power."[30]

The late nineteenth- and early twentieth-century European-born Hebrew writer Haim Nahman Bialik was not as confident as the Romantics in the ability of the poet to restore harmony between humanity and God. Nevertheless, he saw the poet as a kind of hero of words who is able to negotiate the complexities of the relationship between human beings and the mysteries of existence. In his 1915 essay "Gilluy vekhissuy balashon" ("Revealment and Concealment in Language"), Bialik writes of poets as "the masters of allegory, of interpretation and mystery [who] spend all their days in pursuit of the unifying principle in things. . . ."[31] They are uniquely qualified to do so, according to Bialik, because they have the ability to reinvent language and thereby put us in touch as much as is humanly possible with the divine mysteries lying behind that which separates us from ultimate reality. "[These] masters of poetry," he writes, "are forced to flee all that is fixed and inert in language, all that is opposed to their goal of the vital and mobile in language. On the contrary, using their unique keys, they are obliged themselves to introduce into language at every opportunity never-ending motion, new combinations and associations."[32]

Writing in the spirit of Bialik's essay, Yochanan Muffs has argued more recently that poets are uniquely qualified to come closest to ultimate truth and convey some sense of that truth to others. "The poet," he writes, "is essentially a visionary who strives to penetrate the outer core of reality, to enter its holy of holies and to see reality in all its clarity and horror. To do this, he converts his being into a sensitive instrument capable of reacting to every nuance of reality, of every insight hidden in stereotyped words and everyday speech."[33] In seeking to discern the reality which lies beyond existing language, the poet undertakes what most people avoid doing, according to Muffs. "He realizes ever so painfully that man is afraid of confronting existence in all of its grandeur and horror and that words are more often used to block out reality instead of transmitting it; that the palliative of words may be necessary for others, but not for him: he wants to feel directly, to see immediately, to strip words of their protective coverings in order to penetrate the very core of reality—to behold the vision of reality in all of its intensity."[34]

Of course, much theological reflection has been expressed in prose form. Nevertheless, as Jakob Petuchowski suggests in a series of rhetorical questions, prose formulations of theology are of limited value: "What if [religious] experience transcends the capacity of rational discourse? What if it involves aspects of the human personality which lie beneath the level of consciousness? What, finally, if, by its definition, the very subject matter of theology eludes the human grasp?"[35] It is poetry, not prose, argues Petuchowski, that best conveys the human understanding of God. "[T]heology is compelled to rely on intimations," he writes. "When we speak of something *of* which we only have hints and intimations, we can speak of it likewise only *in* hints and intimations. We can allude to it, and we can suggest it; but we can hardly formulate it in propositions which will pass muster before the bar of logical rigor. We had, therefore, best express it in the images and the nuances of poetry."[36]

Since poetry, suggests Petuchowski, is to a large extent closer than prose to the primary experience of God, he calls on theologians to admit "that the data with which theology is working are data derived from a realm of poetry and myth."[37] Like Bialik and Muffs, Petuchowski believes that poetry has an important role to play as a renewer of theology. "If poetry is the medium through which 'normative' theology ('normative' at least for its time and place) best expresses itself," he argues, "then poetry becomes a still more fitting medium for the expression of theological views which, even if they are not fully heretical, nevertheless represent a challenge to what has become normative and conventional."[38]

The free play of imagination in poetry is a key to its effectiveness as a vehicle for expressing religious insight. As Gordon Kaufman argues, there is a universal human need to exercise the imagination in order to develop a conception of God. "The mind's ability to create images and characterizations, and imaginatively to weld them together into a unified focus for attention, contemplation, devotion, or address, is at work in the humblest believer's prayers as well as in the most sophisticated philosopher's speculations,"[39] writes Kaufman. "In this respect," he declares, "all speech to and about God, and all 'experience of God,' is made possible by and is a function of the constructive powers of the imagination."[40]

Since metaphors have always played a central role in this process of imaginative construction, poets have much to contribute to any culture seeking to express its relationship with the divine. "Metaphors . . . ," writes T. R. Wright, "provide perhaps the most important means by which language is stretched beyond the literal in order to talk of God. They play an important role in the Bible and in traditional doctrinal discourse. But they are absolutely central to poetry . . . . They abound in Gerard Manley Hopkins, who stretches language to the breaking point, and in the metaphysical poets, who violate expectations by linking sacred and profane in a series of striking metaphors."[41] Like Bialik, Muffs, and Petuchowski, Wright looks to literature in general and poetry in particular to renew religious language. "It is this [ability to devise new metaphors]," he writes, "which gives poetry its potential to generate new meaning."[42] It is essential for poets to keep inventing new metaphors, argues Wright, because "[i]t is . . . only too easy for metaphors to become over-familiar."[43] Once they do, they lose the multi-dimensional complexity that is crucial for a fully expressive religious language.[44]

This focus on poetry as the most profound conveyer of theological understanding would seem to distance religious discourse from the rational scientific thinking that is so central to Western culture. In recent decades, however, there has emerged a growing appreciation of the similarities in the ways that literature, religion, and science engage in the apprehension of reality. Robert Schaible has observed that these three modes of human discourse are connected by the fact that they depend on metaphors "to construct and tell the truth they *keep on finding* to tell."[45] This is so because, as Schaible puts it, "metaphor is at the very core of the conceptual system with which we get a grasp on the world."[46] Whether we are engaged in the writing of works of literature, theology, or science, metaphor is the best means available to us, because it is impossible to know absolute truth, and thus all we can do is to approximate reality in metaphorically based language. "[R]eligion, literature *and* science . . . ," writes Schaible, "are vehicles for rowing us out to the thick darkness, each exploring its own particular kind of darkness, each providing its own kind of metaphors and its own kind of *provisional* clarity. Each is a field of exploration useful for cutting through particular kinds of ignorance so that we can then confront the mystery that inevitably lies just on the other side of our forever opaque language."[47]

Poetry and Religion in Our Time

Poets seeking in the context of our secular era to fulfill their role as renewers of the language of religious discourse have faced special challenges. As is well known, contemporary Western culture is the product of a series of cultural upheavals: the scientific revolution, the Enlightenment, the industrial revolution, and the emergence of such secular ideologies as democracy, socialism, and nationalism. Religious faith has been further undermined by the anxieties evoked by the carnage of two world wars, the threat of annihilation by weapons of mass destruction, and, more recently, acts of terror that have taken many innocent lives.[48] Ours is the post-Nietzchean era of the "death of God," in which much of humanity no longer feels bound by transcendental truths and denies the existence of any dimension beyond what people can see, touch, or control.[49]

The poets in this study, however, like numerous other poets in Western culture, write as if God is anything but dead. Derek Stanford's observations on the writing of poetry in our post-Nietzchean era do much to explain how contemporary poets are able to write about God, even though they have been deeply affected by the theologically skeptical ethos of our time. "When Nietzsche, in the eighties of the last century, proclaimed the death of God," writes Stanford, "his statement helped to change the Western world. Naturally enough, it did not change God, but played its part in changing man's awareness of Him. It helped, as do all negative expressions, to injure and impede the means by which we find access to what is positive. In other words, the declaration of God's death assisted in a very real sense toward the decay and decrease of vision."[50] Nevertheless, some twentieth-century poets, notes Stanford, have tried to come to terms with the loss of God and have explored the human desire to reconnect with the divine. "What teases and haunts [these poets]," he argues, "is the dim sense of a God who cannot be located; a God, as it were, beyond the mind's horizon; a God sought for but undiscovered. . . . For such poets a mood of undiagnosed homesickness is the emotion they are most aware of. . . . [These poets have] been disturbed and made uneasy, filled with profound nostalgia for an object remaining in the dark."[51] The result is a body of poetry that reflects the religious doubts and affirmations that play themselves out in the human soul even in our time. As Stanford puts it, "a poet may write at one moment as if his revelation had made him a believer and at another moment as if a second revelation had quite reversed this process for him. Then, in addition, there will be revelations that cause the poet to occupy varying positions along the line between faith and disbelief."[52]

For poets of our time, religious affirmation emerges in the midst of radical doubt out of a longing for a sense of God's presence that will allow them to transcend despair and, at times, out of an actual sense that they have reconnected with God. Nathan Scott writes of the longing for God as "the primordial drive of the human spirit to find opposite itself an otherness, which is available on the terms of intimacy, which is under the law of participation, and whose rhythms join our own mortal music to make some true counterpoint."[53] We long, writes Scott, for "the conception of reality as ultimately personal, as ultimately possessing the same kind of steadiness belonging to personal relationships characterized by mutuality of trust and love."[54] Langdon Gilkey writes of the ways one can rediscover God precisely as one confronts the abyss of meaninglessness: "[We] begin to notice, to see, and to feel the immense creativity of the 'given' in life, those aspects of our being which neither we nor anyone else can create and yet which are the foundation of all that we are and love." He then goes on to observe that "[i]t is this creativity of the given that other cultures have celebrated as the main positive or to-be-loved side of the ultimate or the sacred."[55]

Poets in our time wish to express the possibility of reconnecting with the divine by means of the kinds of mythic imagery that have always served to express the nature of religious experience. For those like some contemporary poets who, in the words of George Steiner, have "found agnostic secularism more or less unendurable,"[56] the answer has been to reconnect with the power of religious myth from which modern culture has been so distant for far too long. As explorers of mythic imagery, poets are well equipped to contribute to this necessary process of what Steiner calls "remythologization."[57] The frequent tendency of poetry to allude to the world of myth helps to reverse what Colin Falck refers to as the "mythic decline [that] took place in the modern world in the face both of the rational thought-systems of seventeenth-century philosophy and science and of the manipulative or technological thought-habits which were their inseparable accompaniment."[58]

Myth has always served as the basis for religious experience, and poetry reconnects us with an appreciation for the centrality of mythic thinking in matters of religious faith. "Since there is little reason to suppose that human biological nature has significantly changed during the period in which our more rational and intellectual modes of comprehension have come about," writes Falck, "it seems likely not only that myth and mythic consciousness must lie at the origin of our subsequently more fully-articulated linguistic awareness, but also that the most important structures of our fully-articulated linguistic awareness will continue to fall within the outlines of myth and will be most satisfyingly open to 'explanation' through an assimilation to mythic patterns—some at least of which we share with the mythic consciousness of the ancient world."[59] Falck does not advocate the abandonment of rational thought. Instead, he calls for "an integrated mode of vision which comprises both the perceptual and the subjective or spiritual, and which we can recapture from the viewpoint of a later cultural stage only through a unifying and metaphorical effort of poetic imagination."[60] Like the Romantics, who reacted so strongly "against the mechanistic philosophies of the seventeenth and eighteenth centuries . . . ," argues Falck, "it is to the poetry or literature of our own culture (and to what is . . . accessible to us from other cultures) that we have increasingly found ourselves looking for a re-mythologizing of our spiritual landscape."[61]

The body of poetry I will consider in this book reflects the radical break from religious tradition that was so characteristic of the twentieth century and continues to have a strong impact on us at the beginning of the twenty-first century. Nevertheless, as each poem explores the range of possible orientations between the two extremes of skepticism and faith, it makes a significant contribution to the search for a religious discourse appropriate to the religious crisis of our time. Whether these poems speak of God's presence or absence, they always have much to say about the contemporary search for the divine, and, being of our time, these poems speak in uniquely direct ways to our most central spiritual concerns.

CHAPTER ONE

Zelda Mishkovsky
"The small garden showed me signs that His mercies never cease."

ELDA SCHNEURSON MISHKOVSKY (1914–1984), known to the Israeli reading public simply as Zelda, was born during the waning years of Czarist rule in Russia, the only child in a family that had been devoted to the Habad school of Hasidism for several generations.[1] Her father was a direct descendant of Schneur Zalman of Liadi, the founder of the Habad dynasty, and one of her mother's forebears had been a disciple of Schneur Zalman. When Zelda was four years old, her father was fired from his rabbinical position in the aftermath of the Bolshevik Revolution, and the family moved to a modest apartment which they shared with her grandparents and two unmarried aunts. Despite the anti-religious orientation of revolutionary Russia, Zelda's family maintained their loyalty to traditional Judaism, and although Zionist activities were outlawed by the Communist regime, Zelda was active in the establishment of a Zionist youth group. After living through the turmoil of the Russian Civil War, at the age of eleven Zelda immigrated with her family to the Land of Israel and settled in Jerusalem. During their first year of residence there, her grandfather and father died within a month of each other. Although it was not common then in Orthodox Jewish circles for a woman to regularly recite the Mourner's Kaddish in the synagogue, Zelda did so for her grandfather and father during the year following their deaths.

Zelda continued to live with her mother. They eventually moved to Tel Aviv, and after her mother remarried, to Haifa. The only time Zelda did not live with her mother was during a period when she attended the Bezalel Art Academy in Jerusalem. She eventually interrupted her studies at Bezalel to care for her mother in Haifa when she became ill. When her mother's second husband died, Zelda returned with her to Jerusalem. Zelda married Hayim Mishkovsky at the age of thirty-six. The couple continued to live with Zelda's mother until she died in 1965. They had no children, and Hayim died in 1971. Zelda first gained widespread recognition as a poet when she was in her early fifties. She then spent the last decade and a half of her life as a curious cultural anomaly: an Orthodox Jew who wrote poetry accepted by the secular literary establishment and popular with Israeli readers.

Throughout her life Zelda remained religiously observant, yet she was also involved in culture outside the framework of traditional Judaism. Even as a child raised in a pious Jewish family, Zelda was exposed to Russian culture. Her parents sent her to a gentile school, which she attended as long as one of the teachers arranged for her to be absent on Saturdays. After that teacher left, Zelda stopped attending the school. As Hamutal Bar-Yosef reports, "Her young aunts spoke among themselves and with the children in Russian and also told the children the contents of the Russian books that they read. Her mother, Rachel, would amuse the children with card games and translated detective stories of Conan Doyle and Pinkerton, so that they would not disturb the [traditional] learning of her grandfather and father."[2] Zerubavel Gilad notes that, as an adult living in Israel, Zelda developed a wide range of cultural interests, including "Hebrew poetry of all periods . . . Russian . . . literature, . . . the poetry, art, and culture of the Far East, . . . [and] music, especially classical music . . . [and in particular] religious music of the classical composers."[3] Furthermore, according to Gilad, her religious concerns were far from parochial: "She had a great interest in learning about other religions, and she was open to discussions on faith with pious Jews, with secularists, and with people of other religions."[4] In an interview by Rachel Hollander-Steingart, Zelda declared, in a tone of voice in which one could sense her ongoing "affection for the language,"[5] that she still spoke Russian.

Although Zelda began publishing poetry in periodicals in the early 1940s, it was only following the publication of her first collection of poems in 1967 that she rose to prominence in the Israeli literary scene. The publication of that collection made her an instant success. Bar-Yosef attributes the rapid acceptance of Zelda's poetry in the late 1960s to the fact that her style of poetry met certain cultural needs of the time. The Six-Day War of 1967, with its seemingly miraculous outcome and its re-establishment of the connection between Jews and their biblical roots in Jerusalem and the West Bank, gave rise to a new openness to religious categories that made the Israeli reading public more willing to consider the spiritual dimensions at the heart of Zelda's poetry. In addition, argues Bar-Yosef, by the late 1960s a reaction had set in against the emotionally controlled poetry of the 1950s and early 1960s, characterized by the work of such leading poets as Yehuda Amichai and Nathan Zach. Indeed, notes Bar-Yosef, one can see in the poetry of the 1970s and 1980s (for example that of Yona Wollach and Meir Wieseltier) a style more in keeping with "the emotional heights, spirituality, [and] the world of legend and dream"[6] that are so central to Zelda's poetry.

Zelda was well aware of the difficulties facing anyone who seeks to embrace traditional Jewish belief. As she once said to Gilad, "There are those who think that if a person is religious, his faith is all set [*kemunaḥat bequfsah*, literally as if it were placed in a box], but they don't understand that day by day the believer must renew his faith."[7] Her God is one to whom a person can turn for help in providing comfort, companionship, and good fortune in life, but often He does not appear to play that expected role. Although in many of her poems the speaker relates her sense of the presence of God, in a number of works the speaker calls desperately to an apparently absent God for help, either for herself or for others. At certain points in her poetry, one even senses the speaker's anger at God for distancing Himself from humanity, although this anger is typically expressed in an understated manner.

The issue of God's presence and absence is frequently correlated in her poetry with inner psychological experience. "God as an object of thought," observes Bar-Yosef, "is conceived throughout Zelda's poetry as an existential anchor for consciousness and as a psychological support needed by human beings in order not to sink into a cognitive or moral void or into torments of the soul that paralyze the ability to live."[8] Particularly in her later poetry, writes Bar-Yosef, "faith in God is presented as the opposite of moral and spiritual chaos."[9] In the poetry that I will consider, the speaker tends to be alone facing existential anxiety. In some poems, she sees in nature signs of the void of meaninglessness that alternate with signs of God's reassuring presence. In other poems, she is virtually cut off from normal human experience, alone with the terrifying thoughts evoked by her confrontation with mortality. Even when people occupy a poem, the speaker sometimes plays the role of spectator or outsider, detached from human contact and haunted by inner stress. One speaker feels alienated from a noisy market ("I Am a Dying Bird"), another observes a wedding rather than fulfill the commandment to gladden the hearts of the bride and groom ("The shadow of the white mountain . . ."), and yet another stands at a distance from a mourner she has come to comfort ("Be Not Far").

There is a tendency in these poems to refrain from portraying a direct divine response to the speaker's spiritual needs. In poems when the speaker calls out to God and in poems when she experiences a religious malaise that could be cured by God's revelation to the speaker, divine comfort comes from subtle expressions of God's presence in the world around her. As Marcia Falk observes, "It is to [the traditional male God] that the speaker [in Zelda's poetry] turns for help in her weakness, her dependency, her despair. Yet her rescue most often seems to come from the world itself as it enters her ordinary life."[10]

Signs of God's reassuring presence appear to the speaker in ways that are gentle and unassuming: in silence, a garden, a butterfly, the speaker's mind. "The sensual-aesthetic experience, such as observing nature, enjoying the beauty and aroma of flowers, tasting food," writes Bar-Yosef, "has without doubt an important role [for Zelda] . . . but contact with the world of the senses does not have an absolute value in itself, unless the concrete object is perceived as a symbolic reflection of holiness, as a crack through which it is possible to glimpse the upper worlds."[11]

Zelda's speakers are frequently conscious of the danger of the void of mean-inglessness, and experience is often presented as a narrative whose plot is based on the suspense of whether God will appear to the speaker to rescue her from such spiritual chaos. Bar-Yosef attributes Zelda's affinity for narratives to her exposure in childhood to Hasidic tales and Russian folk narratives.[12] The prev-alence of narrative allows for a concrete situation with which readers can iden-tify. It also provides an opportunity to tell a story in which change occurs, from the experience of God's absence to the revelation of God's presence.

In general, references to God and allusions to traditional liturgy are under-stated in Zelda's poetry. It is typical for God to be referred to only once in a poem, and that reference is often delayed until the middle or end of the poem, a delay, notes Bar-Yosef, "that creates an unexpected turn in the rhetorical situ-ation that has been portrayed throughout the poem."[13] The effect is to empha-size the pervasive nature of religious doubt as one awaits a sense of God's pres-ence, which is typically fleeting in nature.

Although Zelda often makes use of expressions from the traditional Jewish prayer book, she does so sparingly. In fact, she rarely refers to God with the two most dominant terms in classical Jewish texts, the Tetragrammaton (tradition-ally pronounced *Adonay*) or *Elohim*.[14] She chooses instead less commonly used, albeit traditionally authentic, divine names from biblical and rabbinic texts. As Bar-Yosef notes, the terms for God that Zelda prefers include those that refer to "God's creating and providential involvement in the world," as well as those that refer to "his existence beyond the limits of human perception."[15] Examples of both types of terms include two terms that refer to God as creator of the universe, *yotser* and *borei*, as well as the terms *ḥay olamim* (Eternal One), *ribbono shel olam* (Master of the Universe), *yodea ta'alumot* (Knower of Mysteries), and *yah tamir venelam* (Hidden and Concealed God). The de-emphasis on the more fre-quently used names of God would seem to reflect a desire to write of religious experience in a way somewhat independent of conventional religious imagery. This has the effect of making the contemporary reader view Zelda's poetry as

more authentic precisely because she has liberated herself from the more preva-
lent clichés of the tradition. It is as if the poet has chosen to put aside the overly
used concepts of God that have lost their vitality and is attempting to discover
the presence of God from a new perspective.

Zelda's religious worldview was colored by her Hasidic upbringing, whose
teachings were important to her throughout her life.[16] In addition to the Habad
teachings she learned in her family circle, Zelda, like so many contemporary
Jewish writers, was drawn to the fascinating Hasidic leader Nahman of
Bratslav.[17] A number of scholars have discerned echoes of Hasidic and other kab-
balistic theology, as well as elements of supernatural folk beliefs, in her poetry.[18]
Examples of mystical terminology and supernatural folk beliefs in the poetry I
selected for this chapter include *yah tamir venelam* (Hidden and Concealed
God) and *shedim umazziqim* (demons and evil spirits).

Throughout her work, Zelda creates refreshing new images not found in clas-
sical Jewish devotional literature, by means of which she conveys a range of ex-
periences from the depths of existential despair to the heights of religious cer-
titude. The false security that masks an inner anxiety of being separated from
God is likened to shipwrecked sailors standing on the back of a whale that they
think is an island ("Island"). The rediscovery of God's presence is represented
by a dying bird that is suddenly revived and begins to hop and sing ("I Am a
Dying Bird"). God is referred to with modern, scientific terminology as being
"light-years" from humanity ("Be Not Far"). An uttered prayer gives rise to a
leafy plant that provides shade ("The shadow of the white mountain . . .").
Death brings a silence as heavy and strong as a bull, which obliterates language
that is used to create human categories ("A Heavy Silence").

Zelda's poetry combines simple, down-to-earth language with words of a high
stylistic register, especially expressions from the Bible and Jewish liturgy and
other rabbinic texts, including *gei tsalmavet* (valley of the shadow of death), *gan
eden* (Garden of Eden, or paradise), *tehom* (the abyss), *mesos ḥatan vekhallah*
(the joy of the bride and groom), *ki lo kalu raḥamav* (that His mercies never
cease), and *shaḥarit* (the morning prayer). Biblical expressions do more than
raise the stylistic register of the poetry: they link the experiences of the speaker
with those of such biblical figures as Jonah and Job. Traditional liturgical ex-
pressions connect Zelda's poetry to the faith of past generations embodied in
the traditional Jewish prayer book.

If I were to include poems by Zelda that have traditional ritual observance as
central imagery, the selection would be much larger. A number of her poems
evoke imagery of Sabbath observance, such as lighting candles and reciting Kid-
dush (the blessing over the wine). In the context of this study, the most relevant
poems are those in which the speaker either addresses God or refers to issues of
faith and doubt. One can discern in such poems three distinct literary strategies
that Zelda adopts when writing about religious experience: (1) the speaker

explores issues of faith and doubt in a concrete, natural setting, with nature im-
ages representing and evoking sometimes spiritual turmoil and anxiety, and
sometimes the tranquility of faith (with the exception of one of this type of
poem, there are no direct references to social relations between the speaker and
other human beings, and the speaker does not address God directly); (2) the
speaker portrays herself as being on the margins of society, and from that stance
she turns to God; and (3) the speaker is alone with her thoughts, and she calls to
God to help her to come to terms with her mortality.[19]

Signs of God's Presence within Nature

הָאוֹר הַדַּק שֶׁל שְׁלוֹמִי

פַּרְפַּר יָמָיו בְּגַן־עֵדֶן
דָּבַק בַּפֶּרַח שֶׁזָּרַעְתִּי
בַּסְּתָו
אוֹתִיּוֹת שֶׁל מַעְלָה בִּכְנָפָיו הַכְּתֻמּוֹת
סִימָנִים שֶׁל יָהּ.   5

בַּסִּימָנִים הָאֵלֶּה
שֶׁנֶּגֶד עֵינַי טָבְעוּ בֶּחָלָל
רִפְרֵף הָאוֹר הַדַּק
שֶׁל שְׁלוֹמִי.

THE DELICATE LIGHT OF MY PEACE

A butterfly hailing from paradise
clung to the flower I planted
in autumn
letters from on high on its golden wings
5 signs of God.

In these signs
that before my eyes sank into space
fluttered the delicate light
of my peace.[20]

The butterfly that the speaker observes facilitates contact between God (*yah*
in the original Hebrew, 5), whose message it bears, and the human speaker, to

whose flower it clings. The butterfly displays black designs on its golden wings, which the poet takes to be "letters from on high" (4).[21] In contrast to the biblical notion of revelation in Exodus, which speaks of God actually engraving the letters of the Ten Commandments on the tablets He gave to Moses on Mount Sinai (Exodus 32:16), here communication between God and humanity takes the shape of naturally formed visual designs. Specific verbal content is less important than a more abstract sense of the divine presence reflected in the wonders of nature.

The Hebrew term that is used to describe the butterfly clinging to the flower (*davaq*, 2) has a long history of signifying a close relationship between human beings and God, from the biblical verse *ve'attem hadeveqim bAdonay Eloheikhem* ("but you who cling to the Lord your God," Deuteronomy 4:4) to the mystical term *devequt*, which suggests some form of human communion with God. In the traditional sense of the term *davaq*, human beings are the ones who cling to God. In the poem, the relationship is reversed; it is God's agent, the butterfly, that clings to the flower, which had been planted by humanity.

Of particular significance is the fact that the speaker planted the flower in the autumn. Her act of planting just before winter can be seen as an expression of faith performed in defiance of the winter, in confident anticipation of the renewal of life in the spring, when the flower will emerge in preparation to meet the butterfly. This act of faith is emphasized by the placement of the Hebrew word that signifies "in autumn," *basetav*, as the only word in line 3. There is also a meaningful connection between God's paradise, *gan eden* (literally "the Garden of Eden," 1), and the garden planted by the speaker. Her act of creating a garden in this world helps to link her to the divine spiritual garden which is God's domain.

The speaker does not refer directly to the butterfly in the second stanza. Nevertheless, elements of the butterfly remain to signify the content of this divine revelation. As the butterfly flies away, God's signs appear to sink into space. When they do, it becomes clear to the speaker that in those signs she can discern a light that represents, or one might say reveals, to the speaker a moment of tranquility. It is significant that the qualities of that revelation of light share some of the physical characteristics of the butterfly: the light is "delicate" (literally "thin" [*daq*], 8), and it "flutter[s]" (*rifref*, 8). A trace of the butterfly can be seen in the word *rifref*: since the same letter in Hebrew represents the sounds "p" and "f," the speaker has in effect reversed the consonants of each syllable in the Hebrew word for butterfly, *parpar*. Thus, a concrete, physical manifestation of nature undergoes a process of progressive abstraction; the designs on the butterfly's wings are transformed into an ethereal vision of light that belongs more to the world of the spirit than to that of material existence.

אִי

אֲנִי דוֹרֶכֶת עַל הָאֲדָמָה
כְּמוֹ עַל גּוּף חַי
כְּאוֹתָם פְּלִיטֵי אֲנִיָּה
שֶׁעָמְדוּ עַל גַּבּוֹ שֶׁל לִוְיָתָן
כִּי טָעוּ בְּמַרְאֵה הָעֵינַיִם.   5

אֲנִי דוֹרֶכֶת עַל הֶעָפָר
שֶׁתַּחְתָּיו מְדַבְּרִים הַמַּיִם
מְדַבְּרִים שָׁרָשִׁים
מְדַבְּרוֹת מַתָּכוֹת
קוֹל הֲמוֹנָם מַחֲרִישׁ אֶת אָזְנִי   10
מְסַחְרֵר אֶת לִבִּי
גַּם הָאֲוִיר מִתְנוֹעֵעַ וְשָׁר
וּבַגְּבָהִים מִתְפּוֹצְצִים עוֹלָמוֹת.

רַק הַמַּחֲשָׁבָה עַל אֱלֹהִים
הִיא אִי בַּמְּעַרְבֹּלֶת.   15

ISLAND

I tread on earth
as if on a living body
like those shipwreck survivors
standing on the back of a whale
5   for their eyes had failed them.

I tread on soil
under which the waters speak
roots speak
metals speak
10   their multitude of sounds deafens my ears
dizzies my heart
the air too sways as it sings
and worlds on high explode.

Only the thought of God
15   is an island in the vortex.[22]

The speaker's strong sense of spiritual vulnerability as she walks is evoked by an image derived, apparently, from a talmudic legend: shipwreck survivors assuming they have arrived at an island without realizing that they are really seeking refuge on the back of a whale (3–5).[23] This image also has a more ancient mythological dimension. The Hebrew word that refers to the sea creature which the survivors mistakenly take to be an island is *livyatan* (4), which is used in modern Hebrew to signify a "whale." In the Hebrew Bible, *livyatan* (known to readers of the Bible in English translation as "Leviathan") is a sea monster associated with the chaos that God had to bring under control at the time of creation (Psalms 74:14). Leviathan also represents the forces of evil with which God must struggle to bring about the final redemption (Isaiah 27:1).[24] Thus, to be unknowingly located on the back of such a creature is to be dangerously close to a void that could drag one down to perdition.

The imagery then shifts from the sea back to the land on which the speaker is walking. In this set of images, unlike the shipwreck survivors who are unaware of the impending danger to their existence, the speaker has a special sense of how threatened she is. She hears a dizzying collection of sounds emitted from the underground elements of waters, roots, and metals (7–9). Unsure of what is reliable on land, she turns her attention to that which is above ground, only to discover once again a threatening chaos: "the air too sways as it sings / and worlds on high explode" (12–13). Just when it appears that there is no way out of the existential anxiety she is experiencing, suddenly "the thought of God" (14) enters her mind, providing a reliable refuge ("an island," 15) in the spiritual "vortex" (15) that threatens to completely undermine her spirit.[25] Thus, when the world outside of herself feels overwhelming, the speaker discovers inside herself the power of the human imagination to conceive of a God who can stop the descent into spiritual chaos.

הָיָה מַשֶּׁהוּ מַבְהִיל
בְּגוֹן הַשָּׁמַיִם
הִשְׁתּוֹמַמְתִּי שֶׁצַּמְּרוֹת הָעֵצִים
מִתְנַדְנְדוֹת בְּקַלִּילוּת
בְּלִי צֵל שֶׁל חֲרָדָה.   5
רָצִיתִי לִבְרֹחַ מִן הָרָקִיעַ הַלָּבָן
אַךְ הַגִּנָּה הַקְּטַנָּה
הֶרְאָתָה לִי סִימָנִים
כִּי לֹא כָּלוּ רַחֲמָיו.

There was something alarming
in the color of the heavens
I was horrified at the tree tops
swaying so easily
5   with not a shadow of anxiety.
I wished to flee from the white sky
but the small garden
showed me signs
that His mercies never cease.[26]

In this poem, nature has the capacity to evoke both anxiety and comfort. Not unlike the speaker in "Island," this speaker possesses a highly sensitive aware-ness of the possibility that chaos could erupt at any time. The white color of what is presumably a cloud-covered sky (2, 6) and "the tree tops / swaying so easily" (3–4) do not suggest, on the face of it, that there is anything about which to be concerned. For the speaker, however, these are subtle early signs of a storm during which the white clouds will turn to gray and emit a driving rain, and what are now light winds will be transformed into strong destructive gusts.

As alarming as the impending storm is, with its potential to tear off branches or even uproot trees, the fact that the trees do not anticipate the coming danger is even more frightening. The speaker makes the horrifying observation that the branches appear to be incredibly oblivious to their vulnerable state as they sway "so easily / with not a shadow of anxiety" (4–5). The expression "with not a shadow of anxiety" (*beli tsel shel ḥaradah*) signifies that the trees have abso-lutely no awareness of how vulnerable they are and also alludes to mortality: after all, a tree that cannot cast a shadow (or shade, as the Hebrew word *tsel* connotes both) is one that, having lost its leaves, is in a death-like state. The expression also sounds like a play on the Hebrew expression *beli tsel shel safeq* (without the shadow of a doubt). The speaker's experience of anxiety, of course, is the opposite of the experience of certitude that both of these Hebrew expres-sions signify. In a more symbolic sense, the trees' confident lack of awareness may represent other people who do not share with the speaker her hypersensi-tivity to dangers inherent in human existence.

The speaker is finally redeemed from her anxiety by the revelation of a "small garden" (7) that reminds her of the presence of a God of mercy. This is a very subtle revelation of God's presence, for it consists only of "signs" (8) that God is reliably merciful. Even as the speaker finds comfort in sensing God at the end of the poem, God is not mentioned directly. Instead, His presence is evoked by a reference in line 9 to His quality of mercy found in the "Modim" prayer of thanksgiving traditionally recited by Jews in the "Amidah" prayer three times a day: "that Your mercies never cease" (*ki lo kalu raḥamekha*).[27] The beauty of the garden toward the end of the poem provides a comforting aesthetic pleasure that stands in marked contrast to the earlier threatening images of the storm clouds and the winds pushing on the trees. Furthermore, a garden is designed and maintained by human beings, thereby suggesting that people can take their destinies into their own hands and create a harmonious world in spite of all that evokes their anxiety. The garden imagery recalls the flower planted in autumn by the speaker in "The Delicate Light of My Peace," a human act of faith that draws into this world the spiritual dimension of God's reassuring presence.

בְּמַלְכוּת־הַשְׁקִיעָה

בְּמַלְכוּת־הַשְׁקִיעָה
אֲפִלּוּ קוֹץ מֵפִיק נֹגַהּ.

פִּתְאֹם נְמוֹגִים כְּתָרִים
וְקוֹץ חוֹזֵר לִהְיוֹת קוֹץ
וְהַר שָׁב לְגָלְמִיּוּתוֹ,   5
נֶחְשָׂפָה מִדַּת־הַדִּין
וּמְבַצְבֵּץ שֶׁלֶד הַיְקוּם.

אַךְ אֵינֶנּוּ מֵתִים מִפַּחַד
כִּי מַגִּיעַ חֶסֶד הַלַּיְלָה
וְהַנֶּפֶשׁ מַמְרִיאָה לְהַשָּׂגָה חֲדָשָׁה   10
שֶׁל הַבּוֹרֵא.

In the Kingdom of Sunset

In the kingdom of sunset
even a thorn brightly shines.

Suddenly crowns melt away
and a thorn turns back into a thorn
5   and a mountain returns to its crude form,
the attribute of justice is revealed
and the universe's skeleton bursts forth.

But we do not die of fear
for the grace of night arrives
10   and the soul soars to a new perception
of the Creator.[28]

From the speaker's point of view, sunset temporarily transforms the appearance of the world into a glorious manifestation of royalty.[29] The colors of the sunset cast on nature a glow that creates the illusion of nobility, so that even the lowly thorn has its dignified bearing as it "brightly shines" (*mefiq nogah*, an expression found in the Sabbath morning prayer "El adon" in reference to the light shining from the sun, moon, and stars, 2). As sunset gives way to dusk, however, the nobility of that kingdom disappears and the world appears again as it did before the sunset ennobled it. Now it is once again undignified and insignificant, as captured by the speaker's statement, "and a thorn turns back into a thorn / and a mountain returns to its crude form" (4–5). Accompanying the transition from the beauty of sunset to the dullness of dusk is the realization of the existence of God's "attribute of justice" (*middat hadin*, 6), which, when it is not tempered by His attribute of mercy (*middat harahamim*), can be most frightening to human beings. The expression "the universe's skeleton bursts forth" (7) would seem to signify what we might refer to as a "bare bones" look at the nature of things, as if examined by a moral X-ray machine applied by the divine attribute of justice in an effort to discern all infractions of God's law. The skeletal image prefigures the reference in line 8 to the real possibility of dying from fear induced by the unmitigated wrath of God's judgment.[30] As in other poems by Zelda in which a sense of God's presence rescues the speaker from existential despair, here too the speaker is saved by a divine revelation of sorts, referred to as "the grace of night" (9), that saves the speaker from death and allows the soul to soar "to a new perception / of the Creator" (10–11).

This experience, which lasts from sunset until nightfall, provides a lesson in how to move from the delusions of inflated pride (the thorn that brightly shines only because it temporarily reflects the colors of the sunset), through deflating guilt (evoked by the revelation of divine justice), to the comforting realization that God's grace can eventually overcome the fear we experience when we feel judged ("the grace of night"). That which looks to be dignified and glorious, the poem suggests, may in fact be an illusion, and the real existence of divine justice to which we might be subjected need not arouse our fear. In "The Delicate Light of My Peace" and "There was something alarming . . . ," the speaker sees in nature imagery hints of God's presence. In "Island," the discovery of God comes more from a willed effort of the human imagination to become once more aware of a reassuring sense of God's presence. In this poem, the revelation of God appears to operate on both levels: night itself is reassuring, but it is the mind that must arrive at "a new perception / of the Creator."

Turning to God from the Margins of Society

אֲנִי צִפּוֹר מֵתָה

אֲנִי צִפּוֹר מֵתָה,
צִפּוֹר אַחַת שֶׁמֵּתָה.
צִפּוֹר עוֹטָה מְעִיל אָפֹר.
בְּלֶכְתִּי, לֵץ מַפְטִיר לְעֻמָּתִי.

פֶּתַע אֲפָפַתְנִי שְׁתִיקָתֵךְ–   5
חַי עוֹלָמִים.
בְּשׁוּק שׁוֹקֵק עוֹף מֵת יָשִׁיר–
רַק אַתָּה קַיָּם.
בְּשׁוּק שׁוֹקֵק מְדַדָּה צִפּוֹר עִם שִׁיר
נִסְתָּר.   10

I Am a Dying Bird

I am a dying bird,
one bird who is dying.
A bird wrapped in a gray coat.
As I walk, a fool heaps scorn on me.

5   Suddenly Your silence surrounds me —
Eternal One.
In a bustling market dying fowl will sing —
only You exist.
In a bustling market a bird hops with a song
10   concealed.[31]

The speaker's sense of waning vitality is captured poignantly in the image of "a dying bird" (1) no longer able to exercise its freedom to fly. The Hebrew word for bird used here, *tsippor*, is of feminine gender, thereby making clear that, as in other poems by Zelda, the speaker is a woman. One may safely assume that death here refers metaphorically to the speaker's psychological, emotional, and spiritual life. As Bar-Yosef notes, "the gray coat of the bird (3) symbolizes the depressing monotony of the [speaker's] life, and it is a metonymic projection of her inner death."[32] The seeming redundancy of line 2, "one bird who is dying," emphasizes the centrality of loneliness in the speaker's experience of her uniqueness as one individual cut off from others.[33]

Lines 3 and 4 turn the poem away from death toward life. A walking bird is very different from one that is listlessly dying. The reference to the bird being wrapped in a gray coat serves to connect the animal imagery more directly to human experience. It also suggests that the bird has some comforting protection against hostile elements in her environment. The last expression of line 4, *lets maftir le'ummati*, is difficult to translate because there is more than one possible meaning for the first two words. It is likely, as Bar-Yosef suggests, that Zelda uses *lets* here to indicate a person who makes fun of the speaker, as in the biblical expression *moshav letsim* ("the company of scoffers," Psalms 1:1). The word *maftir* is apparently taken from the biblical expression *yaftiru vesafah* ("they open wide their lips," Psalms 22:8). Both the expressions "the company of scoffers" and "they open wide their lips" appear in Psalms in the context of mockery. The translation "a fool heaps scorn on me" fits well with Bar-Yosef's observation that "[t]he primary human situation in Zelda's poetry is often the situation of an inner death as a result of serious emotional harm, a mixture of bereavement, loneliness, and the consciousness of being mocked."[34] Alternatively, the expression "heaps scorn" might be replaced by the word "sneers," with its connotation of the physical action of contorting one's face, in keeping with the biblical image of opening wide one's lips. The alliterative repetition of the sound "ti" in line 4 (*belekhti, lets maftir le'ummati*), noted by Bar Yosef,[35] serves to reinforce the repetitive annoying mocking to which the speaker is subjected.

In lines 5 and 6, the speaker discovers God's presence and thereby is able to escape the gloom in which she has been immersed. The suddenness of God's revelation to the speaker is reinforced by the choice of the word *peta* to express "suddenly" (5), with its accent on the first syllable and its relative shortness in length. Synonyms such as *lefeta* or *pitom*, or the combined expression *lefeta pitom*, would lack this effect. The speaker's reference to God as "Eternal One" (*hay olamim*, 6) links God to the reaffirmation of life (*hayyim*) and the negation of death in eternity (*olam*).[36] Significantly, the speaker's ability to overcome a spiritual death is evoked not by human contact with the life of the noisy market, but rather by an encounter with God's silence (5–10). As God's affirming presence in silence surrounds the speaker, she is represented not by the image of a bird walking around in a gray coat, but rather by the image of a bird hopping around singing to itself.[37] The speaker has discovered that God's eternal existence is the only true existence and that, therefore, her spiritual death is not as real as she had imagined it to be (6, 8). The single word in the final line, *nistar* ("concealed," 10), is heavy with mystical associations. On a literal level, the word *nistar* functions as an adjective modifying the word immediately preceding it, *shir* ("song," 9). Bar Yosef, however, has proposed another possible interpretation of *nistar*. If the alternating lines 6 and 8 in the second stanza ("Eternal One" and "only You exist") are expressions addressed to God, she suggests, perhaps the next alternating line (10) can also be seen as an address to God, something like "You, Concealed One," as if the speaker concludes the poem affirming her relationship with this God who had been hidden from her.[38]

אַל תִּרְחַק

הַמְנַחֲמִים בָּאִים אֶל הֶחָצֵר
הַחִיצוֹנָה
עוֹמְדִים עַל יַד הַשַּׁעַר
אֲשֶׁר פָּנָיו אֶל גֵּיא צַלְמָוֶת
וְאֵימָתוֹ סָבִיב סָבִיב.   5
עֲמִידָה עַל יַד הַשַּׁעַר כָּל יְכָלְתָּם
שֶׁל מְנַחֲמִים לָשֵׂאת.
גַּם נַפְשִׁי בְּמֶרְחַק פַּרְסָאוֹת
מִן הָאֲנִי שֶׁל הַבּוֹכֶה. גְּזֵרָה הִיא.

יוֹצֵר לֵילוֹת וָרוּחַ   10
הֲלֹא נֶגְדְּךָ בְּכִי אִים זֶה,
אַל תִּרְחַק–
אַל יַעַמְדוּ כְּחַיִץ
מִילְיוֹנֵי שְׁנוֹת אוֹר
בֵּינְךָ וּבֵין אִיּוֹב.   15

BE NOT FAR

The comforters arrive at the outer
courtyard
and stand by the gate
that faces the valley of the shadow of death,
5   its terror all around.
Standing by the gate is all
the comforters can bear.
My soul too is miles
from the "I" of the weeper. It is fate.

10   Creator of nights and spirit
this dreadful cry is surely directed at You,
be not far—
don't let millions of light-years
stand as a barrier
15   between You and Job.[39]

The title of the poem, "Be Not Far," alludes to the biblical expression "be not far from me (Psalms 22:12; 35:22; 38:22; 71:12),[40] which appears in the "Shema qolenu" prayer of Yom Kippur as "be not far from us." Here the sense of God's distance is not related to the speaker's personal dread of divine abandonment, as it is in the classical sources, but rather to her feelings of empathy for a man who feels abandoned by God as he mourns the death of a loved one. (The gender of the mourner is indicated by the masculine form of the Hebrew word for "weeper," *bokheh*, 9.) Yet it is not only God who is distant: the pain of the mourner is more than the human comforters can appreciate or bear, so they stand at a distance "at the outer / courtyard" (1–2) confronting the reality of mortality, represented by the image of "the valley of the shadow of death" (4) of Psalms 23:4. The speaker also declares that her "soul," or inner being, "too is miles / from the 'I' of the weeper" who mourns (8–9). The word translated here as "miles" is *parsa'ot*, an Aramaic measure of distance found in rabbinic literature.[41] By not using the contemporary Israeli measure of distance, the kilometer, the poet takes the speaker's experience out of an immediate contemporary context and connects it to the world of traditional Jewish values. In so doing, she emphasizes the degree to which those who have come to visit the mourner have failed to live up to their traditional religious obligation to comfort mourners (known in rabbinic sources as *niḥum avelim*). The reference to the "'I' [*ha'ani*] of the weeper" (9) emphasizes the utter loneliness of the mourner confronting the death of a loved one.[42]

In the second stanza, the speaker turns directly to God, pointing out to Him that the "dreadful cry" of the mourner is "directed at" Him, literally "against" Him (*negdekha*, 11). The speaker, in effect, criticizes God for the role He played in causing the mourner's suffering by taking away the life of his loved one. She also suggests that God appears to be no more capable of comforting the mourner than the people who visit him. This challenge directed at God is underscored by an allusion to the book of Job. The comforters' inability to understand the mourner's grief and to relieve him of the pain of his loss resembles the failure of Job's friends to comfort him. God's silence at this time of mourning recalls that, for most of the book of Job, He does not appear in response to Job's cries for contact with Him. Yet at the end of the biblical account, God does reveal Himself to Job. Here, however, He does not. He remains, in a figurative sense, "millions of light-years" (13) away from the mourner. Like Job himself, who pleaded with God to explain his suffering to him, the speaker demands that God overcome that distance: "[D]on't let millions of light-years / stand as a barrier / between You and Job" (13–15).[43] The speaker's idiosyncratic use of the term "light-years" (*shenot or*) from physics to refer to metaphysical matters is effective in that it takes the poem beyond theological clichés and provides an image from science with which readers can readily identify.[44] It also stands in marked contrast to the ancient term for distance, *parsa'ot*, used in the first

stanza, suggesting a gap between the attempt of the human comforters to pre-
serve the traditional rituals of mourning and the contemporary scientific per-
spective that raises serious questions about the presence of God in our lives.

צֵל הָהָר הַלָּבָן
כִּסָּה אֶת פָּנַי וְיָדַי
וְדִמִּיתִי שֶׁנַּפְשִׁי חָפְשִׁית
כַּמֵּת.
צֵל עָצוּב כִּסָּה אֶת הַבַּיִת   5
וְאֶת עֲלֵי הַגֶּפֶן
אַךְ כַּאֲשֶׁר
בְּאֶרֶץ זָרָה
שֶׁהִיא רְחוֹבִי
נִגֵּן כִּנּוֹר   10
יָצָאתִי אֶל מְשׂוֹשׂ חָתָן וְכַלָּה
וְרָאִיתִי
כִּי הֵם שׁוֹזְרִים
תִּקְוָה עֲדִינָה עַד מְאֹד
וְרָאִיתִי   15
כִּי הֵמָּה שׁוֹזְרִים
תִּקְוָה אֲמִתִּית,
וְכָךְ בִּקַּשְׁתִּי בַּחֲשַׁאי:
יוֹצֵר הָאָדָם־
שֶׁלֹּא יִסְתָּעֲרוּ שֵׁדִים וּמַזִּיקִים   20
עַל דִּמְיוֹנָם
שֶׁיִּהְיֶה בִּנְיָנָם
בִּנְיָן עֲדֵי־עַד.
תְּפִלָּתִי הַצְמִיחָה
עָלִים יְרֻקִּים.   25
יָשַׁבְתִּי בְּצֵל הַקִּיקָיוֹן
וְלֹא יָדַעְתִּי עוֹד
מַה שֵּׁם הַתַּחֲנָה
שֶׁהִגִּיעוּ אֵלֶיהָ חַיַּי.

The shadow of the white mountain
covered my face and my hands,
I imagined my soul released
like the dead.
5   A sad shadow covered the house
and the leaves of the vine
but when

in a foreign land
that is my street
10   a violin played
I went out to the joy of the bride and groom,
I saw
them weave
a most delicate hope,
15   I saw
them weave
a true hope,
and thus I quietly pleaded:
Creator of Man—
20   may demons and evil spirits not assault
their imagination
may what they build
be everlasting.
My prayer brought forth
25   green leaves.
I sat in the shade of the gourd plant
not yet knowing
the name of the station
at which my life had arrived.[45]

In the first nine lines of this poem, images of alienation and death prevail: a mountain's shadow covering the face and hands of the speaker, the speaker's soul released from her body, a sad shadow covering her immediate surroundings, and her street experienced as a foreign land. The expression "released / like the dead" (*hofshit / kamet*, 3–4) may derive, as Bar-Yosef notes, from a biblical passage that refers to being left to lie among the dead (Psalms 88:5–6).[46] However, in addition to the association with the image of complete abandonment found in Psalms, one might also understand the expression to convey the promise of the soul's freedom at the time of death. This alternative interpretation is underscored by the appearance of the word "released" on its own at the end of line 3 before the eye perceives "like the dead" at the beginning of line 4. This enjambment creates within the reader a momentary sense that the speaker thinks of death as a positive experience in which her soul will be freed from its confines in her body. This apparent death wish is then interrupted by the life-affirming sounds created by the wedding musicians.

The speaker relates that she "went out to the joy of the bride and groom" (11). The expression "the joy of the bride and groom" (*mesos hatan vekhallah*) alludes to the biblical expression "the joy of the groom upon the bride" (*mesos ḥatan al kallah*, Isaiah 62:5),[47] which also appears in the traditional prayer for welcoming the Sabbath, "Lekhah dodi." In both contexts, God's relationship to the people of Israel after exile is compared to that of a groom and his bride. Thus, when the speaker comes across the wedding, it is as if she has undergone an experience of divine redemption from the depths of her death-like state of alienation.

It is significant, however, that she only observes the couple from a distance and does not partake in the traditional Jewish obligation to bring joy to the bride and groom (*lesameaḥ ḥatan vekhallah*). As the bride and groom celebrate their union, it is as if they have woven a cloth of hope (11–17) that can counter the gloomy images with which the poem began. Although this is a vulnerable "delicate hope" (14), it is one that is "true" (17). Being so preoccupied with that which can bring sadness into the world, the speaker cannot help but be concerned that the joy of the bride and groom might not last, so she prays to God that this couple's dreams for a good life together not be frustrated (18–23). Her prayer is laced with traditional images and expressions: the supernatural folk image of "demons and evil spirits" (*shedim umazziqim*) assaulting their imagination (20–21) and the expression of hope for their everlasting security, which makes use of two terms from the traditional seven blessings recited at a Jewish wedding: "Creator of Man" (*yotser ha'adam*, 19) and "an everlasting building" (*binyan adei ad* [translated in the poem as "what they build / be everlasting"], 22–23).[48]

While the speaker never receives a direct response to the petition she presents to God, the act of prayer provides her with a measure of comfort. Her declaration "[m]y prayer brought forth / green leaves" (24–25) suggests that words of prayer can lead one to a new emotional state; by asking for the good fortune of others—and not for one's own good fortune—one experiences inner tranquility and security and discerns the beauty of life that was not evident before. This tranquility is analogous to that of the prophet Jonah, who gained refuge from the sun under a gourd plant ("I sat in the shade of the gourd plant," 26). The allusion to Jonah's gourd plant, which disappeared overnight (Jonah 4) suggests that the effects of the speaker's prayer will only be temporary.[49] Life, the poet suggests, is a continuous alternation between despair and joy. The bride and groom are at a stage of life that brings joy, but at what stage along the oscillating continuum of despair and joy, asks the speaker, is she herself? (27–29). The ephemeral nature of emotional states and human fate is captured in the poem's structural device of short lines, often of only one or two words in the original Hebrew. This choppy progression from expression to expression creates an atmosphere of tentativeness by means of which the poet avoids creating the illusion that one can ever arrive at a final state of satisfaction and self-fulfillment.

Asking for God's Help in Confronting Mortality

כָּל הַלַּיְלָה בָּכִיתִי

כָּל הַלַּיְלָה בָּכִיתִי
רִבּוֹנוֹ שֶׁל עוֹלָם
אוּלַי יֵשׁ מָוֶת שֶׁאֵין בּוֹ
אַלִּימוּת
מָוֶת שֶׁדּוֹמֶה לְפֶרַח.   5
כָּל הַלַּיְלָה הִפַּלְתִּי תַּחֲנוּנִי
אֲפִלּוּ אֲנִי עָפָר
תִּהְיֶה בִּי מְנוּחָה
לְהַבִּיט אֶל גָּבְהֵי שָׁמַיִם
עוֹד וְעוֹד וְעוֹד   10
לְהִפָּרֵד מִיָּפְיָם,

כָּל הַלַּיְלָה חָשַׁבְתִּי
בְּרִיּוֹת רַבּוֹת גָּרוֹת
בְּחָזִי הַכּוֹאֵב
וְסִפּוּרִים שׁוֹנִים,   15
צָרִיךְ לְהַדְלִיק נֵר
וּלְהַבִּיט עֲלֵיהֶם
בְּטֶרֶם אִישַׁן הַמָּוֶת.

ALL NIGHT I WEPT

All night I wept
Master of the universe
perhaps there's death without
violence
5   death that resembles a flower.
All night I offered my entreaties
even if I am dust
may I have the tranquility
to look at the heights of the heavens
10   again and again and again
to separate from their beauty.

All night I thought
many creatures dwell
in my aching breast
15   and many stories,

I must light a candle
and look at them
before I sleep the sleep of death.[50]

In this poem, as in the following two poems, the speaker beseeches God to help her to come to terms with her mortality. In the first stanza, terrified of death, she pleads with God for the opportunity to experience her passing in a peaceful and aesthetically pleasing manner. She wonders if it is possible to die without experiencing any degree of violence, and she prefers a death that resembles a flower, beautiful in its delicate appearance (1–5). Echoing the divine curse placed on Adam and Eve—"for dust you are and to dust you will return" (Genesis 3:19)—she pleads with God to allow her to transcend her return to the dust of the earth and cling for an extended period of time to the pleasant sight of the sky, thereby departing from the world in a gradual and peaceful manner ("even if I am dust / may I have the tranquility / to look at the heights of the heavens / again and again and again / to separate from their beauty," 7–11).

Death raises another set of concerns for the speaker. She is painfully aware of her memories of all that has happened to her in her lifetime ("many creatures dwell / in my aching breast / and many stories," 13–15), and these she realizes will be lost upon her death. She thus feels impelled to revisit those memories. She examines them by the light of a candle that she has kindled (16–17), thereby associating this act with an atmosphere of traditional piety embodied by the ritual lighting of candles on Sabbath and holidays. Although, by the second stanza, God's presence has faded from the poem, the speaker's reference to death at the end of the poem is one which indicates that she has made her peace with mortality. The "sleep of death" (18) to which she refers is a biblical expression (Psalms 13:4), which is also found in the traditional Jewish bedtime prayer. In the original biblical and liturgical contexts, this expression refers to a lack of desire to die, but in the poem the expression brings a welcome degree of resolution to the tension she had experienced. The poem begins with the speaker unable to fall asleep, spending the whole night praying to God for an ideal death, and concludes with a vision of death as sleep. In one sense, such a death provides welcome relief from the insomnia of her night-long supplications. In another sense, such a death signifies the peaceful demise for which she has so urgently prayed to God.

The transition from a focus on the contrast between a violent and a peaceful death in the first stanza to a focus on the narrative content of the speaker's life in the second stanza is significant. As long as the speaker is focused on her fear of how death will affect her, she is in a state of panic which induces her to call upon God to save her from the effect of death. Once she shifts her focus to the

life she has led, she no longer has the same need for God. She realizes that the
most important issue is not the kind of death she will have, but rather how she
is to come to terms with all creatures with whom she has interacted throughout
her life. If she is able to arrive at a satisfying conclusion to such a confrontation,
she will receive the peaceful death which she seeks, for once one has come to
terms with one's past, one no longer needs to fear one's mortality.

בְּשָׁעָה מְהֻרְהֶרֶת זוֹ

בְּשָׁעָה מְהֻרְהֶרֶת זוֹ
מְנֻתֶּקֶת מִכֹּל
הִתְעַנַּגְתִּי עַל יְפִי עֲלֵי הַגֶּפֶן־
רַק כַּאֲשֶׁר צֵל שֶׁל שָׁלוֹם
שָׁרוּי בְּהָרֵי יְרוּשָׁלַיִם   5
וְקוֹלוֹת יְקִיצָה שֶׁל צִפֳּרִים
וְתִינוֹקוֹת מַקִּיפִים אוֹתִי,
וְלֹא בָגַדְתִּי
וְלֹא דִבַּרְתִּי דֹּפִי,
וְאֵימָה חֲשֵׁכָה לֹא כִסְּפָה   10
אֶת חוּשַׁי־
קוֹלֶטֶת נַפְשִׁי רֶטֶט רָפֶה עַד מְאֹד
שֶׁעוֹבֵר בֶּעָלִים בְּפָגְשָׁם
אוֹר שֶׁל שַׁחֲרִית.

יָהּ טָמִיר וְנֶעְלָם   15
הַצִּילֵנִי מִשְּׁמוּעוֹת רָעוֹת
שֶׁהוֹדְפוֹת לָאֹפֶל
אֶת הַשֶּׁקֶט הַדַּק
שֶׁל לֵב מִסְתַּכֵּל מִן הַצַּד.
כִּי מַה בֵּיתִי וּמַה חַיַּי   20
בְּיוֹם שֶׁל אֲהָהּ
זֶה הַיּוֹם הַפִּרְאִי
שֶׁמַּשְׁלִיךְ לָאָרֶץ
בְּחֵמָה מְעֻוֶּרֶת
אֶת עֶדְנַת הַגֶּפֶן   25
וְכָל הֶגְיָגַי.

AT THIS THOUGHT-FILLED HOUR

At this thought-filled hour
disconnected from everything
I took pleasure in the beauty of grape leaves—
Only when a shadow of peace
5   lies on Jerusalem's hills
and waking voices of birds
and infants surround me,
and I have not betrayed
and I have not slandered,
10   and a dark dread has not bewitched
my senses—
my soul perceives a very faint tremor
passing among the leaves as they meet
the morning light.

15   God hidden and concealed
save me from evil tidings
that thrust to obscurity
the delicate quiet
of a heart observing from the side.
20   For what is my house and what is my life
on the day of woe,
the savage day
that casts to the earth
in blinding fury
25   the delightfulness of the vine
and all my meditations.[51]

At the beginning of this poem, the speaker is "disconnected from everything"
(2) and experiences the moment in which she lives as if she is immersed in an
atmosphere of thoughtfulness (1). As she undergoes this experience, she feels
fully capable of enjoying the natural "beauty of grape leaves" (3), sitting in the
tranquility and security symbolized biblically by the vine ("each person under
his vine and under his fig tree," 1 Kings 5:5; Micah 4:4). Beginning with line 4,
the speaker relates that under certain circumstances she can discern a reassur-
ing presence from a realm beyond the vision of the naked eye. This presence
comes to her only when certain elements are in place: there is "a shadow of
peace . . . / on Jerusalem's hills" (4–5), she is surrounded by the inspiring "wak-
ing voices of birds / and infants" (6–7), she can convincingly claim that she is

free of the sin of disloyalty to her fellow human beings ("and I have not betrayed / and I have not slandered," 8–9), and she is freed of any feelings of terror that might interfere with her ability to sense the divine ("and a dark dread has not bewitched / my senses," 10–11).

In lines 8 to 11, the speaker appears to distance herself from two types of religious experience found in traditional sources. The speaker presents a kind of negative Yom Kippur confessional: "and I have not betrayed / and I have not slandered" (8–9). In defiance of the traditional notion that one must confess one's sins in order to achieve spiritual purity, the speaker seems to be saying that she need not submit to the self-negating process of the confessional; she knows she has not betrayed or slandered others. She also distances herself from the overwhelming experience of "dark dread" (*eimah hashekhah*, 10) that Abraham underwent when God put him into a deep sleep in preparation for a divine revelation (Genesis 15). Her rejection of "dark dread" signifies not only her distance from the intensity of the revelation that God granted to Abraham, but also her assertion that her discovery of God will not come at a time of fearful thoughts.

The "very faint tremor / passing among the leaves as they meet / the morning light." (12–14) that her soul then senses is, on a naturalistic level, the effect of the wind blowing through the leaves. On a spiritual level, however, the tremor indicates the speaker's awareness of an invisible divine dimension that is beyond what the physical senses can perceive. The use of the name of the traditional prayer service, *shaharit*, to signify morning (14) reinforces the sense that this is a spiritual experience. The tremor that the speaker senses as the leaves and light meet is expressed by means of the Hebrew word *retet*, which typically connotes the physical trembling of a person gripped by intense emotions, as in the biblical description of the "trembling" (*retet*) that seizes Damascus in anticipation of divine judgment (Jeremiah 49:24). Being "very faint," however, the trembling of the leaves is present, yet not overwhelming.

Having experienced a muted expression of God's presence in the trembling of the leaves, the speaker now refers to this God as "hidden and concealed" (*tamir venelam*, a mystical expression found in the traditional Jewish liturgy, 15). She calls on God to save her from "evil tidings" (16) that threaten to completely undermine the tranquility of her current experience. Since she maintains a distance from the world in which she seeks the presence of God ("a heart observing from the side," 19), there is always the danger that her awareness of God will be undermined, that the quiet of her experience will be dashed to obscurity when she is reminded of the presence of evil on earth. Evil recalls human mortality, and, thus, she beseeches God to save her not only from evil, but from the frightening experience of complete destruction on the day of her death. The description of "the savage day / that casts to the earth / in blinding fury" (22–24) would appear to refer to a notion of death similar to the violent death that the speaker fears in "All Night I Wept." It is a force that violently cuts the speaker off from

her capacity to contemplate nature and consider its significance ("the delightful-
ness of the vine / and all my meditations," 25–26). The threatening "evil tidings"
(16) and "the day of woe" (21) allude to frightening forces mentioned in biblical
texts (Psalms 112:7 and Joel 1:15, respectively). The link established between these
two disturbing elements is reinforced by the way that both are described as force-
fully disposing of the speaker's ability to take pleasure in the world: the evil tid-
ings "thrust to obscurity / the delicate quiet / of a heart observing from the side"
(17–19), and the day of woe "casts to the earth / in blinding fury / the delightful-
ness of the vine / and all [of the speaker's] meditations" (23–26).

שְׁתִיקָה כְּבֵדָה

הַמָּוֶת יִקַּח אֶת הַשֹּׁנִי הַמַּרְהִיב
שֶׁבֵּין אֵשׁ לְמַיִם
וְיַשְׁלִיכֵהוּ לַתְּהוֹם.

שְׁתִיקָה כְּבֵדָה כְּפַר
תִּרְבַּץ עַל הַשֵּׁמוֹת   5
שֶׁנָּתַן הָאָדָם לְעוֹפוֹת הַשָּׁמַיִם
וּלְחַיַּת הַשָּׂדֶה
לִשְׁמֵי הָעֶרֶב
לַמֶּרְחַקִּים הָעֲצוּמִים בֶּחָלָל
וְלִדְבָרִים סְמוּיִּים מִן הָעַיִן.   10

שְׁתִיקָה כְּבֵדָה כְּפַר
תִּרְבַּץ עַל כָּל הַמִּלִּים.
וְקָשָׁה תִהְיֶה עָלַי הַפְּרִידָה
מִשֵּׁמוֹת שֶׁל דְּבָרִים
כְּמוֹ מִן הַדְּבָרִים עַצְמָם.   15

יוֹדֵעַ תַּעֲלוּמוֹת
הֲבִינֵנִי מַה לְבַקֵּשׁ בְּיוֹם אַחֲרוֹן.

A HEAVY SILENCE

Death will take the astounding difference
between fire and water
and cast it to the abyss.

Silence heavy as a bull
5   will crouch on the names
that Adam gave birds of the sky,

beasts of the field
the evening sky
the vast expanses in space
10   and things hidden from sight.

Silence heavy as a bull
will crouch on all the words.
And separating from names
will be as hard for me
15   as separating from the actual things.

Knower of mysteries
let me understand for what to plead on the last day.[52]

Mortality means something different in this poem than in the previous ones. Here the poet is preoccupied with the ability of death to obliterate the distinctions between elements of life. Even the difference between two of the most opposite elements, fire and water, will be obliterated by death ("Death will take the astounding difference / between fire and water / and cast it to the abyss," 1–3). As the poem develops, the speaker declares that death will be difficult for her not only because she will part from elements in this world, but also because the distinctions conceived of by humans that give meaning to life—a process which began when, as recounted in Genesis 2:19–20, the first human named the animals ("the names / that Adam gave birds of the sky, / beasts of the field / the evening sky / the vast expanses in space / and things hidden from sight," 5–10)—will be eliminated when we die. All the names, all the words that humanity has conceived to create the categories of life, will be reduced to silence. This process is conveyed by means of the curious metaphor of silence as a bull crouching on names and words (4–5, 11–12). This blurring of verbal distinctions is particularly painful to the speaker, a poet sensitive to the nuances of language. She declares, "And separating from names / will be as hard for me / as separating from the actual things" (13–15). She knows, however, that she cannot escape the power death holds over language, and so she turns to God and asks Him for the wisdom to know what she can ask of Him on her final day on earth (16–17).

The speaker addresses God here as *yodea ta'alumot* ("Knower of mysteries" [an expression found in Psalms 44:22], 16). God's consciousness transcends the visible world which humans endow with meaning. His transcendent world, to which we go when we die, is one in which the human categories of meaning do not operate. Thus, the poem may suggest that what the speaker needs to learn from God is how to transcend her preoccupation with the loss of categories of meaning at the end of life, for those categories are a humanly created structure of meaning that has little to do with ultimate reality.

CHAPTER TWO

Yehuda Amichai
"Footprints of birds in the sand by the sea."

Y EHUDA AMICHAI (1924–2000) was raised in an Orthodox Zionist Jewish home in the city of Würzburg in the German state of Bavaria.[1] Both his maternal and paternal grandfathers owned farms, and his father was a traveling salesman who marketed buttons, fasteners, and various other sewing accessories. Although Amichai's family was traditionally observant and Zionist, like most pre-Holocaust twentieth-century German Jews, they felt closely connected to German society and culture. A significant indicator of that connection was the fact that Amichai's father served in the German army in World War I. Hitler rose to power the year that Amichai turned nine, and three years later, in 1936, Amichai and his family immigrated to the Land of Israel. After first living in Petach Tikva, which was an agricultural settlement at the time, the family settled in Jerusalem, where Amichai spent the majority of his adult life.

In 1942, Amichai's senior year at the Orthodox Jewish high school he attended was shortened so that he and his fellow students could enlist in the Jewish Brigade of the British armed forces and fight against the German army that was threatening at the time to invade the Land of Israel. The historical irony of Amichai fighting against the country for which his father had so loyally fought in the previous World War was not lost on him, as he wrote in his autobiographical story, "Mitot avi" ("My Father's Deaths"): "It's good that I didn't fight in [World War I], otherwise [my father and I] would have killed each other, because he wore the uniform of Kaiser Wilhelm and I that of King George, but God put between us a space of twenty-five years."[2]

After the war, as a member of the Haganah, he engaged in illegally smuggling weapons to the Jewish forces in the Land of Israel. It was during this period that he first began to write poetry. During the Israeli War of Independence in 1948–1949, he served in the Palmach fighting force of the newly created State of Israel. He later served in the Israeli army in the Sinai Campaign of 1956 and in the Six-Day War of 1967. Following the War of Independence, Amichai pursued an undergraduate course of study in Hebrew literature and biblical studies at the Hebrew University in Jerusalem. For much of his adult life, Amichai earned his living as a teacher. Amichai was married twice; he had one son with his first wife and a son and a daughter with his second wife.

Amichai's poetry was very popular with the Israeli reading public for many decades. His works were widely translated into a variety of languages, and he frequently traveled abroad, becoming over time Israel's best-known poet. Ortsion Bartana's understanding of Amichai's popularity touches on an important aspect of his work and public image. Bartana characterizes Amichai as having been "a likable rebel [mored simpati] who [was] not dangerous and not threatening."[3] He was very compatible with the anti-heroic, ironic mood that developed in Israeli culture in the 1950s and persisted, to varying degrees, in subsequent decades. As Bartana puts it, many Israelis could easily identify with Amichai: "[L]ike us, a Jew, but modern, ironic, Western, knowing alternative concepts, not wanting heroism or sacrifices, but rather the quiet existence of a high school teacher of literature."[4] His appeal, Bartana explains, was as "a revolutionary who knew how, by means of his poetry, to find acceptance by the majority, by those who wanted a revolution and also those who did not at all know that a revolution was taking place."[5] Bartana, however, criticizes Amichai's poetic stance as a "likable rebel," because, from Bartana's point of view, it constituted an abdication of his responsibility as a poet to be a prophetic presence in his society. Nevertheless, by taking a publicly appealing stance, Amichai may have had more influence on Israeli culture than he would have had if he had presented himself as a fiery prophet. It is not, as Bartana argues, that Amichai impoverished the power of poetry, but rather he embraced the anti-heroic celebration of the everyday that was so much needed as an antidote to the highly ideological trends of pre-state Zionism, religious orthodoxy, and forms of Israeli nationalism that have struggled for the hearts and minds of Jews in Israel for so many decades. Well-liked for his unassuming, easy-going manner and respected for the wisdom of his observations on life in his poetry and in public utterances, Amichai was greatly mourned by those who knew him personally and by his readers when he died after a protracted illness at the age of seventy-six.

Most readers of Israeli poetry view Amichai's poetry as fundamentally secular and even anti-religious. One observer of the public reaction to Amichai's death noted that "there were many eulogizers throughout the city who emphasized that Amichai was the bearer of the flag of the secularists."[6] Bartana laments Amichai's role as "the most moderate but also the most consistent representative of the removal from Hebrew poetry of its metaphysical values."[7] Boaz Arpaly argues that Amichai's search for God "taught him that there is no God in this world [and that there] is no point in searching for him, or for any other entity that may possess the qualities attributed to God in the religious tradition."[8]

Shlomo Sadeh presents a more nuanced understanding of Amichai's relationship to secularism and religiosity, arguing that Amichai's poetry must not be read as only conveying an attack on traditional religious beliefs. Sadeh discerns in Amichai's poetry a kind of "secular faith"[9] in "the 'holiness' of modern, secular humanism as a kind of 'new religion.'"[10] Rather than seek religious experience in the realm of the transcendent, argues Sadeh, Amichai's poetry elevates the everyday to the level of a kind of religious experience. "It is precisely the simple, routine, home-based, everyday world that is in the eyes of the speaker-poet the more transcendent world," writes Sadeh, "[a]nd thereby is wondrously concretized the 'holiness' of secular-humanistic existentialism, according to Amichai."[11] While Sadeh gives credence to an ongoing religious impulse in Amichai's poetry, he does not sufficiently appreciate the degree to which Amichai was neither rejecting religious faith nor inventing a new secular religion, but rather continuing to struggle with the God of Israel to whom he had been introduced as a child.

There is much evidence in Amichai's poetry and public persona for this image of the poet as secular agnostic, even atheist, or at best creator of a secular substitute for traditional religion. By the time he was an adult, Amichai had abandoned the traditional Jewish beliefs and practices in which he had been raised. Furthermore, there is little in his poetry that can be taken as an unqualified affirmation of traditional faith. Nevertheless, Amichai's poetry has consistently explored the metaphysical dimension of human experience. As Eliezer Cohen notes, "[T]he question of God troubled Amichai and he often dealt with it in his poetry, from the beginning [of his poetic career] to its end. God is found in Amichai's work more than in that of the other poets of his generation, and in effect more than in the poetry of the newer generations that followed him . . . with the exception perhaps of some of the religious poets of recent times."[12] As Rafi Weichert observes, "From its beginning in the late 1940s and early 1950s, Yehuda Amichai's poetry conducted a constant dialogue with God: speaking to Him, telling about Him, . . . searching for Him, expressing fury at Him."[13] In a certain sense, however, as Weichert notes, what one finds in Amichai's poetry is not really a dialogue with God, because only the human speaker expresses himself: "Amichai's God is mainly a silent God, who hides His face [and] does not answer humanity which seeks Him in despair from the depths of war-weary sadness, at moments of the pain of bereavement, both national and private, in the grayish corridors of the everyday."[14]

Dan Miron notes that, due to his upbringing, Amichai was "saturated with the language of prayer and synagogue" and, in effect, God became "a household member in his poetry."[15] When Miron goes on to say that, despite Amichai's frequent use of religious language, "religious faith was beyond him,"[16] he misses the true significance of the presence of God in Amichai's poetry. An important distinction must be made between poetry that affirms faith and poetry that struggles with God in ways that are actually not foreign to the Jewish tradition. As Admiel Kosman has observed, despite the rebellious attitude toward the Jewish tradition that is so prevalent in his writings, Amichai's poetry can be seen as "a completely legitimate part of the interpretive tradition of past generations."[17]

Amichai's public statements about his relationship to traditional Jewish faith have presumably contributed to the critical debate about whether there is any religious significance to his poetry. Amichai saw himself as very much in the tradition of Jewish textual commentary. "In my poems," he once stated, "I try to recreate and re-interpret. In this sense my writing is genuinely Jewish. In my opinion, Jewish literature consists of the endless interpretations of the source. This is what [the medieval Jewish commentator] Rashi did, and this is what modern Zionism did."[18] Amichai, however, also played down the personal religious significance of references to the Jewish tradition in his poetry, suggesting that they were primarily part of a cultural heritage that he received in childhood that was not relevant to his current identity. "Though I am not religious," he has stated, "it is a marvelous treasure, and I use it."[19] In this interview, he compared his use of traditional Judaism to the way that the Irish writer James Joyce drew on the Catholic tradition against which he had rebelled. "Catholicism was always a presence for [Joyce], so, for me, our classical literature, the Bible, the rabbinic writings, the prayers, are always a presence for me. Like Joyce I did my own thing, but I used my religious background as he used his religious background."[20]

When Amichai said in this English-language interview that he was not "religious," he presumably had in mind the Hebrew term *dati*, which in the Israeli cultural context signifies being traditionally observant. Thus, his statement that he was not "religious" did not preclude his preoccupation with issues of religious faith. Indeed, in another interview, we can see that the Jewish religious tradition was, for Amichai, more than just material on which to draw. While, as he declared to the interviewer, he no longer practiced Judaism, the basic religious belief in a transcendent dimension of meaning was still very much a part of his worldview. "To believe in some greater power—," he asserted, "everyone believes in it. But we don't believe that we can understand everything. Nothing is purposeless. There must be some reason for everything, which we don't understand."[21] Here Amichai indicated that, despite his abandonment of traditional Jewish practice and his dissent from theological explanations of existence put forth by the Jewish tradition, he could not help but share with those of religious faith the assumption that there is a hidden dimension of meaning beyond what is immediately evident to humanity. His rebellion against the Jewish tradition did not lead him to a nihilistic atheism, but rather to a continuing search for a way to replace the religious certainty of his childhood that there is a purpose to life.

The degree to which Amichai continued to link himself with traditional religious concerns is suggested in a published passage from his diary reflecting on the celebration of Israel Independence Day:

> Independence Day, with some old friends we decided to have a picnic . . . .
> It was hot; we ate and drank. I must admit that every year I feel a growing
> depression on this holiday. Perhaps because my generation is the generation
> of independence. Then we were young and with the maturing and growing
> state [Israel] we are growing old. In effect I transfer qualities of Yom Kippur
> and Rosh Hashanah to Independence Day: soul searching (heshbon nefesh)
> and guilt feelings. I did not participate in the creation of Rosh Hashanah al-
> most three thousand years ago, but I did take part in Independence Day; I
> helped to create it. So, the birthday of the state is also my birthday. It is a day
> of reckoning (heshbon) and a day of comparison and a day of weighing and
> a day of judgment, in a personal and in a general sense.[22]

The picnic on Independence Day is the quintessential secular ritual of the Israeli civil religion. Yet note the degree to which Amichai felt compelled to turn it into a contemporary form of the Days of Awe, permeated by an atmosphere of self-examination. It is true that he did not mention God in this passage, but he clearly expressed the need to measure himself and his society by some sort of transcendent standard that resembled the expectations of the God of judgment on Rosh Hashanah and Yom Kippur.

What is most striking about Amichai's religious poetry is his playful, often ironic use of the language of classical Jewish texts, especially the Bible and the traditional Jewish prayer book. As Arpaly puts it, "Amichai does not dispose of words and concepts that are part of the linguistic and cultural inheritance; on the contrary, he uses them and exploits them, he even makes use of them to organize in a dialectical manner his poetic world, and that way he positions himself in relationship to the tradition and in relationship to the previous generations (a position that in certain respects is rather revolutionary)."[23] Barukh Kurzweil observes that "[p]recisely the relationship and positive affinity to [his] childhood, [to his] parents' home, led [Amichai] to a natural dependence on metaphors, on images whose origin is in the *siddur* [prayer book], the *mahzor* [holiday prayer book], and the Bible."[24] As Amichai began to lose the childhood certainties of religious faith, he was driven to establish a different relationship with the language of liturgy than he had had when he was young. "[T]he collapse of a secure and protected world," writes Kurzweil, "forced on the poet the need to reconsider the accepted expressions that characterized the elements of reality."[25] This reconsideration was conveyed in Amichai's early poetry by means of irony, which, Kurzweil observes, "allowed the preservation of the linguistic inheritance by means of a change in its status and significance."[26] In consonance with Amichai's comparison of his relationship to religious tradition with that of James Joyce, Kurzweil relates Amichai's poetry to a central dimension of modern literature, which he refers to as "the unceasing struggle with the whole cultural, artistic, and linguistic inheritance."[27] In effect, argues Kurzweil, "[t]rue modern poetry from its beginnings, from the German Romantics, from Baudelaire [and] Rambeau until Eliot and Brecht, is notable for its surprising expertise in the sources, in the poetic inheritance, against which it rebels in order to reconquer it, in order to bring it to a new integration into the new reality."[28]

Amichai's approach of playful irony allows him to maintain a relationship with the language of traditional Jewish faith even as he critiques its inadequacy as the basis for a contemporary worldview. "The imputation of blasphemy in [Amichai's] poetry . . . ," writes Glenda Abramson, "is avoided only by its penetrating irony, which serves to alter the implication of the biblical or liturgical texts while still acknowledging their essential presence in Jewish thought. By building secular structures on sacred foundations Amichai does not reject the original but debates with it and scrutinizes it with the logic born of twentieth-century experience."[29]

The interconnection of the sublime and the mundane often functions in Amichai's poetry on the level of language. Amichai excels in the ability to blend the high style of classical Hebrew found in the Bible and in post-biblical classical Jewish literature with the lower style of contemporary Hebrew speech. Amichai attributed this ability to the way he learned Hebrew as a child in Germany. "My first contact with the Hebrew language was . . . with 'the language of God,' when I was three years old,"[30] he has recounted. "Since our household was Zionist, we also learned the songs of the ḥalutsim [Zionist pioneers] of that period . . . . I have a dual relationship to the language, which is both a holy language and a spoken language."[31]

In his poetry, Amichai seeks to come to terms with the metaphorical expressions and mythic narratives that the Jewish tradition has developed to articulate the relationship between humanity and God. He adapts metaphors and myths, sometimes turning them on their heads, and thereby invents new forms of verbal expression more in keeping with his understanding of the nature of the divine. In some of Amichai's poems, biblical stories undergo changes that undermine their lessons of faith and intensify the tension between the promises of God's providence and the realities of human suffering. In "And For This You Merit Praise," the speaker reverses the Garden of Eden story. It is not God who calls to Adam hiding in shame after committing the first sin, but the opposite: "But this time God hides and man cries, 'Where are You?'" In "I Am the Last of Them," the speaker is a Job figure who pleads with God not to bet against

Satan, because in contemporary experience the speaker cannot discern a clear victory for either God or Satan ("You've won / and he too has won").

Some poems assume characteristics of actual traditional Jewish prayers, only to undermine by means of parody the religious faith expressed in those prayers. The title and opening line of one poem, for example, are composed of the beginning of the traditional Jewish memorial prayer, "God Full of Mercy," but then the poem proceeds to critique God for being so full of mercy and not sharing that mercy with the world ("if God were not so full of mercy / there'd be mercy in the world, not just in Him"). The title of the poem "And For This You Merit Praise" is taken from the refrain of a liturgical poem (*piyyut*) recited on Yom Kippur, and the poem is even subtitled "From a *Piyyut* for the Days of Awe." This is a rather heretical *piyyut*, however, which ironically praises God for hiding from humanity.

Arpaly notes that Amichai's references to God are a means to express at times the human sense of the limitations of existence and at other times the human hope to overcome those limitations. These concerns are, in effect, essential elements of all religious quests, and, thus, for all intents and purposes, God is a reality with which Amichai struggles in much of his poetry.

In Amichai's poetry, Arpaly observes, God can serve as "a term for the fundamental facts of the world, for 'eternal' forces like time, the cycle of the year, and death, and for (arbitrary) 'laws' that cause him to act. These facts set the fate of the individual and define the limits of his existence, but from his point of view they are without meaning, arbitrary, destructive, and in the best case, irrelevant to his hopes and aspirations."[32] God in such poems is indifferent and, as Glenda Abramson writes, "capricious and often cruel,"[33] unable or unwilling to intervene in human affairs. While in some of Amichai's poems one can discern a rebellious anger against this cruel God, in other poems one can discern what Abramson calls a "tone of resignation [that] implicitly recognize[s] God's position of eternal authority, [the speaker's] rebellion [having] changed to submission . . . ."[34] At times, this submission is accompanied by the speaker "entreat[ing] God to give not only him but the world a rest . . ."[35] In "God Full of Mercy," the speaker's suffering forces him to declare that he "can say for sure the world's empty of mercy." In "God's Hand in the World," God's relationship to the world is compared to the image of the speaker's mother cleaning a chicken while she absentmindedly gazes out of the kitchen window. In "And For This You Merit Praise," God relates to the world like a garage mechanic constantly fixing a car that tends to break down, while His relationship to humanity is one of obliviousness ("God lies on His back under the world, / always busy fixing, something's always breaking. / I wanted to see Him whole, but I see / only the soles of His shoes and I cry"). In "After Auschwitz there's no theology . . . ," God's silence during and after the Holocaust is conveyed by the speaker's statement, "The numbers on the arms of the prisoners of destruction / are the phone numbers of God / numbers never answered / and now they are disconnected, one by one." The years of pain unallevi-ated by God lead the speaker in "I Am the Last of Them" to declare, "Leave me alone, God, I am tired now." In "Our Father our King . . . ," the speaker expresses the alienation between God and humanity with the disturbing notions that human beings are God's "orphans" and that God is like a father "whose children died."

"The concept of God and related concepts," writes Arpaly, "serve in Amichai's poetry . . . as the embodiment of human . . . aspirations, hopes, meaning . . . that have been invested in [these concepts] for generations, and as such they serve as symbols for phenomena that still exist today in the world of the individ-ual."[36] Yet, for Amichai, God is more than just a symbol for the elements of human existence that provide hope. In his poetry, Amichai concludes that people's longing for hope and meaning indicates that there is some fundamen-tal human need that drove traditional believers to seek a relationship with God, and that need must be met today, even if its expression must assume new forms. As is suggested by the title of his poem cycle "Gods Change, Prayers Remain Forever," an underlying assumption of Amichai's poetry is that we will always need a God to turn to in longing. In "God's Fate," the speaker suggests that the modern skepticism about God resembles the period when people turned from worshipping nature to worshipping a transcendent God, and so, just as nature did not leave humanity when that transition took place, God will not leave us ("But He must stay with us: / at least like the trees, at least like the stones / and like the sun and the moon and the stars"). In "Footprints of birds in the sand by the sea . . . ," God's presence in the world can be discerned by His effect on the world, just as we know that footprints in the sand during the day indicate that birds walked on the sand the previous night. In "Our Father our King . . . ," the speaker writes of "[l]ongings for God / and for a better world," and in "God is steps that ascend . . . ," God is declared to be steps on a ladder that represent both "faith" and "disappointment."

In some poems, Amichai makes use of traditional liturgical phrases in order to reconnect with religious experience in an authentic contemporary manner. One poem, "My Father, My King," an adaptation of the penitential liturgical expression "our Father our King" is, in effect, a prayer to God that reflects the mid-twentieth century concerns of a secularized man. Another poem adapts the formulaic expression in Maimonides' principles of faith, "I believe with per-fect faith." The contemporary faith statement that follows is the notion that "prayers preceded God." Far from being blatantly blasphemous, the poem ex-presses an attempt to understand the human drive to pray as the genesis of reli-gious experience.

Many readers of Amichai's poetry have noted the associations the poet makes between his experience of God's distance and the absence from his life of his father, who died of a heart attack at a relatively young age. In Amichai's poetry, observes Abramson, the speaker's relationship to God is very much intertwined with his relationship to his father, "a tender, loving, devoted, and pious man"[37] toward whom the speaker feels guilty for having rebelled against the Jewish tradition. "It is difficult to separate Amichai's images of God and the father," writes Abramson, "since their function . . . is so similar. This function seems to radiate from the focal point of all of Amichai's verse, which is the father's death and the consequent assumption of having murdered him by rejecting his world, committing the dual sin of patricide and deicide."[38] Evidence for this association between God and his father may be found in the poem "My Father, My King." In this poem, the speaker turns to God as a child asking his father to make everything right in the world: "My Father, my King, make it so that whatever happens to me / between desire and sadness / will not afflict me." In "Even private prayer needs two . . . ," the speaker's father actually becomes godlike, with a spiritual strength that forces God to pray to him. In "Our Father our King . . . ," the speaker identifies less as a son and more as a father who can understand God's frustration at being unable to fully protect His people: "What does a father do / whose children died and he'll be bereaved unto eternity?"

One can find many images of dichotomies in these poems: silence–crying and water–fire in "And For This You Merit Praise"; faith–disappointment in "God is steps that ascend . . ."; love–hatred, laughter–crying, and desire–sadness in "My Father, My King"; and forgetfulness–memory in "Our Father our King. . . ." In many poems, a central issue is the suffering of the individual who feels pulled in these opposite directions. It is typical that the pain of human existence is captured in very personal images, in what Chana Kronfeld refers to as a "rhetoric of autobiography . . . [that] suggest[s] the poems are nothing but the attempts of one ordinary man to come to terms with his experiences."[39] Often, the images mix the grandiose and heroic with the mundane through the autobiographical narrative that points to fundamental existential struggles of human existence. "I've been in Jerusalem and in Rome. Perhaps I'll be in Mecca," declares the speaker in "And For This You Merit Praise." In one sense, this is a simple statement of the history of a typical Israeli, who is able to visit Jerusalem and Rome, but not Mecca, from which Jews and other non-Muslims are barred. Yet, in a more symbolic sense, this is a statement of how modern Jews find themselves moving back and forth between the Jewish and Christian civilizations, while, for political reasons, they are still cut off from the Arab and Muslim worlds. Later in the same poem, the speaker mixes modern realities with images of the grandiose battles of medieval warriors as he turns to his lover and declares, "Remove from me the armor of my yellowing undershirt, / I've fought all the knights till the electricity went out." In two poems, suffering is presented ironically as a kind of profession, simultaneously raising its significance and undermining the position of a person so experienced in calamity. In "God Full of Mercy," the speaker says that his "heart lifted weights of pain / in the awful competitions." The speaker in "My Father, My King" declares, "The years have turned me into a taster of pain. / Like a wine taster I can distinguish / between different kinds of silence." In "God's Hand in the World," rather than refer to suffering as a profession, the speaker relates to it as if it were a family inheritance passed on from generation to generation: "My pain is already a grandfather: / It gave birth to two generations / of pain like it."

Amichai's poetry on religious themes emphasizes the unheroic nature of human existence in his time. In "And For This You Merit Praise," the speaker seems to completely give up on the value of heroism when he declares, "Perhaps like an ancient statue without arms / our lives too are more beautiful without heroic deeds." It is the frustration from the pain of self-division and the inability to have a major impact on the world that drive the speakers in Amichai's poems to despair and to a longing for the help of God in restoring people to wholeness, as the speaker in "My Father, My King" declares: "My Father, my King, make it so my face is not torn apart / by laughter or crying."

As one surveys Amichai's poetry, it is clear that he continued to wrestle with the nature of religious experience throughout his life. God never died for Amichai, even if the poet's commitment to traditional Jewish practice did. His engagement with God, or whatever God represented to humans in the past, was always very real, even as it was very problematic. In poems from the cycle "Gods Change, Prayers Remain Forever" included in this chapter, the speaker attempts to reconnect with the prayer experiences of his youth. As he recalls his father's private prayer, public prayers for peace, and the traditional morning introductory psalms known as "Pesuqei dezimra," the urge to pray is taken very seriously, even if the results of prayer are questionable. In one poem, God has to pray to humanity; in another poem, those who pray cannot decide whether shouting for peace or praying quietly for peace will sway God; in yet another poem, the introductory psalms might affirm the existence of God or of pagan gods. Amichai pushes the language of tradition nearly to the breaking point. In so doing, however, he makes an important contribution to the spiritual growth of his readers by undermining the worn-out expressions of classical Jewish literature and, thereby, facilitating his readers' engagement in a more honest confrontation with the transcendent dimension of existence.

Amichai wrote poetry about God throughout the greater part of his career, from his early collection *Bemerḥaq shetei tiqvot* (At a Distance of Two Hopes, 1958) to the last collection published in his lifetime, *Patuaḥ sagur patuaḥ* (Open Closed Open, 1998). It is interesting to note, however, that the highest percentage of poetry about God appears in the final collection. In commenting on this fact, Weichert writes, "It would appear that the poet felt, even before the revelation of his [fatal] illness, that he was standing before the conclusion of his life and literary work, and that it was incumbent upon him to summarize his relationship with divinity."[40] A careful reading of Amichai's poetry reveals that, for

the most part, his wrestling with God did not have defined periods of develop-
ment. There is a higher concentration of poems that ironically critique God's
lack of intervention to relieve human suffering in his earlier poems of the 1950s,
yet he does return to that critique in the 1990s. Although he focuses more on
religious themes in the 1998 collection than in any other collection, this is, in
actuality, an intensification of an obsession that preoccupied him throughout
his poetic career. In considering the facets of Amichai's relationship to the di-
vine in the poetry he published over a period of forty years, one can discern three
categories: 1) poems that explore the nature of divine–human relations in the
context of human suffering; 2) poems that explore the underlying experiences
that religious tradition has called the divine–human encounter; and 3) poems
that take the form of a prayer or explore the nature of the prayer experience.[41]

God and Human Suffering

יַד אֱלֹהִים בָּעוֹלָם

[א]
יַד אֱלֹהִים בָּעוֹלָם
כְּיַד אִמִּי בִּמְעֵי הַתַּרְנְגוֹל הַשָּׁחוּט
בְּעֶרֶב שַׁבָּת.
מָה רוֹאָה אֱלֹהִים מֵעֵבֶר לַחַלּוֹן
בְּעֵת יָדָיו נְתוּנוֹת בָּעוֹלָם?   5
מָה רוֹאָה אִמִּי?

[ב]
כְּאֵבִי כְּבָר סָב:
יָלַד שְׁנֵי דּוֹרוֹת
שֶׁל כְּאֵבִים הַדּוֹמִים לוֹ.
תִּקְוֹוֹתַי הֵקִימוּ שְׁכוּנִים לְבָנִים   10
הַרְחֵק מִן הַדֹּחַק שֶׁבִּי.
נַעֲרָתִי שֶׁכְחָה אֶת אַהֲבָתָהּ עַל הַמִּדְרָכָה
כְּמוֹ אוֹפַנַּיִם. כָּל הַלַּיְלָה בַּחוּץ וּבָטֵל.

יְלָדִים רוֹשְׁמִים אֶת תּוֹלְדוֹת חַיַּי
וְאֶת תּוֹלְדוֹת יְרוּשָׁלַיִם   15
בְּגִיר יָרֵחַ עַל הַכְּבִישׁ.
יַד אֱלֹהִים בָּעוֹלָם.

God's Hand in the World

[A]
God's hand in the world
like my mother's hand in the guts of a slaughtered chicken
on Sabbath's eve.
What does God see through the window
5   while His hands are placed in the world?
What does my mother see?

[B]
My pain is already a grandfather:
It gave birth to two generations
of pain like it.
10   My hopes have erected white neighborhoods
far from the stress within me.
My girl forgot her love on the sidewalk
like a bicycle. All night outside and in the dew.

Children record the history of my life
15   and the history of Jerusalem
in moon-like chalk on the road.
God's hand in the world.[42]

This work appears to be two poems with very distinct features. In the first poem, the speaker plays with a comparison between God and his mother preparing a chicken for the Friday evening Sabbath meal. In the second poem, the speaker explores images of pain, loss, and hope. Structurally, the poems are united by the fact that the first line of poem A and the last line of poem B are identical with the title, "God's Hand in the World." The repetition of this line emphasizes the centrality of the speaker's desire to understand the nature of God's involvement in the world of human experience.

The comparison between God and the mother (1–6) suggests a number of facets of God's relationship to the world. This is a reassuring image recalled from childhood: God relates to us like a Jewish mother in her traditional role of taking care of her family by preparing the Sabbath meal. There is, however, a disturbing dimension to this image. The speaker refers to the chicken as "slaughtered" (*shahut*, 2). Although on one level this is literally true—a kosher chicken would have undergone ritual slaughter (*shehitah*)—the reference to this obvious fact is jarring. If the chicken represents the world and the mother represents God, the fact that the chicken has been slaughtered by another figure, the ritual slaughterer (*shohet*), suggests that the world is subject to forces of violence out of divine control. Furthermore, the analogy suggests that God perhaps condones the existence and effects of these independent forces of violence, just as the mother accepts the killing of the chicken by the ritual slaughterer that allows her to serve it to her family. All God can do is clean up the world's mess, just as the mother cleans out the guts of the chicken. Another concern is raised by the image in lines 4–6 of God resembling a mother absentmindedly gazing out of the window as she cleans the chicken, which suggests that God does not always pay full attention to the world He is supposed to rule. Like the mother's well-rehearsed weekly act of preparing the chicken, God's involvement in the world has become routinized and not particularly caring. After all, how emotionally involved is the mother in the chicken she is cleaning? The use of the expression "His hands are placed [*netunot*]" in line 5 conveys the notion of a passive divinity who is merely present and not driven to actively interact with the world.

The first stanza of the second poem (7–13) explores the speaker's pain and hopes. His pain has persisted for so long in his life that it feels as if it has lasted for three full generations. Like the unfolding of generations in a family, pain has become a kind of natural process in which the fact that one has undergone distressing experiences in the past makes it difficult to experience life subsequently as free of pain. The speaker's hopes, in contrast, are envisioned by the poet as white *shikkunim* (10). This term, translated here as "neighborhoods," may be more literally understood as "dwelling places" or "housing projects." During the 1950s, when the poem was written, many brand new projects consisting of apartment buildings arranged into neighborhoods sprang up throughout Israel. The *shikkunim* provided a significant rise in the standard of living for recent immigrants to Israel, who had been housed in shacks and tents in transit camps (*ma'abarot*) upon their arrival in the late 1940s and 1950s.[43] In addition, for many young Israelis, an apartment in these *shikkunim* was their first home in which they began to build a family. The hope for a better life that the *shikkunim* represent, however, is still felt by the speaker to be too remote to assuage his anxiety ("My hopes have erected white neighborhoods / far from the stress within me," 10–11).

The poem then makes use of images related to childhood: forgetting a bicycle outside and writing in chalk on pavement (12–16). The girlfriend falling out of love with the speaker comes across as careless and wasteful: she was as wrong to forget her love for him as a child would be if she left her bicycle outside at the mercy of the elements. The children's chalk writing is also not very stable or reliable: it is easily erased. Nevertheless, the image of children is much more hopeful than the previous images of a mother cleaning a chicken or pain likened to a grandfather. When the speaker declares, "Children record the history of my life / and the history of Jerusalem / in moon-like chalk on the road" (14–16), he conveys the sense that they are in closer contact with the true significance of life than are the adults. In contrast to the absent-minded image of "God's hand in the world" at the beginning of the poem, represented by the mother contained within her house gazing out the window while she mechanically cleans a chicken, the image of "God's hand in the world" is associated at the end of the poem with the more engaging and empowering image of children playfully expressing themselves in the open air.

אֵל מָלֵא רַחֲמִים

אֵל מָלֵא רַחֲמִים,
אִלְמָלֵא הָאֵל מָלֵא רַחֲמִים
הָיוּ הָרַחֲמִים בָּעוֹלָם וְלֹא רַק בּוֹ.
אֲנִי, שֶׁקָּטַפְתִּי פְּרָחִים בָּהָר
וְהִסְתַּכַּלְתִּי אֶל כָּל הָעֲמָקִים,   5
אֲנִי, שֶׁהֵבֵאתִי גְּוִיּוֹת מִן הַגְּבָעוֹת,
יוֹדֵעַ לְסַפֵּר שֶׁהָעוֹלָם רֵיק מֵרַחֲמִים.

אֲנִי שֶׁהָיִיתִי מֶלֶךְ הַמֶּלַח לְיַד הַיָּם,
שֶׁעָמַדְתִּי בְּלִי הַחְלָטָה לְיַד חַלּוֹנִי,
שֶׁסָּפַרְתִּי צַעֲדֵי מַלְאָכִים,   10
שֶׁלִּבִּי הֵרִים מִשְׁקָלוֹת כְּאֵב
בַּתַּחֲרֻיּוֹת הַנּוֹרָאוֹת.
אֲנִי, שֶׁמִּשְׁתַּמֵּשׁ רַק בְּחֵלֶק קָטָן
מִן הַמִּלִּים שֶׁבַּמִּלּוֹן.

אֲנִי שֶׁמֻּכְרָח לִפְתּוֹר חִידוֹת בְּעַל כָּרְחִי   15
יוֹדֵעַ כִּי אִלְמָלֵא הָאֵל מָלֵא רַחֲמִים
הָיוּ הָרַחֲמִים בָּעוֹלָם
וְלֹא רַק בּוֹ.

GOD FULL OF MERCY

God full of mercy,
if God were not so full of mercy
there'd be mercy in the world, not just in Him.
I, who picked flowers on mountains
5 and observed all the valleys,
I, who brought corpses from the hills,
can say for sure the world is empty of mercy.

I, who was king of salt by the sea,
who stood undecided by my window,

10   who counted steps of angels,
        whose heart lifted weights of pain
        in the awful competitions.
        I, who use just a small portion
        of words in the dictionary.

15   I, who must solve riddles against my will,
        know that if God were not so full of mercy
        there'd be mercy in the world,
        not just in Him.[44]

The speaker in this poem is struck by the contradiction between the traditional Jewish image of a merciful God and the prevalence of human suffering. The position of traditional Jewish faith is presented in the opening words "God full of mercy" (*El malei rahamim*) of the memorial prayer recited at funerals, on designated Jewish holidays, and on the anniversary of a death. The death of a loved one is perhaps the greatest challenge to faith in God's mercy, for after such a death one may feel completely abandoned by a God who did not intervene to preserve that life. By means of this memorial prayer, the traditional liturgy inspires Jews to renew their faith in the mercy of God, despite the emotional upheaval caused by death, and it provides a way to verbalize an appeal to God to grant eternally peaceful rest to the soul of the departed.

For the speaker, however, the truth of the traditional liturgical expression is contradicted by what actually happens in the world. He refers in the poem to very personal sets of experiences, each of which begins with the formulation "I, who" (4, 6, 8, 13, 15) as he challenges the belief that God grants mercy to the world of the living and to world of the dead.[45] The joys of picking flowers on a mountain (4) are overwhelmed by the contrasting image of bringing the corpses of dead soldiers from the hills (6). Therefore, the meaning of the phrase "God full of mercy" must be transformed, the speaker suggests, from the notion that the merciful God will share His mercy with us to the notion that God keeps all the mercy to Himself and shares none of it with the world He has created. The irreverent nature of this ironic challenge to God's way of relating to the world is reinforced by a play on words in lines 1 and 2: the consonants of the two-word expression *El malei* ("God full of") that appear at the beginning of the first line reappear at the beginning of the second line as a one-word expression, *ilmalei* ("were not"), thereby reducing a name of God (*El*, which has the same consonants as *il*) to a mere prefix.

As we see in other poems by Amichai, God's lack of involvement in the world goes hand in hand with the ineffective and painful existence of modern humanity. It is significant that, already in the first stanza, the war imagery is not that of active battle, but of the tragic aftermath of gathering the casualties of war; the glory often associated with war is overwhelmed here by the price in human life that is exacted in battle. In the second stanza, the speaker presents himself as a kind of typical Israeli who must face the fact that he lives an unheroic, perhaps one might say anti-heroic, life. Thus, his inability to improve the world exacerbates the effects of the absence of God's mercy. The speaker is not a king in the fully royal sense of the word, but merely "the king of salt by the sea" (8), a beach bum whose only accomplishment is to become saturated by salt as a result of bathing in the ocean. The ridiculous nature of this supposedly "royal" status is further suggested by the play on words between the Hebrew word for king (*melekh*) and the similarly sounding Hebrew word for salt (*melaḥ*). The speaker is incapable of action and stands "undecided by [his] window" (9). He cannot have completely realized religious visions and is only capable of counting the "steps of angels" (10). Rather than display the physical prowess of a true body builder, in his heart he lifts "weights of pain" (11). He does not even write in a high literary style, choosing instead an everyday style that makes use of "just a small portion / of words in the dictionary" (13–14).

As unheroic as his life is, the speaker cannot escape the need to solve the riddles of human existence (15). The greatest riddle is why God, whom tradition characterizes as merciful, allows so much suffering to exist in the world, and the answer to it is the ironic realization that God really has kept all the mercy to Himself (16–18). When the speaker concludes the poem by returning to the word play of lines 1 and 2 (*El malei* and *ilmalei*), he expresses an even more penetrating critique of God than he presented at the beginning of the poem by dividing the words that originally appeared in line 3 into two lines: "there'd be mercy in the world, / not just in Him" (17–18). By presenting the expression "not just in Him" as a separate line which concludes the poem, the speaker puts greater emphasis on his realization of how selfish God is to keep all the mercy to Himself. It should be noted that, despite the biting criticism of God he expresses, the speaker stops short of declaring God to possess an essentially cruel nature. One can discern in the repeated reference to God as "God full of mercy" a persistent hope that divine mercy may yet be granted to us.

וְהִיא תְּהִלָּתֶךָ

מתוך פיוט לימים הנוראים

בִּשְׁתִיקָתִי הַגְּדוֹלָה וּבְצַעֲקָתִי הַקְּטַנָּה אֲנִי חוֹרֵשׁ
כְּלָאַיִם. הָיִיתִי בַּמַּיִם וְהָיִיתִי בָּאֵשׁ.
הָיִיתִי בִּירוּשָׁלַיִם וּבְרוֹמָא. אוּלַי אֶהְיֶה בְּמֶכָּה.
אַךְ הַפַּעַם אֱלֹהִים מִתְחַבֵּא וְאָדָם צוֹעֵק אַיֶּכָּה.
וְהִיא תְּהִלָּתֶךָ.   5

אֱלֹהִים שׁוֹכֵב עַל גַּבּוֹ מִתַּחַת לַתֵּבֵל,
תָּמִיד עָסוּק בְּתִקּוּן, תָּמִיד מַשֶּׁהוּ מִתְקַלְקֵל.
רָצִיתִי לִרְאוֹתוֹ כֻּלּוֹ, אַךְ אֲנִי רוֹאֶה
רַק אֶת סֻלְיוֹת נַעֲלָיו וַאֲנִי בּוֹכֶה.
וְהִיא תְּהִלָּתוֹ.   10

אֲפִלּוּ הָעֵצִים הָלְכוּ לִבְחֹר לָהֶם מֶלֶךְ.
אֶלֶף פְּעָמִים הִתְחַלְתִּי אֶת חַיַּי מִכָּאן וָאֵילֵךְ.
בִּקְצֵה הָרְחוֹב עוֹמֵד אֶחָד וּמוֹנֶה:
אֶת זֶה וְאֶת זֶה וְאֶת זֶה וְאֶת זֶה.
וְהִיא תְּהִלָּתֶךָ.   15

אוּלַי כְּמוֹ פֶּסֶל עַתִּיק שֶׁאֵין בּוֹ זְרוֹעוֹת
גַּם חַיֵּינוּ יָפִים יוֹתֵר, בְּלִי מַעֲשִׂים וּגְבוּרוֹת.
פִּרְקִי מִמֶּנִּי אֶת שִׁרְיוֹן גּוּפִיָּתִי הַמַּצְהִיבָה,
נִלְחַמְתִּי בְּכָל הָאַבִּירִים, עַד הַחַשְׁמַל כָּבָה.
וְהִיא תְּהִלָּתִי.   20

תָּנוּחַ דַּעְתֶּךָ, דַּעְתֶּךָ רָצָה עִמִּי בְּכָל הַדֶּרֶךְ,
וְעַכְשָׁו הִיא עֲיֵפָה וְאֵין בָּהּ עוֹד עֵרֶךְ,
אֲנִי רוֹאֶה אוֹתָךְ מוֹצִיאָה דָבָר מִן הַמְּקֻרָר,
מוּאֶרֶת מִתּוֹכוֹ בְּאוֹר שֶׁמֵּעוֹלָם אַחֵר.
וְהִיא תְּהִלָּתִי   25
וְהִיא תְּהִלָּתוֹ
וְהִיא תְּהִלָּתֶךָ.

And For This You Merit Praise

From a Piyyut for the Days of Awe
In my great silence and in my meager cry I plough
mixed seeds. I've been in water and I've been in fire.
I've been in Jerusalem and in Rome. Perhaps I'll be in Mecca.
But this time God hides and man cries, "Where are You?"
5   And for this You merit praise.

God lies on His back under the world,
always busy fixing, something's always breaking.
I wanted to see Him whole, but I see
only the soles of His shoes and I cry.
10   And for this He merits praise.

Even the trees went to choose themselves a king.
A thousand times I began my life from here on.
At the side of the road someone stands and counts:
This one and this one and this one and this one.
15   And for this You merit praise.

Perhaps like an ancient statue without arms
our lives too are more beautiful without heroic deeds.
Remove from me the armor of my yellowing undershirt,*
I've fought all the knights till the electricity went out.
20   And for this I merit praise.

Rest your mind, your mind runs with me all the way,*
and now it's tired and has no more worth,
I see you taking something from the refrigerator,*
lit from within by light from another world.
25   And for this I merit praise
        And for this He merits praise
        And for this You merit praise.[46]

*The second person address is in the feminine singular form in these lines.

   The subtitle of this poem declares that it is a selection from a liturgical poem
(*piyyut*) for the Days of Awe. While it is obviously not an authentic *piyyut*,
much of the meaning of the poem derives from the tension between its world-
view and that of traditional *piyyutim*. Glenda Abramson identifies the likely in-
tertext for this poem as a liturgical poem for the "Musaf" service of Yom Kippur
with the refrain *vehi tehillatekha* ("and for this You merit praise").[47] Other ref-
erences to the liturgy of the Days of Awe appear in several images: (a) "water"
(*mayim*, 2) and "fire" (*esh*, 2), alluding to the "Unetanneh toqef" prayer of

"Musaf" on Rosh Hashanah and on Yom Kippur,[48] which speaks of "who [shall die] by fire and who by water" (*mi ba'esh umi bamayim*); (b) "counts" (*moneh*, 13), alluding to the image of God in the "Unetaneh toqef" prayer as counting each person on the day of judgment (*vesofer umoneh*); (c) "fixing" (*betiqqun*, 7), alluding to the expression *letaqqen olam bemalkhut Shaddai* (to restore the world to the kingdom of the Almighty) in the "Aleinu" prayer of "Musaf" on Rosh Hashanah; (d) "king" (*melekh*, 11), a central metaphor of God in the liturgy for the Days of Awe; and (e) the expression "without heroic deeds" (*beli ma'asim ugevurot*, 17), which echoes the plea to God to have mercy on us "because we have no deeds" (*ki ein banu ma'asim*) that would justify ourselves to Him, a plea found in the "Avinu malkenu" prayer of the Days of Awe.

The expressions of faith from the liturgy for the Days of Awe are undermined as the speaker portrays his experience of internal division and distance from God. The first stanza is replete with the dichotomies between which the speaker is caught: line 1 presents silence versus crying; line 2 presents the different species of seeds (*kilayim*)—which, according to the Torah, it is forbidden to plant together (Leviticus 19:19; Deuteronomy 22:9)—as well as water versus fire; and line 3 presents Jerusalem (symbolizing Judaism) versus Rome (symbolizing Christianity) and Jerusalem versus Mecca (symbolizing Islam). These dichotomies do not mix; they cannot be integrated. The sense of division is connected in line 4 with a reversal of the biblical image of God calling, "Where are you?" (*ayyekah*) to Adam, who is hiding after committing the sin of eating the forbidden fruit (Genesis 3:9), to that of God hiding and people trying to find Him.

In the next stanza, the speaker envisions God as a garage mechanic trying to fix the world, which sadly resembles an old, worn-out automobile that keeps breaking down (6–7). This association of God with elements of modern technology is significant, especially in connection with the reference to electricity in line 19.[49] Both passages suggest a close connection between human alienation from God and technological developments that create the illusion of human mastery over the world. In effect, the poet is forced to realize that neither God's supposed supernatural power nor humanity's technological marvels are effective means to transform the world into a better place. In the use of the word *tiqqun* to indicate the work of this divine garage mechanic, we find a prime example of how Amichai exploits the close relationship between sacred and mundane language in Hebrew. In the context of Hebrew as a sacred language, the Hebrew word *tiqqun* means the restoration of the world to the kingdom of God; in the context of contemporary mundane Hebrew, it is used simply to signify fixing things that are broken, such as a car or plumbing.

The contrast between the sacred dimension of the past and the mundane limitations of the present is also captured in an allusion to Moses' request of God that He reveal His *kavod* ("glory" or "presence") to him and God's response that He would only show Moses His back (Exodus 33:18–23). In a parodic replay of this

divine revelation in the Bible, the speaker can only see the soles of the shoes of
the mechanic who represents God (8–9).[50] The image of God's partial revelation
to Moses in Exodus is reduced further when the response of the speaker (here
playing the role of Moses) is merely to cry because he cannot see more of God.

As in "God Full of Mercy," in this poem, the critique of God's limitations is
coupled with a sense of the decline of humanity's ability to take charge of life
and accomplish great deeds. In the third stanza, the speaker recalls Jotham's
parable (Judges 9:7–21) in which the trees set out to choose a king (11). Yet, in
contrast, people cannot set any definite directions for their lives: the speaker
keeps undertaking new ways to live his life (12), and someone keeps counting
endlessly without the ability to establish a clear set of priorities (13–14).

In the final two stanzas, the speaker appears to celebrate, or at least to make
his peace with, the decline of humanity from decisive heroism and meaning to
a more mundane, anti-heroic world. The image of the ancient statue without
arms (16–17) represents the rejection of the aspiration to undertake great deeds,
while the images of the yellowing undershirt which serves as the speaker's armor
as he fights "till the electricity [goes] out" (18–19) and of the refrigerator light
(23–24) completely undermine any illusions of glory that the speaker might
hold. The use of the expression "light from another world" (*or sheme'olam aḥer*,
24) to refer to the electric light in the refrigerator constitutes an ironic under-
mining of the image of divine light found in the Jewish tradition, particularly in
kabbalistic sources.[51]

In the last two stanzas, the speaker, disappointed in God and trying to come
to terms with the limitations of humanity, turns for comfort to the intimacy of
a relationship with a woman, whose "mind runs with [him] all the way" (21) and
who takes "something from the refrigerator" (23), presumably food to provide
them with physical nourishment. Together the speaker and the woman can per-
haps find some relief from the tensions between human aspiration and the
cruel realities of human existence that are the result of the ineffective relation-
ship between the worlds of God and humanity. The speaker's references to his
love relationship however, suggest that life with this woman may not bring full
relief to the existential pain he suffers. The speaker tells her to stop being so
concerned about him. He realizes that she is limited in her ability to empathize
with his situation, and, once she reaches her limits, like a runner who is physi-
cally incapable of continuing to run, her empathy will no longer be effective
("your mind runs with me all the way, / and now it's tired and has no more
worth," 21–22). It is also significant that in his portrayal of their relationship the
speaker does not make use of a more intimate image, such as the sharing of a
meal or love making, but rather the more distant image of his observing her
acting alone as she removes food from the refrigerator.

The poem's refrains that declare that God and humanity (as represented by
the speaker) merit praise must be read as primarily ironic in tone; we praise God

and humanity for great deeds, yet neither is capable of them, and both are responsible for the fact that the world is in such a mess. One could argue, however, that the recapitulation of the refrains at the end of the poem takes some of the edge off of the irony by providing a kind of resolution of the tension of the poem, which is in keeping with the image of supportive human love in the final stanza. At this point in the poem, as he discovers a measure of peace in a comforting relationship with a woman, the speaker is more genuinely ready to praise both humanity and God, despite the imperfections of human existence and the ineffective relationship of God to the world, and so he concludes the poem with three statements of praise: "And for this I merit praise / And for this He merits praise / And for this You merit praise" (25–27).

אָבִינוּ מַלְכֵּנוּ. מָה עוֹשֶׂה אָב
שֶׁיְּלָדָיו הֵם יְתוֹמִים בְּעוֹדוֹ חַי? מַה יַּעֲשֶׂה אָב
שֶׁיְּלָדָיו מֵתוּ וְהוּא יִהְיֶה אָב שַׁכּוּל לְנֶצַח נְצָחִים?
יִבְכֶּה וְלֹא יִבְכֶּה, לֹא יִשְׁכַּח וְלֹא יִזְכֹּר.
אָבִינוּ מַלְכֵּנוּ. מָה עוֹשֶׂה מֶלֶךְ   5
בָּרֶפּוּבְּלִיקָה שֶׁל הַכְּאֵבִים? יִתֵּן לָהֶם
לֶחֶם וְשַׁעֲשׁוּעִים, כְּמוֹ כָּל מֶלֶךְ,
לֶחֶם הַזִּכָּרוֹן וְשַׁעֲשׁוּעֵי הַשִּׁכְחָה.
לֶחֶם וְגַעְגוּעִים. גַּעְגוּעִים לֵאלֹהִים
וּלְעוֹלָם טוֹב יוֹתֵר. אָבִינוּ מַלְכֵּנוּ.   10

     Our Father our King. What does a father do
     whose children are orphans in his lifetime? What will a father do
     whose children died and he'll be bereaved unto eternity?
     He'll cry and won't cry, won't forget and won't remember.
5   Our Father our King. What does a king do
     in the republic of pain? He will give them
     bread and circuses, like every king,
     the bread of memory and the circuses of forgetfulness.
     Bread and longings. Longings for God
10   and for a better world. Our Father our King.[52]

    The expression "our Father our King" (*avinu malkenu*) from the liturgy of the Days of Awe appears in the beginning, middle, and end (lines 1, 5, 10) of this seventh poem of the cycle "Gods Change, Prayers Remain Forever." In its most prominent location in the liturgy, in the prayer "Avinu malkenu," the expression introduces a series of petitionary statements directed at God, who is seen, paradoxically, as both a loving father and a ruling monarch. Each of the first two appearances of "Our Father our King" in the poem, however, are not followed by a petition, but rather by a meditation, first, on what it means in our time to be God in His role of Father and, second, on what it means to be God in His role of King. As the Father of humanity in the twentieth century, a time of unprecedented violence, God has children who have died and children who are the orphans of those who died (1–3). By asking the question, "What does a father do . . . ?" (1), the speaker suggests how impossible a situation God is in as He helplessly observes so much loss of life. The speaker imagines that, in response, God may adopt a variety of stratagems to deal with the painful experiences of ruling over a world of uncontrollable violence, sometimes crying, sometimes not crying, sometimes trying not to forget, and sometimes trying not to remember (4).

The speaker wonders what God can do in His role as the ruler of a "republic of pain" (5–6). God's situation is analogous to that of a monarch who must try to rule over a country that has been transformed from a monarchy into a republic. He is still the king, but He is much less powerful than He once was. Just as monarchs were once absolute, so God could at one time alleviate pain; but now He will not be able to do anything more than throw at the people *lehem vesha'ashu'im* (literally "bread and delights"), the equivalent of the English expression "bread and circuses" (7). The image of "bread and circuses" carries associations with a corrupt Roman Empire that lost all substance as a political entity and felt compelled to deflect any potential criticism from its subjects by providing them with a surfeit of pleasures. Thus, rather than turn to God for aid and comfort, humanity must seek to distract itself from the pain of the present by reveling in the memory of past glories and by engaging in a sensual escape from reality ("the bread of memory and the circuses of forgetfulness," 8).

These "bread and circuses" (*lehem vesha'ashu'im*, 7), however, are then transformed into the similarly sounding "[b]read and longings" (*lehem vegagu'im*, 9), which become "[l]ongings for God" (*gagu'im lElohim*), as well as "for a better world" (9–10). Thus, by the end of the poem, there is more to the relationship between God and humanity than a relatively powerless God who is not sure how to deal properly with His role as father or as king. In the midst of all this suffering, humanity discovers a longing to repair its relationship with the divine and to improve this troubling world in which it lives. The expression "Our Father our King" (10) at the end of the poem carries a different connotation than it does at the beginning and middle of the poem. In the earlier positions in the poem, the expression introduces the dilemmas stemming from God's weakness; in this last position, it is a more loving evocation of divinity for whose presence humanity continues to yearn.

אַחֲרֵי אוֹשְׁוִיץ אֵין תֵּיאוֹלוֹגְיָה:
מֵאֲרֻבּוֹת הַוָּתִיקָן עוֹלֶה עָשָׁן לָבָן,
סִימָן שֶׁהַקַּרְדִּינָלִים בָּחֲרוּ לָהֶם אַפִּיפְיוֹר.
מִמִּשְׂרְפוֹת אוֹשְׁוִיץ עוֹלֶה עָשָׁן שָׁחוֹר
סִימָן שֶׁהָאֱלֹהִים טֶרֶם הֶחְלִיטוּ עַל בְּחִירַת   5
הָעָם הַנִּבְחָר.
אַחֲרֵי אוֹשְׁוִיץ אֵין תֵּיאוֹלוֹגְיָה:
הַמִּסְפָּרִים עַל אַמּוֹת אֲסִירֵי הַהַשְׁמָדָה
הֵם מִסְפְּרֵי הַטֶּלֶפוֹן שֶׁל הָאֱלֹהִים
מִסְפָּרִים שֶׁאֵין מֵהֶם תְּשׁוּבָה   10
וְעַכְשָׁו הֵם מְנֻתָּקִים, אֶחָד, אֶחָד.

אַחֲרֵי אוֹשְׁוִיץ יֵשׁ תֵּיאוֹלוֹגְיָה חֲדָשָׁה:
הַיְּהוּדִים שֶׁמֵּתוּ בַּשּׁוֹאָה
נַעֲשׂוּ עַכְשָׁו דּוֹמִים לֵאלֹהֵיהֶם
שֶׁאֵין לוֹ דְּמוּת הַגּוּף וְאֵין לוֹ גּוּף.   15
אֵין לָהֶם דְּמוּת הַגּוּף וְאֵין לָהֶם גּוּף.

After Auschwitz there's no theology:
From the chimneys of the Vatican ascends white smoke,
a sign the cardinals have chosen a new pope.
From the crematoria of Auschwitz ascends black smoke,
5   a sign that the gods have yet to decide whom to designate
the chosen people.
After Auschwitz there's no theology:
The numbers on the arms of the prisoners of destruction
are the phone numbers of God
10   numbers never answered
and now they are disconnected, one by one.

After Auschwitz there's a new theology:
The Jews who died in the Holocaust
have now become like their God,
15   as He has no form or body
they have no form or body.[53]

In this twenty-seventh and final poem of the cycle "Gods Change, Prayers Remain Forever," the poet explores the effect of the Holocaust on religious faith. Like the poems "God Full of Mercy" and "And For This You Merit

Praise," this poem is replete with an irony that barely masks the speaker's anger at a God who does not seem to care for the world. The statement "After Auschwitz there's no theology," which appears twice in the poem (1, 7), suggests that the Holocaust has created such a rupture in the relationship between humanity and the divine that there really is no point in engaging in an intellectual effort to make sense of that relationship. Each time the statement appears, it is followed by a metaphor that serves to explain the significance of the assertion. In the first metaphor, the image of the white smoke that is released from the Vatican chimney when a new pope is elected by the cardinals is compared to the black smoke of the crematoria at Auschwitz (2–6). This comparison sets up a most disturbing juxtaposition of images from the worlds of Catholics and Jews. Smoke signifies the renewal of the papacy, as well as the murder of six million Jews in World War II. In the Catholic context, the white smoke signifies the decisive choice of the new supreme leader of the religion, whereas in the Jewish context, the black smoke signifies the confusion after Auschwitz about whether the Jews are still God's chosen people.

This juxtaposition of images of the election of the pope in the Vatican and the cremation of Jews in the concentration camps serves to undermine the purity of religious concepts in both Catholicism and Judaism. It calls attention to the scandalous silence of the Catholic Church during the Holocaust, and at the same time it suggests that God's lack of intervention as six million Jews were being killed is even more scandalous. Since World War II, we no longer live with the certainty that the covenant between God and the Jewish people is still valid, and it is as if we have reverted to a pre-covenant pagan world. In line 5, the speaker subtly captures this transition from a world in which God has chosen the Jewish people for a special relationship to a world in which gods cannot choose whom to favor. This transition is conveyed by the use of the word *elohim*, which can mean both God in a monotheistic sense (when accompanied by a singular adjective or verb) and gods in a polytheistic sense (when accompanied by a plural adjective or verb). The beginning of line 5, *siman sheha'elohim* sets up the expectation that the speaker is referring to God, because the word *elohim* with the definite article *ha* is generally used to refer to God, and also because the expression appears in the context of a poem about Jewish faith after the Holocaust. Thus, the expression could be understood to mean "a sign that God." However, with the appearance of a plural verb form for "decided" (*heḥlitu*), readers realize that the speaker is saying, "a sign that the gods."

In the second metaphor following the statement that after Auschwitz there is no theology, the numbers on the arms of the concentration camp inmates are said to be the telephone numbers of God (8–11). A person's telephone number is part of his or her identity, and to know someone's telephone number is to have a means by which to maintain contact with that person. These concentration camp numbers on the inmates' arms speak volumes about the nature of this cruel and indifferent God. When the speaker, in reference to the numbers, states, *she'ein mehem teshuvah,* translated here as "numbers never answered" (10), he may be saying that, just as a disconnected telephone number will not be answered, God will never answer these inmates. For that matter, there will never be an answer to the question of why they suffered as they did. Alternatively, if we translate the expression as "numbers from which there is no return" (*teshuvah* can mean answer or return), one can understand the speaker to be lamenting the fact that most concentration camp inmates died before the camps were liberated, and, therefore, once such a number was tattooed onto their arms, they had little hope of ever returning from the death camps to life. The expression "and now they are disconnected, one by one" (11) can be seen as referring either to the lines of communication with God or to the existence of the inmates. Perhaps the speaker refers here to the increasing skepticism about the possibility of connecting with God after the Holocaust, or perhaps, given the fact that the poem was published in a collection that appeared in the late 1990s, the speaker is reflecting on the fact that the last of the Holocaust survivors are dying out.

In the final stanza, the speaker moves beyond the notion that there is no theology after Auschwitz to the notion that there is a new theology after Auschwitz. The imagery that follows this statement (13–16) bears a striking resemblance to an earlier poem by Dan Pagis, "Edut" ("Testimony").[54] Both poems play on the expression from the "Yigdal" prayer, a poetic rendition of the medieval Jewish philosopher Maimonides' thirteen principles of faith, "He has no bodily form and no body." In the context of "Yigdal," the expression conveys Maimonides' principle that, despite anthropomorphic expressions in the Bible, God has no corporeal form. Both Pagis and Amichai make use of this allusion in a way that departs radically from its original meaning, suggesting that, if the victims of the Holocaust do have a God, it is a God whose essence is connected with the victims' experience of being robbed of their bodies. In both poems, the insubstantial form of smoke into which the victims' bodies were transformed is likened to the insubstantial form of Maimonides' strictly noncorporeal God. In a sense, Amichai follows here the negative theology of Maimonides, according to which one cannot say what God is, but only what He is not. Yet, even as he locates himself in the chain of traditional formulations of Jewish theology, the speaker ironically undermines Maimonides' statement of faith by suggesting that God's insubstantiality actually indicates His ineffectuality as a savior of His people during the Holocaust.

The Nature of Religious Experience

גּוֹרַל אֱלֹהִים

גּוֹרַל אֱלֹהִים
הוּא עַכְשָׁו כְּגוֹרַל
עֵצִים וַאֲבָנִים, שֶׁמֶשׁ וְיָרֵחַ,
שֶׁהִפְסִיקוּ לְהַאֲמִין בָּהֶם
כְּשֶׁהֶחֵלּוּ לְהַאֲמִין בּוֹ.   5

אֲבָל הוּא מֻכְרָח לְהִשָּׁאֵר עִמָּנוּ:
לְפָחוֹת כָּעֵצִים, לְפָחוֹת כָּאֲבָנִים
וְכַשֶּׁמֶשׁ וְכַיָּרֵחַ וְכַכּוֹכָבִים.

GOD'S FATE

God's fate
is now like the fate
of trees and stones, sun and moon,
in whom people stopped believing
5   when they began to believe in Him.

But He must stay with us:
at least like the trees, at least like the stones
and like the sun and the moon and the stars.[55]

   In an earlier stage of human history, the speaker reminds us, when people stopped worshipping elements of nature as gods, they began to worship the monotheistic God. Now, we have arrived at a new stage of human development in which people have ceased believing in the God of monotheistic religion. This loss of faith in the most recent "god," the speaker suggests, need no more lead to an atheistic position than did the earlier loss of pagan faith lead to a rejection of the reality of nature.

   The speaker insists on carrying the comparison of the period when pagan gods were rejected and the period when God was rejected beyond what might be expected. Of course, the natural world, being concrete and visible, continued to play a role in the life of humanity after people stopped worshipping nature, but in today's world it is not so obvious that the rejected monotheistic God, who is invisible, would still play a role in our lives. It is much easier for those who reject God to argue that He does not and never did exist than it was for those who underwent the transition from paganism to monotheism to reject nature. The speaker, however, insists that in some sense we still need God to function in our lives in a way that is parallel to that of elements of nature. Hillel Barzel suggests that in this poem the speaker expresses the need for God not so much as a philosophical conclusion but rather as an emotional drive.[56] This interpretation, however, does not negate the religious insight inherent in the poem. It would appear that the speaker is saying that belief in God is so central a necessity of the human psyche that it must suggest the reality of the claims of religious faith.

The title "God's Fate" would seem to conflict with the traditional Jewish notion going back to the Bible that God controls human fate. Here it is God who would seem to be the subject of fate. In a sense, however, God, as well as humanity, is subject to a fate that is beyond both of them. We could thus understand the speaker as saying that both we and God are fated to remain in our relationship, and, whether we want to rid ourselves of God or God wants to rid Himself of us, we are stuck with each other, for better or for worse.

אֲנִי אוֹמֵר בֶּאֱמוּנָה שְׁלֵמָה
שֶׁהַתְּפִלּוֹת קָדְמוּ לָאלֹהִים.
הַתְּפִלּוֹת יָצְרוּ אֶת הָאֱלֹהִים,
הָאֱלֹהִים יָצַר אֶת הָאָדָם
וְהָאָדָם יוֹצֵר תְּפִלּוֹת   5
שֶׁיּוֹצְרוֹת אֶת הָאֱלֹהִים שֶׁיּוֹצֵר אֶת הָאָדָם.

    I say with perfect faith
    that prayers preceded God.
    Prayers created God,
    God created Man
5   and Man creates prayers
    that create God who creates Man.[57]

Like "God's Fate," this poem affirms the inevitable persistence of religious faith even in an age of skepticism. Its message is consonant with the title of the cycle "Gods Change, Prayers Remain Forever," of which it is the third poem. The cycle's title makes clear the poet's conviction that the existence of a human need for religion will survive any disenchantment with a particular conception of the divine. As the title of the cycle and the poem itself make clear, at the heart of the human need for religion is the persistent urge to pray. If we understand the Hebrew term for prayer, *tefillah*, in its broadest traditional sense, we may presume that, according to the speaker, this underlying urge includes both an instinct to express praise in response to the wonders of nature and human existence, as well as an instinct to express a yearning for the fulfillment of our deepest needs. The speaker, after all, did not choose to focus on either of these two basic aspects of prayer by choosing a word that might exclude one of them, such as *hallel* (praise) or *tehinnah* (supplication).

The first line of the poem plays on the first words of each of the thirteen principles of faith composed by Maimonides, "I believe with perfect faith" (*ani ma'amin be'emunah shelemah*), found in most traditional prayer books at the end of the morning service. Although the speaker sets out in line 1 to make a statement to which he holds "with perfect faith" (*be'emunah shelemah*), he changes a term from Maimonides' principles of faith. He does not state that he *believes* (*ma'amin*), but rather that he *says* (*omer*) the statement. Thus, his words are those of a conclusion that he has personally reached, not a belief he has received from tradition that is affirmed in a ritual context.

The notion that "prayers preceded God" (2) suggests that there is a universal human need to pray, regardless of a particular culture's theological conventions. In fact, the speaker asserts, it was this human need to pray that created the notion that there is a God who created people who need to pray to God (3–7). This statement is based on circular reasoning and, therefore, it fails to prove the existence of God. Nevertheless, there is a comforting dimension to the completeness of this circular process, with people's prayers creating a God who creates people who create prayers that create God who creates people, and so on, which reassures us that our need to pray is built into the nature of reality. The statement "and Man creates prayers / that create God who creates Man" (5–6) may suggest that humanity's urge to pray ("Man creates prayers") introduces into the world a divine dimension ("prayers / . . . create God") that raises humanity to a higher spiritual level ("God . . . creates Man"). Humanity, thus, continuously recreates itself with the religious awareness that it has discovered on its own.

אֱלֹהִים הוּא מַדְרֵגוֹת שֶׁעוֹלוֹת
לְמָקוֹם שֶׁלֹּא קַיָּם שׁוּב, אוֹ שֶׁלֹּא קַיָּם עֲדַיִן
הַמַּדְרֵגוֹת הֵן אֱמוּנָתִי, הַמַּדְרֵגוֹת אַכְזָבָתִי
יַעֲקֹב אָבִינוּ יָדַע זֹאת בַּחֲלוֹמוֹ
הַמַּלְאָכִים רַק קִשְּׁטוּ אֶת מַעֲלוֹת הַסֻּלָּם   5
כְּמוֹ עֵץ אַשּׁוּחַ מְקֻשָּׁט בְּחַג הַמּוֹלָד
וְשִׁיר הַמַּעֲלוֹת הוּא שִׁיר הַלֵּל
לְאֵל הַמַּדְרֵגוֹת.

God is steps that ascend
to a place that again does not exist, or that does not yet exist
the steps are my faith, the steps my disappointment
our father Jacob knew this in his dream
5   the angels merely adorned the ladder's rungs

like decorations on a Christmas tree
and the Song of Ascents is a song of praise
to the God of steps.[58]

In this fourth poem of the cycle "Gods Change, Prayers Remain Forever,"
the speaker explores how to transform the language of traditional Jewish faith
into a verbal expression that will honestly convey his own personal relation-
ship with God. He begins this process by declaring that, in place of any tradi-
tional images of God, the God in which he places his faith may be envisioned
metaphorically as a set of stairs that leads to somewhere else (1–2). This other
place may be one "that again does not exist," or one "that does not yet exist"
(2). The description of the place is paradoxical: it does not exist and has persis-
tently not existed, but it also has yet to exist. God, therefore, does not bring the
speaker to another state of being, but He may be identified with the human
yearning for an alternative existence.

The stairs that metaphorically represent God are both the speaker's "faith"
that he will be transformed and his "disappointment" when he is not (3). Note
the chiastic structure in lines 2 and 3: in line 2, disappointment ("a place that
again does not exist") is followed by hope ("that does not yet exist"), whereas in
line 3, hope ("the steps are my faith") is followed by disappointment ("the steps
are my disappointment"). This structure creates a closed system that conveys
the notion that throughout the never-ending cycle of disappointment and hope
that he has experienced throughout his life the speaker feels a degree of security
in the notion that he is always on those steps that are God.

The speaker then associates this step imagery with two biblical references:
the ladder in Jacob's dream (Genesis 28:12) (4–6), and the series of Psalms of
Ascents that accompanied pilgrimages to the Temple in ancient Israel (Psalms
120–134) (7–8). The connection of God to the image of ascending on steps may
be related in part to these two biblical references, but neither reference pro-
vides a fully adequate way to convey the speaker's relationship with God. Al-
though the image of a ladder between earth and heaven in Jacob's dream con-
nects the speaker's approach to that of the biblical patriarch, in a certain sense
it does not; the biblical angels ascending and descending the ladder are as
significant as angels used to decorate a Christmas tree would be to a Jew who
does not celebrate that holiday. The heading "Song of Ascents" of the biblical
Temple pilgrimage psalms provides a powerful image for the speaker's religious
yearnings. Nevertheless, in order for any of those psalms to accurately convey
the speaker's search for God, it must be reduced to a simple "song of praise / to
the God of steps" (7–8). Despite its reduction to a state of simplicity, this song
of praise (*shir hallel*) makes clear how much the speaker appreciates the process
of yearning for transformation, which he connects directly with God.

עִקְּבוֹת רַגְלֵי צִפּוֹרִים בַּחוֹל אֲשֶׁר עַל שְׂפַת הַיָּם,
כְּמוֹ כְּתַב־יָד שֶׁמִּישֶׁהוּ רָשַׁם, לִזְכֹּר
דְּבָרִים, שֵׁמוֹת, מִסְפָּרִים וּמְקוֹמוֹת.
עִקְּבוֹת צִפּוֹרִים בַּחוֹל בַּלַּיְלָה
נִשְׁאָרוֹת גַּם בַּיּוֹם, אֲבָל לֹא רָאִיתִי   5
אֶת הַצִּפּוֹר שֶׁהִטְבִּיעָה אוֹתָן. כָּךְ הָאֱלֹהִים.

Footprints of birds in the sand by the sea,
like someone's handwriting in a note, to remember
things, names, numbers, and places.
Footprints of birds in the sand at nighttime
5 still remain at daytime, but I didn't see
the bird who made them. God's like that.[59]

In this sixth poem of the cycle "Gods Change, Prayers Remain Forever," the speaker makes use of nature imagery to convey what it means to him to sense God's presence. There are two stages to the use of this imagery. At first, a phenomenon of nature is compared to a human phenomenon: bird footprints by the sea are like a memo someone wrote to himself (1–3). Then, the footprints are compared to evidence of God's existence (4–6). These two stages allow for two ways to talk about God's presence in the world. Working backward in the poem, we can discern two propositions. One proposition is that, even if we cannot see God, there is evidence of His existence, just as, even though we do not see birds at a particular moment, the footprints of the birds provide evidence that they do exist. The other proposition is that there may be a significant content to that sense of God's existence that has something to say to people, just as the memo is a reminder of important information. The problem inherent in the latter proposition is that, just as the language of footprints is not intelligible to us in the way that human language is, so the divine message we discern in the world may be impossible to decipher. In the original Hebrew, the last word of the poem, haElohim, provides the first reference to God in the poem. Thus, on a first reading, we actually have no idea that the poem is about God until it ends. By withholding the reference to God until the end of the poem, the poet fully engages his readers in nature imagery—the reality of which they would not question—before they can marshal any skeptical defenses against faith in God's existence. This increases the possibility that the readers will be more open to make a leap of faith as they read the poem. The delay in referring to God also conveys how elusive the sense of God's presence in the world really is.

It is perhaps not a coincidence that the four poems discussed in this section, in which the speaker senses God's presence, are relatively short. One discerns in the brevity of these poems (the first published in a 1968 collection, and the other three published in a 1998 collection) an underlying method of writing positively about God's presence in the world. It appears that Amichai considered the form of the short reflective poem to be the most effective means to convey to his readers that, despite all of our doubts, we cannot escape the reality of God's presence. In contrast to more developed theological statements in prose or poetry, Amichai chose to make short simple statements, grounded for the most part in very concrete images that would be easily accessible to his readers. Furthermore, it appears that Amichai saw statements of this nature to be the most honest that could possibly be made. Faith is hard to come by, he seems to be saying, but if we can grasp it even in a relatively simple manner, it is worth declaring.

Prayer

אָבִי, מַלְכִּי

אָבִי, מַלְכִּי, אַהֲבַת חִנָּם וְשִׂנְאַת חִנָּם
עָשׂוּ אֶת פָּנַי כִּפְנֵי הָאָרֶץ הַחֲרֵבָה הַזֹּאת.
הַשָּׁנִים הָפְכוּ אוֹתִי לְטוֹעֵם שֶׁל כְּאֵבִים.
כְּמוֹ טוֹעֵם־יֵינוֹת אֲנִי מַבְחִין
בֵּין מִינֵי שֶׁקֶט שׁוֹנִים,   5
יוֹדֵעַ מַה מֵת. מִי.

אָבִי, מַלְכִּי, עֲשֵׂה שֶׁפָּנַי לֹא יִקָּרְעוּ
מִצְּחוֹק אוֹ מִבֶּכִי.
אָבִי, מַלְכִּי, עֲשֵׂה שֶׁכָּל מַה שֶׁיָּקָר לִי
בֵּין תַּאֲוָה וּבֵין עַצְבוּת   10
לֹא יְיַסֵּר אוֹתִי; וְשֶׁכָּל הַדְּבָרִים
שֶׁאֲנִי עוֹשֶׂה בְּנִגּוּד לִרְצוֹנִי,
יֵרָאוּ כִּרְצוֹנִי. וּרְצוֹנִי כִּפְרָחִים.

MY FATHER, MY KING

My Father, my King, baseless love and baseless hatred
have made my face like the surface of this arid land.
The years have turned me into a taster of pain.
Like a wine taster I can distinguish
5   between different kinds of silence,
I know what has died. And who.

My Father, my King, make it so my face is not torn apart
by laughter or crying.
My Father, my King, make it so that whatever happens to me
10 between desire and sadness
will not afflict me; and that all things
I do against my will,
seem to be according to my will. And my will like flowers.[60]

The title of the poem "My Father, My King" ("Avi malki") derives from the expression "our Father our King" (*avinu malkenu*), which is repeated throughout a central prayer recited during the ten days of repentance from Rosh Hashanah to Yom Kippur and also on most traditional Jewish fast days. In choosing to say "*my* Father, *my* King," the speaker departs from the traditional Jewish norm of praying in the first person plural, indicating that he does not feel connected to a community of prayer.

Of central concern to the speaker is his experience of being caught between extremes of human emotions: "baseless love and baseless hatred" (1), "laughter or crying" (8), and "desire and sadness" (10). The first and third dichotomies are particularly striking in that they defy the categories of standard Hebrew terminology. "Baseless hatred" (*sinat hinnam*) appears in the Yom Kippur liturgy in the list of sins in the confessional prayer that begins "Al het shehatanu" ("For the sin that we have sinned"), as well as in a prayer included in the reader's repetition of the standing silent payer ("Amidah") that begins "Our Father our King," which calls upon God to eliminate a list of evils in the world, including "baseless hatred." The expression "baseless hatred" also appears in the Talmudic declaration that it was "baseless hatred" that brought about the destruction of the Second Temple (Yoma 9b). This latter association is suggested by the reference to "this arid land" (2) in which the original Hebrew word for "arid" is *harevah*, which can also mean "destroyed." It is traditional for "baseless hatred" to mean hate that has no justification. "Baseless love," however, is an invention of the poet. It could mean loving someone who does not deserve one's love or who does not return one's love. It thus belongs less to the category of moral failure, to which "baseless hatred" belongs, than to the category of an illusion that causes pain.

The dichotomy between desire and sadness also departs from standard Hebrew terminology. It is typical in Hebrew for desire (*ta'avah*) to be opposed by some form of self control, while some form of joy would be the opposite of sadness (*atsvut*). Like the dichotomy between "baseless love" and "baseless hatred," this dichotomy belongs less to the moral dimension than to that of the vagaries of human desire. The speaker has experienced desire, which is sometimes satisfied and sometimes not, and he has also experienced the sadness that results from thwarted desire or from the realization that the sexual realm is not always the most reliable means to true human intimacy.

Twice in the poem the speaker refers to the effect or potential effect on his face as he is caught between dichotomies. In lines 1 and 2, he informs God that "baseless love and baseless hatred / have made [his] face like the surface of this arid land." In lines 7 and 8, the speaker prays to God to "make it so [his] face is not torn apart / by laughter or crying." The image of arid land (appropriate to the Land of Israel, with its limited rainfall) and the image of being torn suggest abandonment, lack of vitality, and destruction. The Hebrew word for "torn apart" (*yiqaru*) calls to mind the traditional Jewish mourning ritual of rending one's garment (*qeri'ah*). A related expression, which does not refer to the speaker's face, is found in lines 9 to 11, when the speaker asks God that whatever happens to him between desire and sadness "will not afflict" him. The Hebrew word for "afflict" (*yeyasser*) connotes affliction visited upon someone as a punishment, often of divine origin.

The speaker goes on to declare that, just as a wine taster has a well developed palate that allows him to make fine distinctions between excellent and inferior wine, he has become a real expert in distinguishing among the varieties of silences that accompany life's losses, knowing all too well "what has died. And who" (4–6). The connection made here between sadness and wine, which is traditionally associated with times of celebration and referred to in the Bible as that which "gladdens the heart of Man" (Psalms 104:15), is ironic, to say the least.

In lines 11 to 13, the speaker addresses his experience of being called on to act against his will, praying "that all things / [he does] against [his] will / seem to be according to [his] will. And [his] will like flowers." This might refer to the national duty in Israel to fight in war, or to any number of responsibilities from which the speaker may wish to escape. The speaker makes use here of traditional Jewish terminology in an idiosyncratic way that reflects his contemporary perspective. In traditional formulations, the central value is to submit the human will to that of God. Petitions to God in the Jewish liturgy begin at times with the expression, "May it be Your will" (*yehi ratson milefanekha*). In a mishnaic passage, Rabban Gamliel states, "Make His [God's] will (*retsono*) yours so that He [God] will make your will (*retsonakh*) His will" (Pirkei Avot 2:4). The speaker, however, does not even refer to God's will. Instead, he prays that, although it is necessary at times to act against one's will, he would like to be able to appear to be acting in accordance with his own will, so that at least he does not relate outwardly to the world with an attitude of resentment. In the second half of the last line, the speaker beseeches God to help him to transform his will into something beautiful "like flowers" (13). The image of flowers that concludes the poem stands in stark contrast to the image of the arid land in line 2, suggesting a possible way to transcend the dichotomy between life and death and achieve wholeness and integrity.

אֲנִי אַחֲרוֹנָם

כִּי עֵת עַכְשָׁו. הַחֲצֵרוֹת רֵיקוֹת,
וּמַחֲצִית חַיַּי בְּצֵל מַחֲצִיתָם הָאַחֲרוֹנָה.
וְרַק שָׁלוֹם וּשְׁנֵי בְּרוֹשִׁים. דִּבּוּר אֶחָד.
מִי עוֹד יֹאמַר וּמִי יָנוּד וּמִי יָנוּחַ?
אֲפִלּוּ בְּבָתִּים הַנּוֹרָאִים יֶשְׁנוֹ מִתְקָן   5
לְדֶגֶל חַג, שֶׁיִּתְנוֹפֵף וְשֶׁיַּשְׁכִּיחַ.

הַנַּח אוֹתִי, הָאֱלֹהִים, אֲנִי עָיֵף עַכְשָׁו,
אַל תִּתְעָרֵב שׁוּב עִם שָׂטָן. נִצַּחְתָּ
וְגַם הוּא נִצַּח. בֵּרַכְתִּי אֱלֹהִים וְגַם קִלַּלְתִּי
סָבַלְתִּי כָּךְ וְכָךְ. תֵּן לִי שְׁהוּת לָנוּחַ   10
בֵּין "עוֹד זֶה מְדַבֵּר" וּבֵין "זֶה בָּא".

צָרֵף אוֹתִי בְּצֵרוּפִים שֶׁל שְׁמִי הַמְפֹרָשׁ,
פַּזֵּר קוֹלִי כְּאֵפֶר שֶׁשָּׁכַח מַה שֶׁהָיָה
וּזְכֹר אוֹתִי מִזְּמַן שֶׁבּוֹ הָיִיתִי
עוֹד אֲשֶׁר הָיִיתִי, תִּהְיֶה אֲשֶׁר תִּהְיֶה.   15

קַלְסְתֵּר לִבִּי נִכָּר עֲדַיִן בְּפָנָי.
זְכֹר אוֹתִי עִם אַבְרָהָם, יִצְחָק וְיַעֲקֹב,
הוֹסֵף אוֹתִי אֶל רְשִׁימַת מֵתֵי הַמַּכְפֵּלָה
בִּקְצֵה הַמַּדְרֵגוֹת הָאֲפֵלוֹת. אֲנִי אַחֲרוֹנָם.

I AM THE LAST OF THEM

For now it's time. The yards are empty,
and half my life is in the shadow of its final half.
And only peace and two cypress trees. One utterance.
Who else shall speak and who shall wander and who shall rest?
5   Even in the awesome houses there is a holder
for a holiday flag that will wave and cause oblivion.

Leave me alone, God, I am tired now,
don't bet again with Satan. You've won
and he too has won. I blessed God and also cursed
10   I suffered this and that. Give me time to rest
between "while this one was still speaking" and "another came."

Form me in formulations of my fully pronounced name,
scatter my voice like ash that forgot what has been

and remember me from the time I was
15   still who I was, You who are who You are.

The visage of my heart can still be discerned in my face.
Remember me with Abraham, Isaac, and Jacob,
add me to the list of the dead in the Patriarchs' Tomb
at the edge of the darkened steps. I am the last of them.[61]

The first stanza portrays a pause in the middle of the speaker's life, when the final half of his life casts the shadow of mortality on the recently completed first half. This is a period of relative simplicity in the midst of an event-filled life (1–3). In one sense, the images used to portray this period create an atmosphere of minimalist starkness: no one is in the yard, all one can see is two trees, and there is only one statement made. Although there is peace, the speaker also experiences a mood of anxiety as he contemplates his own fate and that of others. The question "who shall wander and who shall rest?" (*umi yanud umi yanuah*, 4) echoes the expression in the "Unetanneh toqef" prayer of the Days of Awe, "who will rest and who will wander" (*mi yanuah umi yanua*). Adding to the anxiety is the fact that, contrary to the spirit of the traditional prayer, it is not clear to the speaker that God or any other being will speak the words that will determine a just human fate (4).

Holidays provide times of reflection and renewal that are congruent with such midlife musings. In the poem, however, the holiday experience that can provide such a break from life's tribulations is lived in "awesome houses" (*babatim hanora'im*, 5, an expression that alludes to the Hebrew term for the Days of Awe, *hayamim hanora'im*), and it proves to be a disappointment. The holiday flag (an apparent reference to the flag of Israel displayed on the occasion of Israel Independence Day) attached to each house can do no more than eliminate the memory of painful experiences, "wav[ing] and caus[ing] oblivion" (6).

In the second stanza, the poet pleads with God to remove him from the Job-like trials of his life that have so exhausted him (7–8). He suspects that, like Job, he is the victim of a cruel bet between God and Satan (Job 1–2). But his situation is worse than that of Job. In the end, because of Job's steadfast relationship with God, the deity won the bet with Satan; the speaker, however, is convinced that both God and Satan have won (8–9). His life has been an endless swing of the pendulum between the good provided by God and the evil provided by Satan. Furthermore, unlike Job, who refused his wife's urging to curse God, the speaker has blessed God, but he has also cursed (9), although it is significant that the speaker does not explicitly say he has cursed God. In lines 10 and 11, the speaker expresses the wish to be spared the experience of relentless suffering that befell Job, of whom it is written that even as he was hearing from a messenger about one calamity another messenger came to inform him of a new calamity (Job 1:16–18).[62]

The speaker then turns to God in what appears to be a paradoxical entreaty to form and scatter him (12–13). Just as some mystics believe they can effect change in the world by means of the divine Tetragammaton that conveys God's essence (*shem hameforash*), the speaker wants God to transform him into a being who clearly reflects his basic essence ("Form me in formulations of my fully pronounced name [*shemi hameforash*]," 12). He also wants God to scatter his voice as if it were an object so transformed by being burned that it turns into ash (*efer*, 13). "Ash" alludes here to the practice, not sanctioned by traditional Jewish law, of cremating a dead body and scattering its ashes, but it also could be seen as an allusion to the ash of the red heifer that served as a vehicle for ritual purification in biblical times (Numbers 19). Ashes also figure prominently in the last words uttered by Job: "dust and ashes" (*afar va'efer*, Job 42:6). The speaker wants God not only to help him to discover a reintegration of self and a purification from past failings and sufferings, but also to return with him to the memory of a time in the past when unity and purity were possible ("and remember me from the time I was / still who I was," 14–15).

In line 15, the speaker addresses God as "You who are who You are" (*tihyeh asher tihyeh*), a play on the expression with which God refers to Himself at the time of His revelation to Moses at the burning bush, *ehyeh asher ehyeh* ("I am who I am," Exodus 3:14). This expression adapted from the Bible reveals the speaker's limited knowledge of God: Whatever You are, You are. Since the imperfect form of the verb "to be" (*tihyeh*) can be understood in modern Hebrew as being in the future tense, this expression can also suggest the speaker's hope that God will indeed be there for him in the future.

The speaker has no desire to hide any of his feelings from God. He declares in the first line of the final stanza of the poem that what he experiences in his heart is as evident as a facial expression: "The visage of my heart can still be discerned in my face" (16). However, not certain of his future relationship with God, he asks to at least be as precious a memory to God as the patriarchs Abraham, Isaac, and Jacob, and to lie with them in their tomb in Hebron "at the edge of the darkened steps" (17–19).

The significance of the title of the poem and its concluding expression, "I am the last of them" (*ani aharonam*, 19) lies in the sense of both continuity and finality in the way the speaker relates to his past. He feels connected to the patriarchs Abraham, Isaac, and Jacob, founders of the people of Israel and initiators of that people's relationship with its Land. He is, however, a lesser descendant of those patriarchs, not sure he can continue their heroic efforts to settle in the Land and to enter into a close relationship with God. As the most recent player in the drama of Jewish existence, he calls on God to release him from the struggle that has been so prominent a feature of life for Jews in Israel, for he is unsure whether he will have the strength to be the newest link in the long chain of Jewish history.

מִתּוֹךְ **אֵלִים מִתְחַלְּפִים, הַתְּפִלּוֹת נִשְׁאָרוֹת לָעַד**

12

גַּם לִתְפִלַּת יָחִיד צְרִיכִים שְׁנַיִם:
תָּמִיד אֶחָד שֶׁמִּתְנוֹעֵעַ
וְהַשֵּׁנִי שֶׁלֹּא נָע הוּא הָאֱלֹהִים.
אֲבָל כְּשֶׁאָבִי הִתְפַּלֵּל הוּא עָמַד בִּמְקוֹמוֹ
זָקוּף וּבְלִי נוֹעַ וְהִכְרִיחַ אֶת הָאֱלֹהִים לָנוּעַ   5
כְּמוֹ סוּף וּלְהִתְפַּלֵּל אֶל אָבִי.

13

תְּפִלָּה בְּצִבּוּר: הַאִם לְבַקֵּשׁ, תֵּן לָנוּ שָׁלוֹם,
בִּילְלוֹת וּבִצְעָקוֹת שֶׁבֶר אוֹ לְבַקֵּשׁ בְּשֶׁקֶט רָגוּעַ.
אֲבָל אִם נְבַקֵּשׁ בְּשֶׁקֶט, הָאֵל יַחְשֹׁב
שֶׁאָנוּ לֹא צְרִיכִים שָׁלוֹם וְשֶׁקֶט.

14

פְּסוּקֵי דְזִמְרָא. הַתְּמִימוּת עוֹלָה מִבְּנֵי הָאָדָם
כְּמוֹ הֶבֶל חֹם מִתַּבְשִׁיל שֶׁעוֹלֶה לְמַעְלָה
וְהוֹפֵךְ לִהְיוֹת אֱלֹהִים וְלִפְעָמִים אֱלֹהִים אֲחֵרִים.

FROM GODS CHANGE, PRAYERS REMAIN FOREVER

12
Even private prayer needs two:
Always one who sways
and the other who doesn't move is God.
But when my father prayed he stood in his place
5   erect and without movement and forced God to move
like a reed and to pray to my father.

13
Public prayer: To request, "Give us peace,"
with wails and cries of despair or to plead quietly and calmly.
But if we plead quietly, God will think
that we don't need peace and quiet.

14
Verse of psalms. Innocence rises up from human beings
like steam of warmth from a cooked dish rising up
and becoming God and sometimes other gods.[63]

The poems numbered twelve, thirteen, and fourteen in the cycle "Gods
Change, Prayers Remain Forever" reflect on the experience of prayer. Al-
though, as we have seen, Amichai often alludes to the traditional Jewish liturgy,
his earlier poetry does not contain the kind of consideration of the process of
prayer one finds in these poems. Here, with references to specific prayer situa-
tions, the speaker attempts to characterize what goes on when Jews pray.

In poem number twelve, private prayer (*tefillat yaḥid,* literally "the prayer of
an individual," 1) is a category of Jewish liturgical practice that is distinguished
from public prayer (*tefillah betsibbur*), to which line 1 in poem number thirteen
refers. While the Jewish tradition puts a premium on praying the three daily
obligatory prayers in a congregation of at least ten Jews, those who are not in
such a congregation at the time, pray by themselves. As the speaker recalls see-
ing his father pray by himself, the speaker reminds us that one is not completely
alone when one prays privately, because prayer involves a relationship between
the person praying and God (1–3). It is traditional Jewish practice to sway back
and forth or side to side while praying. However, the speaker's father does not
follow that practice; instead, he stands still (4). In so doing, he reverses the typi-
cal human–divine relationship; instead of a God who seems to be immovable
to whom one sways in prayer, it is the human being who is immovable, thereby
forcing God to sway in prayer toward him (5–6).

The spiritual daring of the father who seeks to reverse the power relations be-
tween God and himself is not completely foreign to Jewish tradition. There are
a number of narratives in biblical and rabbinic literature in which human
figures take strong stands that move God to act. After the Israelites' sin of wor-
shipping the golden calf, Moses argues strenuously with God to spare them
from the destruction He wishes to visit upon them (Exodus 32:11–14). In Talmu-
dic legend, Honi "the circle maker" refuses to move out of a circle he has drawn
until God provides rain (Mishnah Ta'anit 3:8). Yet, in the poem, God does not
really actively intervene in human affairs. Instead, He does whatever people do
to relate to Him: he sways in prayer. The comparison of God's swaying to that
of a reed (6) would appear to diminish God's power, even as it suggests that, just
as it is natural for a reed to sway, so it is natural for God to sway as He prays to
humanity.

The issue in poem number thirteen is how to approach God: in a forceful
manner ("with wails and cries of despair," 2) or in a gentle manner ("quietly and

calmly," 2). It would appear appropriate to pray for peace calmly and quietly. However, such a tone might create the false impression for God that we do not desperately need peace ("But if we plead quietly, God will think / that we don't need peace and quiet," 3–4). A prayer for peace, the speaker suggests, in fact must be shouted if we are ever to convince God how much we really need it. This second possibility is very much in keeping with the portrait of the father praying in the previous poem. Prayer in both poems provides an opportunity to forcefully assert one's needs and declare one's refusal to accept one's fate.

Poem number fourteen expresses a very different understanding of the nature of prayer. Here prayer is not the occasion to be forcefully assertive before God, but rather to make an offering to God of one's innocence (*temimut*, 1). The term "verses of psalms" (*pesuqei dezimra*, 1) refers to the psalms that are traditionally recited in the introductory section of the daily morning prayers. In the poem, these psalms are a figurative dish being cooked for God, and the innocence of their expressions of faith rises up to Him like warm steam from delicious food (1–2). This image recalls the aroma of the sacrifices that rise toward God in the biblical conception of worship, as, for example, in the passage which tells that "God smelled the pleasing odor" of Noah's sacrifice (Genesis 8:21). As the figurative steam of prayer rises, it is transformed into God (3), a notion congruent with the statement in poem number three of the cycle that prayers create God. Not one to be tied to a single, eternally fixed image of God, the poet has his speaker declare rather playfully that, as the steam rises, it may not be the one God of Israel that will emerge, but one of many possible alternative gods ("and sometimes other gods," 3) that might be even more appropriate for the spiritual needs of humanity in our time.

CHAPTER THREE

Asher Reich
"Perhaps He'll answer me this time."

ASHER REICH (1937–) was raised in a Yiddish-speaking, Ultra-Orthodox family in Jerusalem.[1] When he was sixteen years old his father died. During the period of his transition from adolescence to young adulthood, Reich lost his traditional religious faith and his commitment to Jewish ritual observance. At the age of eighteen he cut off his traditional sidelocks, left the yeshiva in which he was studying, and, in defiance of prevailing Ultra-Orthodox practice, enlisted in the Israeli army. Following an early discharge from the military, granted so that he could provide material support for his widowed mother, he began to publish poetry in the Hebrew daily press.

At the yeshiva Reich had not received the secular education necessary to pass the matriculation examinations that would allow him to enter college. Nevertheless, after his army service, he began to audit courses at the Hebrew University. Eventually, Dov Sadan, the leading professor of Yiddish at the time, encouraged him to enroll there for a B.A. degree, which he completed in the fields of Hebrew literature and philosophy.

In spite of his connection to Dov Sadan, Reich chose not to study Yiddish literature at the Hebrew University because, as he reports, he felt too alienated from the spoken language of his childhood. He describes that childhood in rather unappealing terms: "without kindergarten or a [secular] elementary or high school education, without children's books, without acquaintance with the world of plants and animals, without nature hikes or youth group experiences or sports."[2] He recalls that the *ḥeder* (Orthodox elementary school) he attended was characterized by poor educational methods, corporal punishment, and a lack of tolerance for the expression of ideas deemed to be heretical. He considers the Ultra-Orthodox community in which he grew up to have been excessively strict in its religious demands, while at the same time quite hypocritical in its practice: "All of my childhood and youth was a kind of door that led me to the confinement of a kingdom of prohibitions and a holy people [an ironic play on the designation God gave the Israelites at Mount Sinai, "a kingdom of priests and a holy people," Exodus 19:6], which I wanted to desert. What wasn't done in our neighborhood in the name of God? They procreated, gossiped, cursed, told on others, insulted, lied, fornicated, had sinful thoughts, beat their wives, harassed the weak—all in the name of [God] whose power and might fill the world."[3] As negative as his feelings about his Ultra-Orthodox upbringing are, he feels indebted as a poet to the wealth of language to which he was exposed in his youth: "[T]he treasure of my memories is fortified by words and sounds that I absorbed [*yanaqti*, literally "suckled"] from the prayers and the Torah of my days in *ḥeder*, which to my mind is a kind of special school for the Hebrew language. [Hebrew] is not only a verbal structure, but a bottomless well of poetry."[4]

From his earliest awareness, Reich was conscious of the centrality of God in the life of his family and community. He claims to remember that, even before he was one year old, he had learned to say the word "God" (*Eloqim*, according to the Ultra-Orthodox practice). "With the name of God," he relates, "I went to bed. With it I fell asleep in the evening and with it I arose in the morning. God was always alive on my lips not only during prayer, not only when we sat down to eat meals, but also at study time, and in my house I heard His name all the time from my father and mother."[5]

For Reich, the writing of poetry is a way to compensate for the spiritual deprivation he began to feel when he abandoned religious observance and no longer had a framework within which to pray. "I came to poetry," he has stated, "out of a longing for prayer."[6] Over time, he relates, "I discovered that to me poetry is like prayer. I have noticed that I write a lot precisely on the holidays, instead of praying, which I had been accustomed to do for many years."[7] Reich believes that poetry and prayer "have a clear common denominator."[8] This relationship between poetry and prayer is, according to Reich, particularly true for those who write in Hebrew. "Even today," he has declared, "it is not possible to completely secularize the Hebrew language. For it was always a holy language both for prayer and for other religious rituals. That is the good fortune of Hebrew, that it has interacted with our history for thousands of years, and with all of the changes that have occurred in it, it has remained true to its origins. Thus, for example, if King David would suddenly visit us, we would be able to speak with him in our language and he would understand us."[9]

Reich's affinity as a poet for the language of traditional Jewish prayer can be discerned in the frequency with which he alludes to liturgical expressions in his poetry. Indeed, of the six poets I am considering, Reich has the highest percentage of liturgical expressions in his poems. This use of liturgical language and related allusions to biblical and rabbinic texts are a function of his preference for the language of traditional Jewish sources in general. "The past is located in language," he has stated, "in the language of the sources on which I was raised. I relate to the Hebrew language that developed over the generations. I do not like 'slang' in poetry; it suggests showiness and cheap pandering."[10] To the extent that he is willing to use newly invented language, his preference is for words that "derive from within the roots of the language."[11] Reich's frequent use of the language of tradition reflects also his understanding that "for the poet there is no such thing as past-present-future; from my point of view they exist together."[12] The origin of this would appear to be his childhood consciousness of the biblical stories as present occurrences: "In the course of days I would pass through the Garden of Eden daydreaming, passing in horror by the quarrel between the brothers Cain and Abel, shocked at the murder of Abel, drunk from the story of Lot's wife and daughters, astounded at the cruel test by God in the story of the binding of Isaac, amazed at the deeds of Jacob, observing with disgust the selling of Joseph to the Ishmaelites, and celebrating his success in Egypt."[13] On the basis of this approach, one can imagine that at the moment he is writing a poem with expressions from the traditional liturgy Reich returns, in some sense, to the consciousness he had as a child praying fervently in synagogue. Yet, because he frequently plays with traditional language, substituting words, changing the context of an expression, or transforming the worldview that lies behind a verbal construct, one senses that he is also testing the viability of traditional religious ideas and, in particular, of traditional notions of prayer. One thereby discerns in Reich's poetry a constant movement between a stance of critical alienation from the world of tradition and a nostalgic longing to return to that world.

The God of Reich's poetry is distant from humanity. He does not regularly respond to prayer, nor does He intervene effectively in the affairs of the world in order to save people from trouble. Human beings come across in a number of these poems as burdened by feelings of guilt and unsure whether there exists a means to gain God's forgiveness of their sins. These two factors of God's inaction and humanity's unforgiven sinfulness give rise to persistent doubts about the basic axioms of religious faith, namely that God cares for humanity and that there are ways for human beings to relate to God. Indeed, a high percentage of the poems I am considering have the word "perhaps" (*ulay*) in them, for the most part in connection with speculation about whether God will respond to human needs. Often the word "perhaps" precedes an expression from traditional Jewish liturgy that affirms God's concern for humanity, for example, "perhaps He'll answer me this time" (*"Piyyut* for Nights of Awe"), "[p]erhaps we will be answered" ("A voice . . ."), "perhaps for a moment He'll pity us" ("In-stead of a Prayer"), and "perhaps Your right hand is still / outstretched to receive those who turn back" ("Ne'ilah"). By adding the word "perhaps," the speaker expresses an ambiguous relationship to religious faith; he is not sure he can trust God, yet he holds out the possibility that God will respond to his needs. In the poem "*Piyyut* for Days of Awe," the speaker makes use of the word "perhaps" not to hold out the possibility that God will respond, but rather to suggest how ineffective a relationship God has with the world. God in this poem does not fit the traditional image of the divine judge who in the new year grants people a fate which they deserve, but rather He is envisioned as old and weak, as the speaker ironically states, "perhaps not as great not as mighty not as awesome / as the prayer ads tell of Him." Here the speaker comments pointedly on the dis-crepancy between theology and human experience; it is difficult to take seri-ously the traditional image of an omnipotent God who is committed to justice when there is so much evil in the world.

Biblical religion and later rabbinic Judaism consistently envisioned mecha-nisms for human beings to gain forgiveness from God for sins. In a number of Reich's poems, those mechanisms have apparently broken down, and all the speaker can do is to ask God's forgiveness, with no assurance that He will grant it. The speaker in "If There Are" yearns for "forgiveness," lest he be "stricken by sin," and a pervasive question in the poem is whether there is any source of water that would symbolically purify him. "*Piyyut* for Nights of Awe" refers to "a prayer to purify the blood / in every vein within me." The speaker in "How Shall I Come" contemplates someday approaching God "with the silence of my sins." In "Take My Thoughts," there is a reference to people vomiting out their sins. Yet none of these imagined ways of a sinful person approaching God—yearning, praying, immersion in water, expulsion of sin—definitively relieve any of the speakers of their guilt.

Despite the challenges to his faith in a God who cares for humanity and for-gives people's sins, in his poetry Reich never seems to completely give up on the possibility of prayer. Even with all of the doubts that his poetry expresses, he suggests in the titles of a number of poems that they are a kind of prayer: "*Piyyut* [liturgical poem] for Nights of Awe," "*Piyyut* for Days of Awe," "Travel Prayer," and "Ne'ilah [the final prayer on Yom Kippur]." One poem bears the title "In-stead of a Prayer," and another is titled "Kind of a Prayer," as if to suggest that even if one cannot pray one needs to do something to make up for this lack of ability to address God.

As he seeks to explore the possibility of religious experience, the poet finds it necessary to modify the traditional language of prayer, as well as that of biblical and rabbinic texts, by changing the wording or the context of the appearance of expressions. These modifications have the effect of freeing God from tradi-tional images that are difficult for the poet to accept. In a number of cases, the

poet departs from images of the God of Israel as a supernatural being and re-
conceives Him in more universal, human, and naturalistic terms. In "*Piyyut* for
Nights of Awe," the speaker writes of praying "to Him who answers on judg-
ment night those who call," an expression which is very close to the traditional
liturgical expression "to Him who answers those who call to Him on judgment
day." The fact that God is never mentioned by name in this poem, however,
lends a new significance to the use of the pronoun "Him" in this expression.
Rather than referring to God, "Him" now becomes a more ambiguous term
that could refer to a source of response conceived of differently than the tradi-
tional God of Israel. The poem "Kind of a Prayer" begins with the words "Praise
to Him who granted the sky / its endless color / with patience so clear," a reason
to praise God that does not appear in the traditional liturgy. The title of the
poem "*Piyyut* for Nights of Awe" ("*Piyyut* leleilot nora'im"), is a play on the tra-
ditional expression "a *piyyut* for the Days of Awe" (*piyyut leyamim nora'im*).
This connects the concerns of the poet with themes of Rosh Hashanah and
Yom Kippur, but individualizes it and puts it in a universal human context by
suggesting that the poet refers not to any period in the holiday cycle, but rather
to difficult nights that he and others have experienced. In addition, it is
significant that, in this poem, the speaker writes of the physical gesture of his
"hand groping in the world" as a necessary substitute for the words of prayer that
he is incapable of uttering. He goes on to declare that it is not the merits of the
ancestors or an angelic advocate, as tradition would have it, but rather a new
path in life chosen by the speaker that "perhaps / now will defend [him] at the
judgment."

An approach that Reich adopts in a number of poems is to replace references
to God in religious expressions with images of nature and natural occurrences.
In two poems, night takes the place of God as a source of understanding and
forgiveness. In "*Piyyut* for Nights of Awe," the speaker prays for "a night that will
understand my dreams." In "Take My Thoughts," the liturgical expression "God
full of mercy provide perfect rest under the wings of the Shekhinah" becomes
"A night full of mercy will provide the perfect rest / for all who suffer under the
wings of the sky." In "Instead of a Prayer," nature, not God, is the object of praise
and inspiration, when the speaker declares, "I bless the morning with eyes of
splendor and serenity" and "Light excites me / even a single lightning bolt is a
blaze of exultation." Also in this poem, the burning bush in which God was re-
vealed to Moses, which in defiance of the laws of nature is not consumed, be-
comes an image that figuratively suggests anything that keeps going in a power-
ful manner: "I know that in the burning bush / or in anything that burns but is
not consumed / God moves around in goodness." In another part of the poem,
the expression from Psalms "the heavens are the heavens of the Lord" becomes
"the heavens are always the heavens." In "A voice . . . ," the voice of God, to
which Psalms refers as "causing hinds to calve, breaking cedars," is actually the

sound of a ram's horn. The expression from Psalms "may the pleasantness of the Lord our God be upon us" becomes simply "may pleasantness be upon [my feet]" in the poem "Travel Prayer."

Reich seeks to bridge the distance between the divine and the human in his poetry by speaking of humanity with expressions that traditionally refer to God and speaking of God with expressions that usually refer to humanity. In "If There Are," the expression by which God refers to Himself in the revelation to Moses at the burning bush, "I will be who I will be," refers not to God but to the human speaker. In "Ne'ilah," instead of the human Moses turning "here and there" after killing the Egyptian taskmaster, God turns "here and there," only to discover how far He is from humanity. The poem "Instead of a Prayer" makes use of expressions that praise God to praise humanity instead. The liturgical phrase from the Havdalah prayer in which God is blessed as the one who distinguishes between the holy and the profane becomes "Blessed is the man who distinguishes man from wolf." In "Black Holes," the black holes of space are the footprints of God who has left His house and taken a walk in His boots.

In Reich's religious poetry, the significant number of biblical allusions to narratives about Moses, the Exodus from Egypt, and the Israelites' wandering in the wilderness suggests that the poet has been particularly fascinated with these narratives. Expressions such as "the pillars of cloud and fire" which served to guide the Israelites in the wilderness ("Take My Thoughts"), "the burning bush" of God's first revelation to Moses ("Instead of a Prayer"), and "this over-look mountain," a reference to the place from where Moses viewed the Promised Land ("Ne'ilah"), are used to refer to the speaker's longing for some kind of divine revelation along the lines of that which God granted to Moses and the Israelites. Because these expressions are taken out of their original biblical context, they can suggest experiences which are analogous but not identical to that of Moses or the Israelites.

The poems I am considering include those that explore the possibility of relating to God but do not address Him directly, and those in which the speaker seeks to communicate directly with God. Despite Reich's break from traditional observance in his youth, he seems never to have abandoned the search for the experience of God he once found in Jewish ritual and prayer.

On the Possibility of Relating to God

פִּיּוּט לְלֵילוֹת נוֹרָאִים

יַד מְגַשֶּׁשֶׁת בָּעוֹלָם
לִפְעָמִים לִבִּי.
זוֹ תְּפִלָּה לְטָהוֹר הַדָּם
בְּכָל עוֹרֵק שֶׁבִּי.

וְגַם דֶּרֶךְ חֲדָשָׁה שֶׁאוּלַי   5
עַכְשָׁו תַּעֲמֹד לִזְכוּתִי בַּדִּין
וְתַכִּיר בָּאֲפֵלָה אֶת נְעָלַי
וְלַיְלָה שֶׁאֶת חֲלוֹמוֹתַי יָבִין.

שְׁעַת יוֹסֵף עָלַי תָּנוּחַ
וְאֶחְלֹם כָּמוֹהוּ   10
אֵיךְ מֵחַגְוֵי לִבְּךָ יָפוּחַ
הַתֹּהוּ וְהַבֹּהוּ.

זוֹ תְּפִלָּה אֵינָה לַשָּׁוְא
כְּבָר בָּרָק פּוֹרֵץ שָׁמַיִם וָרַעַם–
לְעוֹנֶה בְּלֵיל דִּין לְקוֹרְאָיו   15
אוּלַי יַעֲנֶה לִי הַפַּעַם.

Piyyut for Nights of Awe

A hand groping in the world
sometimes my heart.
It's a prayer to purify the blood
in every vein within me.

5   And a new path that perhaps
now will defend me at the judgment
and recognize my shoes in darkness
and a night that will understand my dreams.

May the hour of Joseph rest upon me
10   and I dream like him
how from the clefts of your* heart will blow
the unformed and the void.

This prayer is not in vain
already lightning is piercing the sky and thunder—
15   to Him who answers on judgment night those who call
perhaps He'll answer me this time.[14]
*The second person possessive is in the feminine singular form.

The title of the poem associates it with the *piyyut* tradition of the Days of Awe, but the expression "nights of awe" (*leilot nora'im*), which comes in place of the traditional expression "days of awe" (*yamim nora'im*), may be taken to mean either the nights of the period of the Days of Awe or any night in which the speaker experiences existential dread. Concepts such as "purification" (*tihur*, 3), "judgment" (*din*, 6), and "prayer" (*tefillah*, 3; 13) link the poem to the traditional Jewish liturgy. Nevertheless, the speaker never addresses God directly, and it is only in the last two lines of the poem that he refers even indirectly to God.

In the spirit of the Days of Awe, the speaker tells of his attempts to pray for a new beginning. In the first stanza, he prays for the purification of his blood "in every vein within [him]" (3–4). Perhaps because the speaker has difficulty relating to the language of the traditional liturgy, at times he expresses his prayer by means of a nonverbal physical gesture, a "hand groping in the world" (1), and at other times his prayer comes directly as a feeling from his "heart" (2), without being translated into words.

Even as the speaker continues to use words in this poem to convey the content of his prayer, he speaks in concrete imagery that transcends a conceptual approach. In the second stanza, the speaker imagines himself embarking on "a new path" (5) in life, a new way of living. He hopes that this path will provide a defense for him "at the judgment" (6). The reference to judgment links this hope to the traditional imagery of Jews standing in judgment before God, yet the lack of reference to God up to this point in the poem leaves open the question of who is actually judging the speaker. The speaker then shifts from a desire for moral justification to a yearning for a transcendent source of understanding and acceptance. There appear to be two possible sources of such acceptance: one is the new path on which he has embarked, which even in darkness will recognize his shoes as they walk on it (5–7); and the other is night itself, which will fully understand the dreams he has (8).

The dreams themselves might constitute a sign that his desire for a new beginning will unfold. The biblical Joseph dreamed of what would happen in the future: his rise to power, the fate of the butler and the baker, and the years of plenty and famine in Egypt (Genesis 37, 40, 41) (9–10). Similarly, in lines 11 and 12, the speaker dreams that his female lover (*libbekh*, "your heart," is in second person feminine singular) will be freed of her inner confusion and experience inner healing. Just as he made use of concrete imagery to convey his hopes for his own renewal, so he refers by means of such imagery to the renewal he wishes for his lover: "how from the clefts of your heart will blow / the unformed and the void" (11–12). The erotic nature of his relationship with this woman is suggested by the use of two expressions that appear in the Song of Songs: "clefts" (ḥagvei, 11 [Song of Songs 2:14]) and "will blow" (yafuaḥ, 11 [Song of Songs 2:17; 4:6]). The expression hatohu vehabohu ("the unformed and the void," 12) alludes to tohu vavohu, the state of the unformed and void out of which God created the cosmos, according to Genesis 1:2. This psychological renewal of the woman released from inner turmoil is, thus, analogous to the divine creation of the cosmos out of chaos. The reference to creation is appropriate in a poem on the Days of Awe, since Jewish tradition teaches that the world was created on Rosh Hashanah.

Although the speaker never indicates that his prayer has been fully answered, in the final stanza, he declares that his address "to Him who answers on judgment night those who call" (15) "is not in vain" (13). He makes this conclusion when he hears and sees thunder and lightning (14). Thunder and lightning are associated with the revelation of God at Sinai (Exodus 19:16), and, therefore, can serve as a sign of God's presence. The loud noise made by the thunder and the forceful way the lightning seems to pierce the sky all point to a power that can transform the inner state of this speaker and his lover. Whether or not the divine response is completely satisfying, it is significant that the nonverbal prayers of the speaker, expressed by means of gesture, feeling, and concrete imagery, are met by a nonverbal response associated with God.

The expression "to Him who answers on judgment night those who call" (15) is based on a line in a piyyut recited on the Days of Awe, "Le'El orekh din": "to Him who answers those who call to Him on judgment day." (In the translation of the poem, the expression "to Him" following the expression "who call" was omitted for stylistic reasons.) Because of the association between the expression in the poem and the traditional piyyut, this is the most direct reference to God in the poem. Nevertheless, the fact that God is not explicitly mentioned anywhere in the poem leaves open the possibility of a nontraditional conception of some kind of response from a realm beyond the speaker that resembles, but is not conceptually identical with, traditional notions of God. The poet also makes a distinction between this line and the line in the original piyyut by making a slight change in the syntax. In the original piyyut, the line reads: le'oneh leqorav beyom din (literally "to Him who answers those who call to Him on judgment day"), whereas in the poem the line reads: le'oneh beleil din leqorav (literally "to Him who answers on judgment night those who call"). The location of the expression "on judgment night" earlier in the line than would be expected calls attention to its particular meaning in the context of the poem. Furthermore, in contrast to the certainty expressed in the traditional piyyut that God responds to prayer, the speaker can only express the hope that "perhaps He'll answer me this time" (16).

קוֹל
וְעוֹד קוֹל
וּבַת קוֹל.
בְּלֵיל זֶה יִבְכָּיוּן כָּל הַקוֹלוֹת
קוֹרְאִים לַקוֹל   5
הַמִּתְהַלֵּךְ בַּגַּן.
אוּלַי יַעֲנֶה לָנוּ
הַקוֹל שֶׁעָנָה לְאַבְרָהָם.
שִׁמְעוּ נָא רַבּוֹתַי דַּיָּנִים מָמְחִים,
אֲנִי מָמְחֶה לִבְדִידוּת.   10
שִׁמְעוּ נָא קוֹל שׁוֹפָר
מְסַפֵּר רָזִים,
מְחוֹלֵל אַיָּלוֹת.
שׁוֹבֵר אֲרָזִים.
קוֹל חָשׁוּךְ וְקוֹל מוּאָר.   15
עַל פִּי שְׁנֵי הֵדִים
יָקוּם הַקוֹל
מוֹלִיךְ אֶת חַיַּי, נוֹשֵׁב אוֹתִי בַּדֶּרֶךְ.
הַקוֹל
בַּקוֹל   20
מִקוֹל
קוֹל.

A voice,
another voice,
the echo of a voice.
On this night all voices weep
5   calling out to the voice
moving about in the garden.
Perhaps we will be answered
by the voice that answered Abraham.
Listen now gentlemen expert judges,
10   I'm an expert in loneliness.
Hear now the voice of the ram's horn
recounting mysteries,
causing hinds to calve.
Breaking cedars.
15   A darkened voice, an illuminated voice.
By two echoes
the voice will arise
guiding my life, urging me along the path.

> The voice
> 20   in the voice
>   from the voice
>   a voice.[15]

As in "*Piyyut* for Nights of Awe," the speaker neither addresses God nor refers to Him directly. The central image of this poem is the voice (*qol*). The poem begins in a haunting manner, with the sound of one voice, followed by the sound of another voice, followed by an echo (*bat qol*, literally "the daughter of a voice," 1–3). The poet conveys the lack of connection among the voices and the echo by placing each on a line of its own. In lines 4 to 6, the collective voice of humanity then unites to cry out to a voice associated with God. This is a special night ("On this night," 4), and the crying of the voices is expressed with the archaic form *yivkayun*, which appears only twice in the Bible in poetic passages in Isaiah 33:7 and Job 31:38. The voices heard that night address "the voice / moving about in the garden" (5–6), an allusion to Genesis 3:8. Since, in the original biblical context of the image, God's voice moves about in the Garden of Eden after Adam and Eve have defied Him by eating the fruit of the tree of knowledge, it would appear that the issue for those who pray in this poem is that of guilt before God. In the Genesis story, God calls out in an angry and accusatory manner to the hiding Adam, "Where are you?" (Genesis 3:9). But, in lines 7 and 8, another allusion shifts the image of a guilt-inducing God to one who is responsive to human need: "Perhaps we will be answered / by the voice that answered Abraham" (7–8). This expression alludes to a line in the Yom Kippur liturgy, which declares, "He who answered Abraham at Mount Moriah will answer us." The God with whom the speaker wishes to communicate is the one who answered Abraham's deeply felt desire not to sacrifice his son (Genesis 22). In the traditional liturgy, the association of those who pray in the present day with Abraham suggests that God is merciful and also that, as descendants of Abraham, Jews can count on God's mercy. But, for the speaker, this conviction must be modified by the word "perhaps."

Reverting back to the sense of disconnectedness conveyed in the first three lines of the poem, the speaker shifts from the power of the collective voice to that of an individual voice. He calls on experts in the law to hear his declaration that his expertise is in loneliness (9–10). He seems to be saying here that there is more to consider on the Day of Judgment than the judges' preoccupation with whether one has fulfilled the law. In other words, there is a deeper personal alienation that must be taken seriously as well. Then he calls on these experts, or perhaps on a larger audience, to hear "the voice [the Hebrew word for "voice," *qol*, can also signify "sound"] of the ram's horn [shofar]" (11), echoing the conclusion of the blessing recited on Rosh Hashanah before the blowing of the shofar, "to hear the sound of the shofar." Drawing on traditional Jewish imagery associating the sound of the shofar with divine revelation, the speaker refers to that sound as "recounting [mystical] mysteries" (12) and as having the effect of the voice of God described in Psalm 29:5, 9 (a psalm which, according to Jewish tradition, describes the revelation at Sinai), a voice that has the ability to "caus[e] hinds to calve" (13) and to "[break] cedars" (14). This sound, furthermore, can sustain itself in darkness and light ("A darkened voice, an illuminated voice," 15).

The shofar blast, which can be seen as an expression of the divine voice, can serve as a powerful guide for the speaker's life ("guiding my life, urging me along the path," 18). Yet, perhaps it is not the voice of God the speaker hears, but only an echo. The expression "By two echoes" (*al pi shenei hedim*, 16) is a play on the biblical expression that refers to the need for two witnesses to convict an accused person in a trial ("according to two witnesses [*al pi shenei edim*]," Deuteronomy 19:15). These two echoes, rather than the voice itself, may be all that the speaker can hear; they are as close as he will get to a reliable testimony to the existence of God and to a divine voice guiding humanity. In traditional imagery, the sound of the shofar can be of human or divine source. Jews blow the shofar before God on Rosh Hashanah, shofar blasts accompanied the revelation at Sinai (Exodus 19:16), and, according to Isaiah 27:13, the shofar will accompany the final redemption. In Zechariah 9:14, it is stated that God Himself will blow a shofar at the final redemption, an image that is carried over to the traditional liturgy in the daily "Amidah" and the "Musaf Amidah" of Rosh Hashanah, in which God is asked to "blow the great shofar of our liberation." This dual nature of the shofar blasts allows the poet to preserve the ambiguity that is prevalent in much of his poetry regarding whether the fulfillment of human needs will take place by supernatural or natural means.

The series of references to voices at the end of the poem, "The voice / in the voice / from the voice / a voice (*haqol / baqol / miqol / qol*, 19–22), is a play on the expression *bakol mikol kol* found in the traditional Jewish grace after meals. In the original liturgical passage, *kol* (spelled with the letter *kaf* and meaning "all"), a homonym of *qol* (spelled with the letter *qof* and meaning "voice"), refers to the many blessings provided by God to each of the patriarchs Abraham, Isaac, and Jacob. This play on words adds to the sense of supportive connection that the divine voice has with the speaker that we saw in line 8, "the voice that answered Abraham." The return to the style of one-word lines in the original Hebrew that was evident in lines 1 to 3 suggests, however, a return to a state of fragmentation presented by a series of disconnected voices that makes one wonder how steadfast the responsiveness and guidance of God can be for humanity.

פִּיּוּט לְיָמִים נוֹרָאִים

שֶׁקֶט בָּאֲוִיר. דְּמָמָה.
הָאֵל חוֹשֵׁב עַל דְּבַר מַה.
צִירֵי לֵדָה. צִירֵי מָוֶת.
מִי יָנוּחַ וּמִי יָנוּעַ
שֶׁקֶט נָא לֹא לְהַרְעִישׁ. 5
בְּנוֹת־קוֹל יוֹצְאוֹת וּבָאוֹת
בִּמְחוֹל הֵדִים הַמּוּמִים.
וְהָאֱלֹהִים הַזָּקֵן וְהַטּוֹב
כָּל־כָּךְ זָקֵן וָטוֹב וְרָגִישׁ.
וְחוּשָׁיו עֲמוּמִים וְהָאָרֶץ עוֹד תָּסֹב. 10
תְּנוּ לוֹ בַּיּוֹם זֶה לְהַרְגִּישׁ
שֶׁהוּא בֶּאֱמֶת מִישֶׁהוּ. אֵל
אוּלַי לֹא גָּדוֹל וְלֹא גִּבּוֹר וְלֹא נוֹרָא
כְּפִי שֶׁתְּפִלּוֹת הַפִּרְסֹמֶת מְסַפְּרוֹת עָלָיו.
אֲבָל אֵין כָּל צֹרֶךְ לְזַלְזֵל. 15
הוּא מִשְׁתַּדֵּל. הוּא בֶּאֱמֶת מִשְׁתַּדֵּל
לְהָכִין לָנוּ שָׁנָה בְּלִימָה חֲדָשָׁה.
לִפְעָמִים גַּם אֲנִי מַרְגִּישׁ רָצוֹן לְהִתְפַּלֵּל
אֵלָיו לְדַבֵּר אִתּוֹ לְמַלְמֵל כַּמָּה מִלִּים אֲרַמִיּוֹת.
יְקוּם פֻּרְקָן מִן שְׁמַיָּא חִנָּא וְחִסְדָּא. 20
אֲנִי מְשַׁעֵר שֶׁיֵּשׁ לַבּוֹרֵא יַחַס טוֹב
וְאַלְמוֹנִי לְרָחוֹק וְלַקָּרוֹב.

Piyyut for Days of Awe

Quiet in the air. Silence.
God is thinking about something.
Birth pangs. Death pangs.
Who shall rest and who shall wander?
5   Quiet, don't make noise.
Heavenly voices come and go
in a dance of terrified echoes.
And the good old God
is so old and good and sensitive.
10   His senses are dulled but the world's still turning.
Let Him feel on this day
that He really is someone. God,
perhaps not as great not as mighty not as awesome

as the prayer ads tell of Him.

15   But there's no need to disparage.
He's trying. He's really trying
to prepare for us a new year out of nothingness.
Sometimes I too feel the desire to pray
to speak with Him to mumble some words in Aramaic.

20   *Yequm purqan min shemayya ḥinna veḥisda.**
I suppose the Creator has a relationship good
and anonymous with all those far and near.[16]

This poem differs markedly from the previously discussed "*Piyyut* for Nights of Awe." Unlike the speaker in that poem, who expresses a yearning for the fulfillment of human needs, the speaker in this poem presents a portrait of God. At the beginning of the poem, the speaker ironically undermines the traditional image of God as the wise ruler of the universe who carefully balances justice and mercy as He judges the fate of humanity at the beginning of the new year. The speaker begins with what could easily set the stage for a scene of religious serenity: "Quiet in the air. Silence" (1). The word for "silence," *demamah*, recalls the biblical expression *qol demamah daqqah*, the "still, small voice" in which God revealed Himself to the prophet Elijah (1 Kings 19:12). This expression also appears in the description of heaven on the Day of Judgment in the "Unetanneh toqef" prayer of Rosh Hashanah and Yom Kippur. The second line, however, greatly undermines the initial impression that we are about to read of a profoundly moving image of God, for here God is brought down to a more human level: "God is thinking about something" (2). We now understand that the reason for the reference to quiet was not to set a scene of heavenly silence, but rather it was a call for all to cease making noise so that God can concentrate on whatever He is thinking. This is a God who is having trouble focusing on the role humanity expects Him to play as the divine judge. It would seem that God's thoughts have something to do with the expressions in lines 3 and 4: "Birth pangs. Death pangs. / Who shall rest and who shall wander?" Although God is supposedly the master of life and death and the one who, according to the "Unetanneh toqef" prayer, determines "who shall rest and who shall wander," the very fact that these thoughts are presented as disjointed expressions suggests that He does not have a firm grasp of what He is supposed to be doing. Then, as if to reinforce the sense that God is having trouble concentrating, the speaker once again reminds his audience to be silent ("Quiet, don't make noise," 5) so that God can concentrate on His thoughts. In lines 6 to 10, the ineffectual nature of God is made clear by the contrast between, on the one hand, the dynamic presence of "Heavenly voices . . . / in a dance of terrified

*Beginning of a traditional prayer in Aramaic: "May salvation come from Heaven, grace, and lovingkindness. . . ."

echoes" (6–7) and the world that is "still turning" (10), and, on the other hand, a God who is described as "the good old God / . . . so old and good and sensitive. / His senses are dulled" (8–10). The terror of the dance of voices is conveyed by the fact that the expression for "dance of echoes," *mehol hedim*, recalls the expression "dance of demons," *mehol shedim*, which is used figuratively in Hebrew to connote an uncontrollable rampage.[17] God, thus, appears to be unable to control the mysterious chaos of His heavenly realm, while the world somehow functions without Him.

After this rather disheartening view of God, the speaker argues in an obviously ironic manner for understanding and empathy for this limited divinity. He admits in lines 13 and 14 that the way tradition portrays God as "great, mighty, and awesome," in the words of the beginning of the "Amidah" prayer, is perhaps just an exaggerated expression promoting God's image, a "prayer ad" that is no more or less accurate than any commercial message. Nevertheless, in an ironic defense of God, the speaker states that He should be given credit at least for trying to play the role of ruler of the universe: "But there's no need to disparage. / He's trying. He's really trying / to prepare for us a new year out of nothingness" (15–17). The expression "a new year out of nothingness" (*shenat belimah hadashah*) alludes to the biblical verse "who suspended earth over emptiness" (*toleh erets al belimah*, Job 26:7), which is also found in the *piyyut* for the Days of Awe which begins "You are our God in heaven and on earth" (*Attah hu Eloheinu bashamayim uva'arets*). In the traditional contexts of these expressions, God conquers the chaos of emptiness that preceded the creation of the world by establishing the world on top of it. God in the poem, however, can only make an attempt to conquer the chaos for us at the start of this new year, with no guarantee of success.

Although this God is not a very impressive deity, the speaker cannot completely dispel his "desire to pray" (18). In keeping with the ironic distance the narrator creates between himself and God, however, this attempt at prayer comes across as rather half-hearted. He refers to it as "some words in Aramaic," a language in which a small percentage of traditional prayers are composed and that may not be as readily understandable to him as would be prayers in Hebrew (18–20). In the translation, the line is kept in the original Aramaic to preserve the sense of strangeness that is conveyed by the contrast between the Aramaic line in the original and the Hebrew of the rest of the poem. The Aramaic expression is from a prayer recited on Sabbath mornings in the section of the service following the reading of the Torah. Its call for "salvation . . . , grace, and lovingkindness" coming to us "from Heaven" contrasts rather ironically with the failings of God conveyed by the poem. The speaker's less than fully enthusiastic approach to prayer is conveyed not only by the more obscure nature of the Aramaic language, but also by the fact that he desires to pray only "sometimes" (18), and when he does, he says the words in the manner of indistinct mumbling (19).

Lines 21 and 22 capture the ambiguity that has permeated the ironic tone of the entire poem. The speaker has the desire to think of God as having a good and constructive relationship with the world, but his affirmation of this desire can only come in the form of a tentative statement. He supposes that one can say God has a good relationship "with all those far and near," but even if this is true, it is an "anonymous" relationship; God does not know our names and we do not know His. Thus, the desire to relate to God remains, but so do the grave doubts about how helpful God can be in fulfilling human needs.

בִּמְקוֹם תְּפִלָּה

מַה יֵּשׁ לְדַבֵּר? הַשָּׁמַיִם הֵם תָּמִיד שָׁמַיִם
וַאֲנִי מְבָרֵךְ עַל הַבֹּקֶר בְּעֵינֵי נֹגַהּ וְרֹגַע
רַק תְּנוּ לִי לְהַלֵּל אוֹתוֹ בַּצָּהֳרַיִם.

בָּרוּךְ הָאָדָם הַמַּבְדִּיל בֵּין אָדָם לִזְאֵב
וּבָרוּךְ הָעוֹף הַמַּבְדִּיל בֵּין דַּחֲלִיל לְאָדָם   5
מַה יֵּשׁ לְדַבֵּר? אוֹר עוֹשֶׂה לִי הִתְפַּעֲמוּת
גַּם בָּרָק בּוֹדֵד הוּא שַׁלְהֶבֶת הִתְרוֹמְמוּת.

אֲנִי יוֹדֵעַ כִּי הַסְּנֶה הַבּוֹעֵר בָּאֵשׁ
אוֹ כָּל דָּבָר שֶׁבּוֹעֵר וְאֵינוּ אֻכָּל
שָׁם אֱלֹהִים מִתְהַלֵּךְ בַּטּוֹב כְּמִלְחַשׁ לוֹ   10
עִם גֶּחָלִים סוֹד גִּצִּים הַד זְרָדִים מִתְפַּצְּחִים
וְאוּלַי לְשָׁעָה יְרַחֵם עָלֵינוּ בְּלִבְלוּבֵי הַלֶּהָבָה.

INSTEAD OF A PRAYER

What's there to say? The heavens are always the heavens
and I bless the morning with eyes of splendor and serenity
just let me praise it at noon.

Blessed is the man who distinguishes man from wolf
5   and blessed is the bird who distinguishes scarecrow from man.
What's there to say? Light excites me
even a single lightning bolt is a blaze of exultation.

I know that in the burning bush
or in anything that burns but is not consumed
10   God moves around in goodness as if uttering incantations
with coals the secret of sparks the echo of crackling sticks
and perhaps for a moment He'll pity us in the blossoming of the
     flame.[18]

To write a poem as a substitute for prayer is to suggest that the need to pray is very real, but the traditional language and forms of prayer are no longer appropriate to the speaker. Twice in the poem, the speaker asks the question, "What's there to say?" (1, 6). This question can be understood as an expression of the speaker's inability to know what words to utter in prayer. There is, however, another connotation to the expression "What's there to say?" (*mah yesh ledabber*), namely that there is no point in saying anything because something is obvious, or unchangeable, or beyond discussion. This could fit well with the sense in the poem that the world, as the speaker observes it, is truly wondrous beyond words.

The way the speaker succeeds in writing a substitute for prayer is by using expressions from which he omits direct references to God that convey emotions associated with religious experience. He transforms the expression "The heavens are the heavens of the Lord" (Psalms 115:16), recited on holidays in the "Hallel" prayer, into "The heavens are always the heavens" (1). Here God is not mentioned, but the reliability of the heavens' existence is an element of religious faith that the speaker can affirm. The speaker then utters a blessing celebrating the morning and asks for the ability to keep praising it until noon. The expression "I bless the morning" (*ani mevarekh al haboqer*, 2) allows for the possibility of God, since the expression *mevarekh al* is used in traditional terminology to mean "to utter a blessing to God in response to something" (e.g., *levarekh al hayayin* = to bless [God] for the wine), and yet the poet does not mention God. What remains of the traditional religious response is the feeling of gratitude for the beginning of a new day. In keeping with the speaker's difficulty in using the language of tradition, he avoids uttering the blessing on the morning in words, but rather expresses that blessing with eyes that reflect "splendor and serenity" (2). Furthermore, the expression in line 3 "to praise it at noon" definitely departs from traditional language, since in this case it is clearly the morning, not God, that is being praised.

The speaker suggests that the optimistic trust that he feels upon wakening in the morning might not last long, although he urgently hopes it will, as he pleads, "[J]ust let me praise it [the morning] at noon" (3). The word for "let" (*tenu*) appears in the second person plural, which would also indicate a departure from traditional formulations of religious faith. In the traditional prayer book, the "Amidah" prayer is introduced with the biblical verse "Lord, open my lips, and my mouth will utter Your praises" (Psalms 51:17). In that verse, it is clear that God is the one who will help us to praise Him. In the poem, however, the speaker does not turn to God, but rather to an unspecified plurality (perhaps other people, perhaps powers beyond him) to allow him to maintain his mood of grateful praise.

In lines 4 and 5, the speaker plays on the traditional liturgical formulation of the Havdalah ceremony at the conclusion of the Sabbath, which blesses God "who distinguishes the holy from the profane, light from darkness, Israel from

the nations, the seventh day from the six days of deeds." Here it is God's crea-
tures who are being blessed; humans are blessed for knowing the distinction
between human and animalistic behavior ("who distinguishes man from wolf,"
4), and birds are praised for knowing the difference between a superficial
representation of humanity ("scarecrow," 5) and the truly human ("man," 5).
These blessings connect the speaker with the religious appreciation of the God-
given powers of moral discernment, but again without mentioning God. The pow-
ers of distinction that are being blessed here are those that ensure self-preservation.
The person who can tell a humane person from an aggressive animal-like per-
son, and the bird who can tell a scarecrow, which does not threaten him, from
a human, who could threaten him, are both indeed blessed with continuing
life. In lines 6 and 7, the speaker returns to the nontheistic religious exultation
of his initial morning experience. Light, even that which he sees quickly in one
lightning bolt, can arouse in him the religious excitement (*hitpa'amut*) and ex-
altation (*hitromemut*) that God, in traditional terms, evokes in those who expe-
rience His presence.

It is not until the third stanza that the speaker refers to God by name. Like
Moses, who discovered God in the bush that burned but was not consumed
(Exodus 3:2), so the speaker declares that he knows that one can find God in such
a sight (8–11). Here the speaker seems to be less interested in the specific mirac-
ulous occurrence of the biblical burning bush and more in any phenomenon—
supernatural or natural—that persists in the face of the threat of destruction
("anything that burns but is not consumed," 9). This possibility of continued ex-
istence despite opposing forces is a sign that there may be a God in the world
who will comfort us and help us to persevere despite that which opposes us. The
crackling fire of the burning bush suggests to the speaker that this is the sound
of God "uttering incantations" (10–11). This God is a far cry from the one whose
voice from the bush commanded Moses to return to Egypt to liberate the Israel-
ites. He is more self-absorbed, even perhaps praying to Himself, but nevertheless
His presence does bring a degree of assurance to the speaker. The speaker does
not expect God to do any act nearly as impressive as the Exodus from Egypt that
He foretold to Moses in the burning bush. Instead, he expresses a more modest
wish that out of the aesthetically pleasing, blossom-like flame of the bush "per-
haps for a moment" God will "pity us" (12).

אִם יֵשׁ

אִם יֵשׁ מַעְיְנוֹת מְחִילָה יִהְיֶה נָא לִי
(בִּמְחִילָה מִכְּבוֹדוֹ) מַעְיָן־מְעַט
יָזוּב לָרֹב מַיִם חַיִּים יְחַטֵּא אוֹתִי
כִּמְסִלָּה זַכָּה לְעַצְמִי לֹא אַכְזָב אוֹ חָתוּם
יִהְיֶה הוּא בִּשְׁבִילִי כְּמַעְיָן הַמִּתְגַּבֵּר   5
לֹא מָהוּל עִם מִישֶׁהוּ שׁוּם אַחֵר

אוֹ אֲפִלּוּ אַךְ פֶּלֶג אִם יֵשׁ
מְבוֹדָד בִּשְׁבִילִי (כַּשֶּׁלֶג יַלְבִּין לִי)
וְלֹא אֶמְעַד מִכֶּה עָווֹן
בּוֹדֵד מֵחֶסֶד בָּאתִי חֶשְׁבּוֹן   10
(עַל הַנִּסְתָּרוֹת וְהַנִּגְלוֹת)

אֲפִלּוּ אַךְ פִּכְפּוּךְ נָמוּךְ אִם רַק יֵשׁ
אֶת נַפְשִׁי יְנַקֶּה אֶת כְּלִי מִכֹּל
וַאֲנִי מִשְׁקֶה מַחֲשָׁבוֹת לִנְאוֹת־מַעְיָן לְעַצְמִי
אוֹ פֶּלַח פֶּלֶג אִם אַךְ יֵשׁ לְמִי   15

אִם אַךְ יִתֵּן בִּי מְעַט מִן הַמְעַט מִמַּעְיָנוֹ,
מִבַּעַד לַמַּבּוּעַ הַפִּלְאִי הַזֶּה אוֹר יַעֲלֶה
(מַעְיָן קָטָן) וְכָל מַעְיָנַי יִפְכּוּ לָהֶן מוֹצָא

אִם יֵשׁ יִהְיֶה
וַאֲנִי, אֶהְיֶה אֲשֶׁר אֶהְיֶה.   20

If There Are

If there are springs of forgiveness let me please have
(with all due respect) a small spring
with abundantly flowing fresh water it will cleanse me
like a pure path for myself not dry or sealed
5   let it be for me like a gushing spring
unadulterated by anyone by any other.

Or even if there's only a stream
singled out for me (may it whiten me like snow)
so I won't stumble stricken by sin
10   separated from grace taking stock
(about the hidden and revealed).

Even if a slow trickle is all there is
it will clean my soul completely of everything
and I, my thoughts watered, will be an oasis spring for myself
15   or a portion of a stream would that someone only had.

If He only gave me a little bit of His spring,
through this wondrous flow a light would rise
(a small spring) and all my springs would gush out.

If there is let it be
20   and I will be who I will be.[19]

This prayer for purification from sin is permeated by a mood of tentativeness
established from the beginning by the title "If There Are." As much as the
speaker longs for purification from sin, he has no firm confidence that the sym-
bolic waters of purification will be provided for him. The first two stanzas of the
poem are replete with expressions that traditionally belong to the realm of sin
and purification from sin: *mehilah* ("forgiveness," 1), *yehattei* ("will cleanse,"
containing the same root letters as a Hebrew word for sin, *het*, 3), *kasheleg yalbin*
("may it whiten . . . like snow" 8, which is an allusion to Isaiah 1:18, "if your sins
be like scarlet they will become as white as snow"), and *mukkeh avon* ("stricken
by sin," 9). As is true of other poems by Reich, God is not mentioned directly,
but only implied as the source of purification, linking the speaker's concerns
with traditional religious categories of experience without tying him too closely
to fixed traditional images of God. The speaker straddles two approaches. One
approach suggests a general desire not directed at any divine entity, for example,
in lines 1 and 2, when the speaker makes a request for a spring to purify him, he
does so with the impersonal expression *yihyeh na li* ("let me please have," 1). The
other approach suggests that he is aware of a divine entity whom he is expected
to respect when he includes the expression *bemehilah mikevodo* ("with all due
respect," literally "with forgiveness from His honor," 2), suggesting that he is
aware that his request might be considered impertinent by the deity.

The speaker makes a series of requests for sources of purifying water. He be-
gins with the grandiose hope for "springs" (*mayenot*, 1), which recall the image
of redemption in the verse "you shall draw waters in joy from the springs of sal-
vation (Isaiah 12:3). However, immediately following this request, he more mod-
estly asks for less impressive sources of water: "a small spring" (*mayan me'at*, 2,
reminiscent of the expression *miqdash me'at* [a small sanctuary] in Ezekiel 11:16,
which rabbinic tradition associates with the synagogue [Megillah 29a]), "a
stream" (*peleg*, 7), "a slow trickle" (*pikhpukh namukh*, 12), "a portion of a stream"
(*pelah peleg*, 15), "a little bit of His spring" (*me'at min hame'at mimayano*, 16),

and "a small spring" (*mayan qatan*, 18), any of which he hopes will have the power of "a gushing spring" (*mayan hamitgabber*, 5) that would purify him of sin with "fresh water" (*mayim ḥayyim*, 3, literally "living water," a biblical expression that is used in traditional ritual law to refer to the naturally flowing water of a ritual bath [*miqvah*]). But, in his desperation, he is so unsure of finding the purifying waters that he will settle for any source, even the most meager one. He speaks not of a communal ritual of purification, but rather of the more personal one of immersion in a ritual bath, emphasizing the solitary nature of the experience "for [him]self" (4), "unadulterated by anyone by any other" (6), and "singled out for [him]" (8).

It is only in lines 9 to 11 that we learn of the sinful state from which the speaker wishes to be saved, a sinfulness that makes him feel as if he is stumbling on a path, separated from divine grace. In this state, he is preoccupied with a moral stock taking in which he seeks to atone for that which he does not know he did ("the hidden [*hanistarot*]") and for that which he does know he did ("[the] revealed [*haniglot*]"). This preoccupation alludes to the Yom Kippur confessional which declares that, whereas we confess that which was revealed to us, God knows all the sins of which we are not aware, in accordance with the verse "The hidden matters [*hanistarot*] are for the Lord our God but the revealed matters [*haniglot*] are for us and our children forever" (Deuteronomy 29:28). Significantly, this image of being purified includes the speaker's freedom not to depend on a deity outside himself anymore. He will then have the inner strength to nurture himself ("and I, my thoughts watered, will be an oasis spring for myself," 14).

The next to last stanza in the poem signals a shift in the nature of the request as the speaker returns to refer, if only indirectly, to God. Here, for the first time he refers to a source of water as belonging to an entity, presumably God's spring (16). A little bit of this divine source of water, he believes, will allow him to see light and open up the internal floodgates of his soul, pouring forth all that is bottled up inside him (16–18). In one sense, the final couplet can be understood as concluding on a note of resignation: if the request is granted, I will continue to exist. In another sense, however, one can discern a more theologically daring statement. The original Hebrew for "let it be" in line 19, *yihyeh*, with the consonants YHYH, closely resembles the Tetragrammaton YHVH, since the letters *yod* and *vav* are graphically and linguistically close. Furthermore, the expression in line 20, "I will be who I will be" (*ehyeh asher ehyeh*), is what God declares to Moses at the burning bush to be His name (Exodus 3:14). Thus, one could read lines 19 and 20 as: "[I am not sure] if there is a God" (*im yesh YHVH*), "[but if necessary] I will be God" (*va'ani, ehyeh asher ehyeh*).

מֵעֵין תְּפִלָּה

תְּהִלָּה לְמִי שֶׁהֶעֱנִיק לָרָקִיעַ
אֶת אֵינְסוֹף צִבְעוֹ
בְּאֹרֶךְ אַפַּיִם צָלוּל.

בַּמְּרוֹמִים
הַשֶּׁמֶשׁ כְּאֵלָה   5
עוֹשָׂה דְּבַר רֵאשִׁית
שֶׁאֵין רֵאשִׁית לְרֵאשִׁיתוֹ.

מַה טֹּבוּ. נוֹפֵי תִּפְאֶרֶת
שֶׁנִּתְּנוּ גְמוּל
לְמִי שֶׁהָיָה   10
הוֶֹה
וְיִהְיֶה.

וְנִפְלְאוֹת אֵינְסוֹף
שֶׁבָּהֶן יְכוֹלָה לְהִוָּלֵד מַחֲשָׁבָה
מִמְּאוֹרוֹת הָאֲדָמָה   15
עַד קְצוֹת הַכּוֹכָבִים.

וְגַם אֱלֹהִים אֲחֵרִים.

KIND OF A PRAYER

Praise to Him who granted the sky
its endless color
with patience so clear.

On high
5   the sun like a goddess
makes a beginning
with no beginning to its beginning.

How goodly. Splendorous views
given in compensation
10   for Him who was
is
and will be.

And infinity of wonders
in which thought can be born
15   from the caves in the earth
to the far reaches of the stars.

And also other gods.[20]

The word *me'ein*, translated in the title as "kind of," is used in traditional Jewish legal literature to refer to a prayer that is a condensed version of a longer prayer. Thus, there is a text known as *sheva me'ein shemoneh esreh* (seven blessings that embody the eighteen blessings of the weekday "Amidah") and another known as *me'ein sheva* (one blessing said on Friday night that embodies the seven blessings of the Sabbath "Amidah"). In certain circumstances, recitation of the condensed version is the legal equivalent of reciting the longer version on which it is based.[21] Thus, the poem is presented as a not quite fully legitimate prayer, but it is still, in some sense, the equivalent of a prayer sanctified by Jewish tradition.

God is not mentioned explicitly in the poem, but He can be understood as the object of the praise in the first stanza. The speaker praises this unnamed God for an action not explicitly mentioned in any of the traditional prayers: "Praise to Him who granted the sky / its endless color / with patience so clear" (1–3). There is an unusual mixture here of the God of nature and the God of morality. God's granting of color to the sky represents His role as the creator of nature, especially since the speaker uses the term *raqia* for "sky," which also appears in the creation story (Genesis 1:6). The fact that God grants color to the sky "with patience" reflects a characteristic of God associated less with creation and more with his ability to forgive people for their sins. In the Bible, this characteristic is known as God being "slow to anger" (*erekh appayim*, Exodus 34:6; Numbers 14:18; Joel 2:13; Jonah 4:2; Nahum 1:3; Psalms 86:15, 103:8, 145:8; Nehemiah 9:17). In the poem, when the speaker refers to God as being "with patience," he uses the expression *orekh apayyim*. The word *orekh* literally means "length" and therefore associates God's quality of patience with the endless sky He created.

In lines 4 to 7, what had appeared to be a praise of the monotheistic God of Jewish tradition starts to seem more like a prayer to pagan deities. The sun, presumably as it has emerged after sunrise to brighten the sky, is likened to "a goddess" (*elah*, the feminine form of a Hebrew word for God, *El*). It is that sun-goddess, not the God of Genesis, who creates a new beginning. That beginning is described with an expression found in the "Yigdal" prayer that poetically conveys Maimonides' principle of faith in God's eternal existence: *ein reshit lereshito* (literally "there is no beginning to His beginning," 7). The poem, thus, appears to be saying that this sun-goddess pre-existed even God.

As the speaker continues to marvel at the beauty of the morning sky, he de-
clares, "How goodly" (*mah tovu*, 8), from the expression "How goodly are your
tents, Jacob" that the prophet Balaam used when he blessed the Israelite en-
campment in the wilderness (Numbers 24:5) and that traditional Jews use when
they first enter the synagogue in the morning. This beauteous appearance of
the sky, the speaker declares, serves as a "compensation" (*gemul*, 9) for our in-
ability to fully believe in the God of tradition, who, as the traditional hymn
"Adon olam" puts it, "was / is / and will be" (10–12). The "infinity of wonders"
the speaker sees can lift one's thoughts from the depths of despair, represented
here by "the caves in the earth," up to the open-ended hopes evoked by the
image of "the far reaches of the stars" (13–16). Indeed, as the poem has sug-
gested, the contemplation of nature may even inspire one to re-conceive of God
in a more pagan manner than tradition allows, pointing to the "other gods" (*elo-
him aherim*, 17) whose worship is prohibited by the Ten Commandments (Exo-
dus 20:3; Deuteronomy 5:7). Thus, all that a religious view of nature can
evoke—wonder, appreciation, and spiritual inspiration—is still possible, but
perhaps only when we see beyond tradition-laden conceptions of God.

חוֹרִים שְׁחֹרִים

כְּשֶׁאֱלֹהִים נוֹעֵל אֶת מַגָּפָיו
וְיוֹצֵא מִבֵּיתוֹ
שְׁמֵי הַשָּׁמַיִם מִתְכַּוְּצִים לִכְבוֹדוֹ.

צְעָדָיו טוֹבְעִים עֲקֵבוֹת,
חוֹרִים שְׁחֹרִים, מַפָּץ   5
גָּדוֹל, קְצוּר דֶּרֶךְ מְכוֹכָב

לְכוֹכָב. הַמֶּרְחָב הַחִיצוֹן
עָקֹם מִשֶּׁנִּדְמֶה לָנוּ –
סוֹפוֹ וְאֵינְסוֹפוֹ הֵם עֵדוּת שְׁקוּפָה
לְקִיּוּמָם שֶׁל יְקוּמִים תְּאוֹמִים.   10

גַּם לֵאלֹהִים אֶחָד
אֵל תְּאוֹם, סוֹבֵל מִטְּחוֹרִים
וּמְלֵחַת אַלְפֵי מַלְאָכִים, חוֹרִים
שְׁחֹרִים: פְּלִיטֵי חֹם פִּתְאוֹמִי,
מִכְרוֹת חֶמְצָה פֶּחָמִית,   15
תְּסִיסַת הַזַּעַם הַשְּׂטָנִית
עַל עוֹלָם וּתְאוֹמוֹ.

BLACK HOLES

When God puts on His boots
and leaves His house
the heavens beyond the heavens contract in His honor.

His steps make footprints,
5   black holes, an explosion
so great, a short cut from star

to star. The external expanse
more crooked than we realize —
its end and its infinity a transparent witness
10   to the existence of twin universes.

And the one God has
a twin god, suffering from hemorrhoids
and from the pus of thousands of angels, black
holes: refugees from sudden heat,
15   mines of carbonic acid,
the fermentation of satanic fury
about the world and its twin.[22]

    The speaker suggests in this poem that there are twin parallel universes: the one we know, ruled by the God of tradition, and another ruled by Satan. A dualistic conception of good and evil gods is not new; it has served in various cultural traditions as an explanation for the existence of both good and evil in the world. Here, however, the speaker makes use of scientific terminology to convey to his contemporary readers that this dualism is not a matter of idle theological speculation, but is actually built into the cosmos as it is conceived by modern science.

    In a rather graphically anthropomorphic statement, the speaker writes of black holes in space as the "footprints" (4) of God. This is a God who is not involved in either the creation and perpetuation of nature or in the events of history. Instead, He is a God who primarily likes to go for walks and receive the adulation due him. He "puts on His boots / and leaves His house" (1–2), and, when he does so, "the heavens beyond the heavens [*shemei shamayim*, a term from medieval Jewish thought] contract in His honor" (3). As God walks, His feet create black holes that open "short cut[s]" (6), including one that connects to the realm of evil.

    Black holes, defined as "cosmic bod[ies] of extremely intense gravity from which nothing, not even light, can escape," are thought to be caused, in many cases, by the death of massive stars.[23] The image conjures up in the popular mind an infinite void that keeps destroying all that enters it.[24] The existence of black holes suggests an unseemly chaotic underside to the cosmos as we know it, not only in the sense of the physically destructive power of black holes, but also in the sense of moral chaos. As the speaker declares, the cosmos is not as perfect and harmonious as we suppose it to be. Its "external expanse / [is] more crooked than we realize" (7–8). Beyond the universe which we inhabit there exists a twin universe much less benign than the one in which we live, ruled by a god who is the twin of the God we know (10–12). That other universe is portrayed by means of images both scatological and immensely destructive in nature. Its god suffers from hemorrhoids and from pus that oozes out of angels, while the black holes flee as "refugees from [the] sudden heat / [of] mines of carbonic acid" (12–15). All these disgusting and destructive elements are the result of "the fermentation of satanic fury" at our world, as well as at the other world (16–17).

   The cosmology suggested by this poem says much about how the speaker views God's relationship to the world. We do not see here the loving compassionate God of Jewish tradition, nor even the God of commandments and justice. This is a God who is honored by the cosmos, but as he trudges around, he opens up passageways to the other Satanic world that is connected with ours and is presumably the source of the evil and suffering we experience. Rather than revert to the more traditional religious imagery of an evil realm ruled by Satan, the poet makes use of the scientific terminology of "black holes" to suggest that evil is as real to us in this sophisticated scientific age as it was to our traditional forebears.

Speaking to God

אֵיךְ אָבוֹא

אֵיךְ אָבוֹא לְפָנֶיךָ הַיּוֹם
וְאַתָּה עָסוּק בְּחֶשְׁבּוֹנוֹת רַבִּים.

אֵיךְ אֲבַקֵּשׁ קִצְבַּת חַיִּים
וַאֲנִי אוֹרֵחַ שֶׁנָּטָה לָלוּן.

מוּטָב וְאָבוֹא בְּפַעַם אַחֶרֶת,   5
יְחִידִי–
עִם דְּמָמַת עֲווֹנוֹתַי.

אַל תַּרְעִיל אֶת אוֹר הַחַלּוֹנוֹת
אַל תַּגִּיף אֶת הַתְּרִיסִים,

חַ כֵּ ה !   10

הֲרֵי אָשׁוּב אֵלֶיךָ
בְּיוֹם מִן הַיָּמִים.

How Shall I Come

How shall I come before You today,
You're busy with so many matters.

How shall I plead for a measure of life
while I am but a guest for the night.

5   It's better if I come another time,
alone—
with the silence of my sins.

Don't veil the windows' light
don't close the shutters.

10   *Wait!*

For I'll return to You
one of these days.[25]

The desire to draw close to God is a central theme in the book of Psalms. In some psalms, this experience is expressed by means of the image of the psalmist himself entering God's house (*avo veitekha*, literally "I come into Your house"), for example, "But I, through Your great love, come into Your house" (Psalms 5: 8) and "I come into Your house with offerings" (Psalms 66:13). In other psalms, it is expressed by means of the image of one's prayer coming before God (*tavo lefanekha*, literally "may it [my prayer or plea] come before you"), for example, "May my prayer come before You" (Psalms 88:3) and "May my plea come before You" (Psalms 119:170). This latter formulation also appears in the introduction to the Yom Kippur confessional: "may our prayer come before You" (*tavo lefanekha tefillatenu*). The speaker combines these two formulations of a person entering God's house and a person's prayer coming before God into the expression "I come before You" (*avo lefanekha*, 1). He is, thus, not exactly like the psalmist who wishes to enter God's house and not exactly like the one who wishes to bring his prayer before God. Instead he *is* the prayer that approaches God. But the desire to come before God is couched in the form of a question: "How shall I come before You today[?]" (1). We gain some insight into what the speaker wants of God in the question he asks in line 3: "How shall I plead for a measure of life[?]" In other words, how can he ask God to continue to grant him the portion of life he would like to have?

Each of the questions in lines 1 and 3 is followed by an explanation as to why the speaker doubts the possibility of drawing close to God. In line 2, it is the speaker's conception of God that seems to elicit this doubt. The speaker assumes that God must be too busy with great cosmic concerns to pay attention to the petty cares of a mere human. In line 4, it is the speaker's lack of commitment to God that would appear to be the barrier. Unlike the psalmist, he has not committed himself to fully enter God's house. Instead, he is merely "a guest for the night" (*oreah natah lalun*, 4). In the original biblical context of this expression (Jeremiah 14:8), it is used to refer to God: the prophet calls on God to help Israel and not be as fleeting a presence as a guest for the night. By reversing its usage, the speaker acknowledges the role he has played in the breakdown of the human–divine relationship.

The speaker's desire to delay confronting God ("It's better if I come another time," 5) would appear to be based on two concerns. He is not yet ready to approach God "with the silence of [his] sins" (7). The word "silence" (*demamah*) may function here to indicate that the speaker has been so overwhelmed by shame that he is not able to even articulate the confession of his sins, as Jewish tradition expects. Furthermore, he cannot seek God's forgiveness in the context of a community, because he has no such community. He approaches God as an individual "alone" (*yehidi*, 6) and overwhelmed by the thought of confronting God. The scary loneliness of this individuality is reinforced by the placement of the word *yehidi* as a single word in line 6.

The speaker decides, therefore, not to force the issue of his forgiveness and to put his approach toward God off till another time. Having declared his reluctance to approach God, however, the speaker fears that God will give up on him and indicate that he is no longer welcome by metaphorically covering the windows of His house. Thus, the speaker cries out, "Don't veil the windows' light / don't close the shutters. / *Wait!*" (8–10). The call to God to wait patiently for him is emphasized by the appearance of the word "wait" (*ḥakkeh*) as the only word in line 10, followed by an exclamation point, and by the graphic technique of placing extra spacing between the letters of the word in Hebrew, which is represented by printing the word in italics in the English translation. Yet one would have to question the determination of the speaker to take the step of approaching God when he states in the last two lines of the poem, "For I'll return to you / one of these days" (11–12). Although in the original Hebrew the expression "one of these days" (*beyom min hayamim*) is in a high literary style, it sounds rather vague and flippant, and thus the speaker seems very far from making a fervent commitment to bridge the gap between himself and divinity.

קַח אֶת מַחְשְׁבוֹתַי

קַח אֶת מַחְשְׁבוֹתַי
לִבְנוֹת מֵהֶן בָּתֵּי תְּפִלָּה
וְתֵן בִּי מִן הַפַּרְפַּר
הַמּוֹסֵר אֶת נַפְשׁוֹ עַל קִדּוּשׁ הָאוֹר
כְּדֵי שֶׁאוּכַל לָמוּת בְּאֵשׁ מִזְבְּחוֹתֶיךָ, רַעֲנָן   5
וְצָלוּל. בַּעֲשַׁן הַקָּרְבָּן
יַעֲלוּ דְמָעוֹתַי לְקַשֵּׁט קִירוֹת הֵיכָלֶיךָ,
וְאַתָּה תִּשְׁלַח חֶמְלָתְךָ עַל פְּנֵי הַמַּיִם
לְמַעַן אֶמְצָאֶנָּה בְּרֹב יְגוֹנוֹתַי.
לֵיל מָלֵא רַחֲמִים יַמְצִיא אֶת הַמְּנוּחָה הַנְּכוֹנָה   10
לְכָל הַסּוֹבְלִים תַּחַת כַּנְפֵי הָרָקִיעַ,
עַד שֶׁנָּקִיא חֲטָאֵינוּ אֶל תּוֹךְ לֵילוֹת אֲחֵרִים.
אַט וּמְפַרְפֵּר יַעֲלֶה הַשַּׁחַר כְּמִתְבַּיֵּשׁ
וּלְפָנֵינוּ יִסְעוּ מַחֲנוֹת וְעַמּוּדֵי הֶעָנָן וְהָאֵשׁ—

TAKE MY THOUGHTS

Take my thoughts
and build from them houses of prayer
and grant me something of the butterfly
that martyrs itself in light
5   so that I can die in the fire of Your altars, fresh

and clear. In the smoke of the sacrifice
my tears will rise to decorate the walls of Your sanctuaries,
and You will cast Your compassion on the face of the waters
so I'll find it in the depths of my sorrows.
10   A night full of mercy will provide the perfect rest
for all who suffer under the wings of the sky,
until we vomit our sins into other nights.
Slowly and fluttering the dawn will rise as if embarrassed
and before us will travel camps and the pillars of cloud and fire — [26]

In lines 1 and 2, the speaker, unable to articulate his spiritual needs in the words of prayer, turns to an unidentified God-like entity with the request that He transform his thoughts into "houses of prayer." It is significant that the speaker does not ask the deity to turn his thoughts into prayer, but rather into whole houses of worship, a more powerful request, for prayer houses are a conduit not only for individual prayer, but also for the prayers of an entire community that presumably would have more effect on God than those of one person.

Beginning with line 3, the speaker shifts to a different way of expressing the desire to draw close to God. He says that he wishes to interact with God by descending into a state of despair, within which he will discover God's compassion. This process is portrayed by means of a convergence between two metaphors: that of the butterfly that "martyrs" itself as it flies directly into a flame to which it is attracted (3–4) and that of a burnt animal sacrifice on God's altars (5–6). The combination of these metaphors conveys the notion that, just as the butterfly's self-destruction is caused by an inbred instinct to fly toward light, so the speaker prays for an unimpeded willingness to sacrifice himself before God. The sacrifice is a metaphor for the speaker's submission to a state of dejection, which, in a certain sense, enhances God's houses of worship: the tears the speaker sheds "decorate the walls" (7) of God's sanctuaries. It is at that moment that humanity and God will meet as the speaker discovers divine compassion "in the depths of [his] sorrows" (9). The speaker refers to God's granting of compassion with the expression "cast Your compassion on the face of the waters" (8), echoing the biblical verse "cast your bread on the face of the waters" (Ecclesiastes 11:1). The biblical expression advises one to be willing to give up one's wealth, and thus the speaker may be urging God not to keep all the mercy only for Himself, a notion also expressed in Yehuda Amichai's poem "God Full of Mercy."

From line 10 until the end of the poem, the speaker portrays an alternative means of finding release from the depths of despair. As he portrays this process, however, he refers even less directly to God than he does in lines 1 to 9. Making use of expressions that are traditionally associated with God, the speaker refers to other non-divine forces that provide him with the relief and security for which he yearns. When he declares that "[a] night full of mercy will provide the perfect rest / for all who suffer under the wings of the sky" (10–11), the original Hebrew *"leil malei raḥamim yamtsi et hamenuḥah hanekhonah / lekhol hasovlim taḥat kanfei haraqia"* plays on the opening of the traditional Jewish memorial prayer *"El malei raḥamim hamtsei menuḥah nekhonah taḥat kanfei hashekhinah"* ("God full of mercy, provide perfect rest under the wings of the Shekhinah"). Thus, night, not God, will comfort those who suffer. This comforting night brings a kind of death-like rest (in the original memorial prayer "perfect rest" [*menuḥah nekhonah*] refers to the eternal repose of the deceased) out of which the sinners may be resurrected to a state of forgiveness.

Having experienced the caring of the night, humanity can now find purification from sin. Like the person whose physical discomfort is relieved by vomiting whatever in his stomach is bothering him, humanity completely casts off all guilt for sinful behavior (12). The relief from guilt, however, would appear to be temporary, since the sins are vomited into "other nights" (12), which the sinners will have to experience in the future. As the night draws to a close, it is followed in line 13 by a dawn whose redness suggests that it is "embarrassed," in keeping with the shame of the speaker who has had to confront his moral failings. This process of self-sacrifice and moral purification will result in humanity seeing a vision of the Israelites traveling in the wilderness under the divine guidance represented by the pillars of cloud and fire (Exodus 13:21–22) (14). The dawn is described as "fluttering" (*mefarper*, 13), a word which has the same root as the word for "butterfly" (*parpar*) in line 3. The semantic connection between these two words hints at the possibility of the revival of the burnt butterfly from the beginning of the poem, as it is transformed into the hopeful image of dawn.

תְּפִלַּת הַדֶּרֶךְ

בִּלְעָדֶיךָ, הַדֶּרֶךְ הַזֹּאת
קִמְשׁוֹנִים וַחֲרוּלִים.

תֵּן לִי לְחַפֵּשׂ דְּרָכֶיךָ וְלִמְצֹא
רַגְלַיִם הַהוֹלְכוֹת בַּתֶּלֶם
וִיהִי נֹעַם עֲלֵיהֶן.   5
הַנּוֹתֵן לַיָּעֵף כֹּחַ
הוּא יִתֵּן לְחַיַּי דְּרָכִים סְלוּלוֹת
לָלֶכֶת וְלָבוֹא וּלְהַגִּיעַ
לַאֲשֶׁר יִשָּׂאֵנִי לִבִּי, כְּשַׁיָּרָה שֶׁל עַצְמוֹ
וְיִשְׁלַח בְּרָכָה בְּמַעֲשֵׂי רַגְלַי.   10

שׁוֹמֵעַ תְּפִלַּת כָּל פֶּה
יִשְׁמַע פְּסִיעוֹתַי.

TRAVEL PRAYER

Without You, this road
is thorns and thistles.

Allow me to search Your ways and to find
my feet walking in a furrow
5   and may pleasantness be upon them.
May He who gives strength to the weary
give my life paved roads
on which to go to come and to arrive
wherever my heart carries me, like a caravan of the self
10   and may He grant blessing to the work of my feet.

May He who hears the prayer of all mouths
hear my footsteps.[27]

The prayer traditionally recited by Jews when they embark on a journey is
known as "Tefillat haderekh" ("Travel Prayer," or literally "The Prayer for the
Path"). In it the traveler asks God to provide a peaceful and successful journey
free from danger. The speaker in this contemporary "Travel Prayer" never re-
fers directly to God, yet he makes use of so many liturgical references that the
connection between what he says and a traditional prayer to God is clear. The
speaker in this version of the travel prayer does not ask for divine protection dur-
ing a particular journey. Instead, images associated with traveling along a path
are used metaphorically to express the speaker's desire for an enjoyable and ful-
filling life.

The speaker follows the metaphor of life as a path by focusing not on his own
words or deeds, but rather on images associated with walking. This approach
provides fresh new imagery that differs from more traditional images. The
speaker begins by acknowledging that, without God, his way in life would be
filled with many obstacles, represented by "thorns and thistles" (1–2). Later he
prays that he be allowed to travel on "paved roads" (7). He asks God to allow
him to be able to search, in a loyal and consistent manner, for the divinely sanc-
tioned way of life, just as one would walk within the confines of "a furrow" (4).
By transforming the biblical expression "May the pleasantness of the Lord our
God be upon us; let the work of our hands be established" (Psalms 90:17) into
the expression "may pleasantness be upon them [my feet]" (5), the speaker
maintains the metaphorical imagery of walking; it is his feet that are important,
not his hands. The elimination of the reference to God in the transformed ex-
pression also distances the speaker from a fixed theological conception and re-
sults in a general desire for pleasantness, without indicating its source as divine.

Addressing God as the one "who gives strength to the weary" (6, a reference to Isaiah 40:29, which also appears in the morning blessings of the traditional Jewish liturgy), the speaker turns away from his earlier request to discover God's ways and asks instead for success "wherever [his] heart carries [him]" (9). This is a significant departure from traditional piety. Based on the speaker's personal inclinations, the path he seeks is independent of God's will and has nothing to do with any commitments he might have to a community. The extreme individualism of this path is emphasized in the image of the individual's heart as "a caravan of the self" (9). The speaker reinforces the consistency of the path imagery by changing two liturgical formulations. In line 10, an expression that appears in the "Mi sheberakh" prayer for a person who has been called to recite blessings on the reading of the Torah in the synagogue, "may [God] grant blessing to the work of his hands," is transformed into "may He grant blessing to the work of my feet." In lines 11 and 12, the speaker presents the expression, found in some versions of the traditional prayer book, "He who hears the prayer of all mouths" (*shomea tefillat kol peh*) and then says that the deity will hear his steps (*yishma pesiyotay*). Thus, just as words and deeds were replaced by walking throughout the poem, prayer, which is normally verbal, is expressed by means of the way the speaker walks on the path of life.

Given the prevalence of theological doubt in Reich's poetry, one is struck by the way the speaker approaches his petition to the deity in lines 6 to 12. In that part of the poem, he uses imperfect forms of Hebrew verbs, which can have the dual meaning of requests of God or as assertions of faith that He will grant the requests. Thus, for example, when, in the concluding couplet, the speaker states *shome'a tefillat kol peh / yishma pesiyotay*, that can be taken as either "may He who hears the prayer of all mouths / hear my footsteps" or "He who hears the prayer of all mouths / will hear my footsteps." If we add the fact that the word "perhaps" (*ulay*) does not appear in the poem to qualify statements of faith, as it does in so many other poems by Reich, we can see this as the most prayerful of the Reich poems we are considering, the one that has the least tension between faith and skepticism and expresses the most confidence that there is a force beyond the speaker that will protect him.

נְעִילָה

בַּחֲלֹף הַשָּׁנִים הַקָּשׁוֹת
אוּלַי יְמִינְךָ תִּהְיֶה עוֹד
פְּשׁוּטָה לְקַבֵּל שָׁבִים
מִדֶּרֶךְ פִּשְׁעָם.
שְׁפוּכֵי עֶרֶב, הַחוֹלְמִים כָּמוֹנִי   5
עַל הַר הָעֲבָרִים הַזֶּה
לַעֲלוֹת וְלִרְאוֹת אֶרֶץ בְּרוּכָה
הַשּׁוֹקֶטֶת עַל שׁוֹמְרֶיהָ.
מִי יַעֲמֹד לָנוּ בְּיוֹם־דִּין
עַל רִיצַת רַגְלַיִם לְהָרַע.   10
הַשֶּׁמֶשׁ יָבוֹא וְיִפְנֶה
מֵעַל חַיֶּיךָ הַשְּׂבֵעִים
וְאַתָּה תִּפְנֶה כֹּה וָכֹה לִרְאוֹת
כַּמָּה רָחֲקָה הַדֶּרֶךְ מִמְּךָ
כְּבָר פָּנָה יוֹם.   15

NE'ILAH

As the difficult years pass
perhaps Your right hand is still
outstretched to receive those who turn back
from the path of their sin.
5   Poured out in the evening, who dream like me
on this overlook mountain
to ascend to see the blessed land
that is tranquil for its guardians.
Who will defend us on judgment day
10   for our eagerness to do evil?
The sun sets and departs
over Your life of great abundance
and You turn here and there to see
how far the way has become from You
15   while day is done.[28]

As in other poems by Reich, while God is not named in this poem, there are enough traditional liturgical expressions to connect the being whom the speaker addresses with the God of Israel. As would be appropriate for a poem named after the final prayer service of Yom Kippur, "Ne'ilah," the speaker is preoccupied at the beginning of the poem with guilt for sins he has committed. In lines 1 to 4, however, we see that he lacks the certainty expressed in the traditional liturgy of "Ne'ilah" that God's hand is "outstretched to receive those who turn back / from the path of their sin" (3–4). Much time filled with difficulties has passed, and there has been no clear evidence of God's desire to reconcile Himself with those, like the speaker, who have sinned, so the speaker can only say that "perhaps" such a reconciliation will happen (2).

In lines 5 to 8, the speaker portrays himself and his fellow sinners as hoping that their prayers will be answered as if they were Moses on *har ha'avarim* (translated here as "overlook mountain," but as some Bible translations indicate, the expression might possibly be the proper name "Mount Avarim"),[29] from where Moses gazed at the promised land before he died (Deuteronomy 32:49). This is a very poignant image: God did not allow Moses to enter the land of Canaan because he did not properly affirm His sanctity before the people of Israel when he produced water by hitting, rather than speaking to, a rock (Numbers 20:12). Despite Moses' entreaties, all God allowed him to do was to view the land from the mountain (Deuteronomy 3:23–27). The use of this image here suggests that those who pray for the "promised land" of tranquility may not have their desires fulfilled. The doubt that they will be forgiven is reinforced in lines 9 and 10 when the speaker wonders, "Who will defend us on judgment day / for our eagerness to do evil?" (*ritsat raglayim lehara*, literally "the running of our feet to do evil," an expression from the Yom Kippur confessional).

In the final section of the poem, the speaker makes use of the imagery of the setting sun found in liturgical poems of the "Ne'ilah" service. In its original context, this imagery helps to reinforce the sense of urgency as those who pray fervently try to complete their process of repentance before the conclusion of the holy fast. The speaker, however, uses this imagery for a very different purpose. The sun is not setting on the lives of those observing Yom Kippur, but rather on the life of the deity the speaker is addressing, suggesting, perhaps, the demise of God's effectiveness as ruler of the universe. The portrayal of God in this part of the poem is quite unflattering. The sun sets over a God who is apparently too preoccupied with His "life of great abundance" (12) to care about humanity. Again the poet alludes to the story of Moses, but this time with the purpose of condemning God. When the speaker tells God, "You turn here and there" (13), he alludes to the description in Exodus of Moses turning "here and there" before burying the Egyptian taskmaster he has just killed (Exodus 2:12). The comparison with this event in Moses' life does more than suggest that God will not forgive people; it suggests that, just as Moses felt compelled to hide his deed, so God attempts to cover up for the way He has mismanaged His interactions with the world.

As God looks around, He becomes aware of something He had lost sight of, namely how distant He is from humanity and its needs ("how far the way has become from You," 14). At the end of the day, it is too late to repair the situation. The speaker weaves together the sunset imagery with that of a confused God by means of the Hebrew root *p-n-y*. This root appears in the expression "and You turn here and there" (*ve'attah tifneh ko vakho*, 13), and also in the expressions from the liturgy of "Ne'ilah," "the sun sets and departs" (*hashemesh yavo veyifneh*, 11) and "day is done" (*panah yom*, 15). Thus, rather than associate the sunset with the final stage of the Yom Kippur ritual of divine forgiveness, this sunset indicates how difficult it may be to effect a reconciliation between God and humanity. The experience is filled with turning points that seem to never arrive at a satisfying destination.

CHAPTER FOUR

Rivka Miriam:
"For a person is a prayer."

R IVKA MIRIAM (1952–) was born in Jerusalem to European Holo-
caust survivors who had immigrated to Israel in 1950.[1] While her parents sur-
vived the war in hiding, all other members of their family died in the war, with
the exception of one of Rivka Miriam's aunts. Rivka Miriam's pen name con-
sists of her first name, Rivka, given to her in memory of her father's mother, and
her middle name, Miriam, given to her in memory of her father's sister; both
women for whom she was named died in the Treblinka concentration camp.
Her father, the Yiddish writer Leib Rochman, was raised in a Hasidic commu-
nity. Shortly after receiving rabbinical ordination at the age of sixteen, he lost
his religious faith. Although he never fully returned to the world of traditional
Jewish belief and practice in which he was raised, he sent his children to schools
in the religious track of the Israeli educational system. This religious education
provided Rivka Miriam with a wealth of classical Jewish textual material on
which to draw for her poetry.

Rivka Miriam had three children with her husband, a clinical psychologist,
from whom she is now divorced. She currently lives in Jerusalem. She does
not define herself as *datiyyah* (religious), in the Israeli sense of observing the
entire body of traditional Jewish ritual law. As she has put it, "There are cer-
tain things I observe and things I don't."[2] Nevertheless, she has maintained an
ongoing interest in traditional Jewish texts, as indicated by her involvement
with Elul, an organization devoted to bringing together religious and secular
Israelis to explore the Jewish tradition. At Elul she has served as *Rosh Beit
Midrash* (Head of the Study House), overseeing the design of the curriculum

of study. She also participates regularly in a private study group devoted to traditional Jewish texts.

Rivka Miriam is attracted to the classical rabbinic belief in the timeless nature of Torah, understood broadly as the entire body of Jewish religious teachings. In an interview I conducted with her during the unsettling period of the second Palestinian intifada, she seemed to take comfort in the rabbinic concept that "Torah preceded the world [*qadmah la'olam*]," and that Torah would survive even if—"perish the thought [*has vehalilah*]"—the State of Israel would be destroyed. As a testament to the staying power of Torah, she told me a story about her father's experience hiding in a bunker during World War II. Cut off from the outside world, he and those with whom he hid thought they were the last Jews in the world. Although he no longer held traditional religious beliefs, he felt an obligation to join the others in an effort to keep Judaism going. They reconstructed the traditional prayer book from memory, fasted on the day they calculated to be Yom Kippur, and refrained from eating bread when they thought it was Passover.

When Rivka Miriam was growing up, her family spoke Yiddish at home. She has described her childhood home as permeated by a strong commitment to Jewish culture. "I grew up in a happy home," she relates, "[that] was a very warm, Jewish home, not religiously observant. The door was always open. Young and old, intellectuals and commoners visited."[3] Her parents made clear to her that, while they mourned their past losses in the Holocaust, they also celebrated their present existence in Israel. "My parents very much loved Israel," she declares, "and they really felt the revival of the Jewish people, no less than they felt the Holocaust."[4]

Jewish identity is of central importance to Rivka Miriam. "I feel very Jewish," she declares, "and that I am part of the flow of Jewish history."[5] Elsewhere, she states, "I feel that my selfhood did not begin in 1952 [the year of her birth] but a long time before that."[6] All Jewish historical memory, she believes, dwells within her. "When I write about the Exodus from Egypt or about the binding of Isaac," she says, "it is not necessarily that I was there at those moments, but I too was there. According to the midrash, all souls were present at Sinai and they are present with us here, in this room. In actuality, the division between periods is not as sharp at it appears."[7] As the bearer of the names of her grandmother and aunt who were murdered by the Nazis, she sees herself as a Holocaust victim who has returned from the dead. "In some sense," she stresses, "I died together with them . . . . I don't rule out the possibility that I have returned. It is likely that I was one of them and I perished there and I am now here. It is likely that one of them came out in me."[8] This identity of a resurrected Holocaust victim gives her a sense of purpose. "It is clear to me," she declares, "that all that I do and every breath that I take derive from the fact that 'I was born for renewal,' after the Holocaust."[9]

With this sense of having gone through the Holocaust, she cannot avoid feelings of existential dread, even though she grew up in a world so much more secure than that which her parents experienced. In the Holocaust, she states, "a complete Jewish world . . . , a multitude of men, women, and children—all kinds of people and all kinds of ideologies—atheistic and religious, beautiful and ugly, fat and thin, all with problems like ours— . . . suddenly . . . [was] erased, and it was as if it never had existed."[10] Having internalized the trauma of sudden unexpected destruction, she cannot escape the feeling "that all that [she] see[s] around [her] is liable to disappear just as that [pre-Holocaust world] disappeared."[11] In general, Rivka Miriam believes that the fear associated with periods of transition is basic to human existence. Our world, she observes, "is a world that is moving toward something, and the moments of rest are few and far between . . . . There are brief periods of time when we feel that we have arrived, but immediately after there is a movement toward something new."[12] As committed as she is to the existence of the State of Israel, she does not believe one can assume that it is the final word on the fate of the Jewish people. "My parents arrived in Israel after the war," she explains, "and as a child I felt as if I had arrived at a final resting point. But . . . the abyss lies at our doorway again and again. On the one hand there is a feeling here of something eternal, fixed, and stable, but along with that there is also absolute chaos and a world of amorphousness, a world of fear."[13] For Rivka Miriam, there is no final answer to life's mysteries. It was significant when, in one interview I conducted with her, she observed that, although she had been personally close to Zelda, the older poet's works bothered her because they seemed to resolve too easily the tensions about which Zelda wrote. "She brings matters to a final conclusion [*hi sogeret et ha'inyanim*]," Rivka Miriam declared. For Rivka Miriam, one must always live with a degree of uncertainty and with an openness to change.

The question of how one can maintain religious faith when the very basis for trust in the world has been completely undermined is central to Rivka Miriam's poetry. For many years, she used to make theological sense of the Holocaust by believing that, for reasons we humans cannot fathom, God found it necessary to bring this great destruction to the Jewish people for the sake of their national rebirth in Israel. In time, she found this explanation to be inadequate and began to feel an impatience with God, who not only allowed the Jewish people to suffer during the Holocaust, but also did not spare them the impact of war even after the establishment of the State of Israel. "[H]ow is it possible . . . ," she asks God, "to force this people to carry so much? How can a woman like my mother, who personally experienced the Holocaust, be allowed to see her son [Rivka Miriam's brother] experiencing wars in the [Israeli] army, while it is likely he will experience other wars in the future . . . ?"[14] Infuriated by God's indifference, which has made all this suffering possible, she declares, "I don't have any more strength to wait for the Messiah. . . . Master of the universe, what is this silence of Yours? What is this hiding of Your face [a biblical image referring to God's apparent absence from human affairs]?"[15]

Despite her anger at God, Rivka Miriam insists that it is as essential to our human existence today to find meaning in absolute truths, myths, and religious faith as it was for our forebears. "In our century more than ever before," she observes, "many concepts that seemed absolute have collapsed. It is likely that there has never before been a period on which there were so many hopes placed like our period, and so the feeling of everything being shattered has been felt sevenfold."[16] According to her, our inability to believe in absolute concepts derives in part from the contemporary tendency to engage in overly analytical rationalism. "When one divides something into its factors," she writes, "and, as happens so often, so much remains at the stage of being taken apart and one is without the ability to reform the divided parts together into a new creation, one is left with emptiness. . . ."[17] Rather than approach the realm of the absolute with skeptical rationalism, she argues, we should realize the possibility of locating the powers of creation in that very realm. "We fear the absolute," she explains, "because it seems to us that it is always pregnant with danger, but we forget that every creation flows from the absolute and exists beyond our powers of perception, including the birth of a child. We are not conscious of the fact that continuity in the world and cultural and artistic creation as a whole are based on a question mark inherent in the absolute itself, within something internal that one should not take apart into elements and which is the only source of our power. A world that destroys itself by dismantling itself [*hamefareq atsmo lada'at*, a play on the expression for suicide, *hame'abbed atsmo lada'at*] cannot derive from within itself power to keep it in existence."[18]

It is in the realm of myth, Rivka Miriam believes, that one can begin to see absolute truths beyond rational perception. However, she notes, "because we are suspicious today of myth, we do not realize that life cannot exist without it. For what is love if not a myth? And the beauty of the sunset and aesthetics and art and perhaps also morality?"[19] She believes that poetry, as well as other forms of art that draw on the insights of myth, can lead us to understand the present in a deeper way. "I think," she declares, "that all art is religious . . . . It seems to me that every artist, even if he denies the existence of God, if his art is great art it is religious art. Because all great art derives from the place that is before thought and after thought; it derives from the place before we were born and after we will no longer live here; it derives from the secret that stands behind everything."[20] From her father she learned how to discover a hidden dimension beyond common experience: "He saw the mythic power not actually in nostalgia or in a utopian vision, but actually in the everyday."[21]

It is this non-rational, mythic thinking, which has always been so central to religious worldviews, that leads her to believe in a force that guides the world. She is hesitant to refer to that force as "God," because, as she puts it, "that is a word that has become almost banal."[22] Whatever one calls it (maybe, as she suggests, "nature" or "the world"), it is the "force that operates everything . . . , [that] causes the trees to be green, some things to wither, and some things to grow."[23] Rivka Miriam finds in the teachings of Judaism a sense of the unity of existence that is central to her religious worldview. "The 'Shema' [Jewish affirmation of God's unity]," she states, "is my source and expresses the essence of my ideas about oneness. I feel that the distance between things is very fragile. Our skins, our bodies are fragile fences, a border between us and others, between inside and outside. And there are times when I don't even feel this border at all; then everything merges into one."[24]

Rivka Miriam's first collection of poems, *Quttonti hatsehubbah* (My Yellow Tunic, 1966), was published when she was only fourteen years old, and she has continued to publish poetry throughout her adult life. The poems selected for consideration in this chapter are from later collections of the 1980s and 1990s, for these collections contain her most mature and aesthetically sophisticated poetic writing about God and prayer. This poetry reflects the tensions within the poet between that which can lead to existential despair and the human need for faith. Some poems are written in first person singular and express a very personal relationship with God, while other poems speak of the divine–human encounter in first person plural, or they refer to humanity in general, conveying the poet's conviction that her religious struggle is shared by others as well.

In Rivka Miriam's poetry, God is sometimes portrayed as very different from humanity. In some poems, His very existence is called into question, whereas in other poems, God is intimately involved with humanity. In three poems I will consider, the poet develops innovative metaphors for God that reflect the difference between the human and divine realms and also explore how, despite those differences, these two realms can interact. In each poem, the distinction and potential estrangement between the divine and the human are clear: in "My God the soul You placed in me . . . ," the deity dwells in an underground realm not immediately evident to human consciousness; in "The God of Pears," the inability of humans to grasp God is presented as analogous to the lack of awareness that a pear has of the person who eats it; and in "Booths," God is ephemeral by nature, while people are fixed and stable. Despite belonging to different realms and partaking of different characteristics, the human and divine do interact in these poems.

Two of these poems explore the potential merging of the human and divine realms by means of images of physical interaction. God is a kind of life force analogous to semen flowing through the speaker's body in the poem "My God the soul You placed in me. . . ." The speaker and God are also seen as having a reciprocally equal relationship, with each considering the other its deity. In "The God of Pears," the pear, which represents humanity, is eaten by God. In contrast, the merging of the human and divine realms is not as intimately physical in the poem "Booths" as it is in "My God the soul You placed in me . . ." and in "The God of Pears." Here it is the experience of being inside a traditional sukkah that provides humanity with evidence for the reality of God's protection.

In four of the poems I present here, the poet deals with the frustrations and satisfactions of the human yearning for a relationship with the divine. The speaker moves back and forth between the two poles of reassurance when sensing God's presence and deep anxiety when sensing that He is absent. In some manner, each poem calls into question the existence of God, His presence among humans, or His ability to function as a viable divinity. In "I'll Go To Present My Plea," the speaker does not even know to whom she would address her concerns. In "My God breathes next to me . . . ," the speaker expresses the anxiety that God might cease to exist. In "In the beginning God created . . . ," while God may exist, the heavens that represent His presence do not exist. In "Who Will Take Us," God is too tired to serve as a spiritual refuge for humanity. Nevertheless, in each poem, a potential for the human–divine relationship is suggested. In "I'll Go to Present My Plea," the very drive to petition a deity suggests that the speaker has not given up on the possibility of discovering the divine. In "My God breathes next to me . . . ," a caring dimension of the cosmos is affirmed despite the human fear that God will cease to exist. In "In the beginning God created . . . ," humanity's ability to pray is the thread that links earth to heaven. In "Who Will Take Us," there is the possibility of humanity sending its prayers as a comfort for the tired God.

Three other poems include short evocations of traditional prayer imagery that reflect the speaker's hope and her disillusionment in her relationship with God. The poem "One" plays on the image of God becoming one at the end of the "Aleinu" prayer. In this poem, God is scattered throughout the world and in need of people to restore His unity. The poem "Sanctification" adapts the Sabbath Kiddush prayer said over wine by expressing the speaker's fears of the destruction of the world, yet the poem also asserts the possibility of approaching the holy even if God turns to nothingness. The poem "Shut" transforms a liturgical poem for the final service of Yom Kippur into the speaker's expression of anger about all of the raised hopes that were never realized. Nevertheless, the very fact that the speaker engages God in this poem testifies to a continuing relationship between them.

Innovative Metaphors for God

אֱלֹהַי נְשָׁמָה שֶׁנָּתַתָּ בִּי
הַנִּגֶּרֶת בְּתוֹכִי כְּבִשְׁעוֹן שֶׁל חוֹל
וַאֲדָמָה שֶׁבִּמְרוֹמַי אֶל עָפָר שֶׁבְּתַחְתִּיתִי תִּגַּע.
לִפְעָמִים, בַּלַּיְלָה, אֲנִי זוֹכֶרֶת
שֶׁבַּקַּרְקַע טָמוּן לִי הַצֵּל   5
שֶׁמִּשָּׁם קוֹרֵא הוּא לִי בְּשֵׁמוֹת רַבִּים
שֶׁמִּשָּׁם הוּא אֵלַי מִתְפַּלֵּל
שֶׁאֲנִי אֱלֹהָיו הַגָּדוֹל וְנוֹרָא
שֶׁאֲנִי בְּרָאתִיו וְאוֹתוֹ מְמִיתָה
וְלִי הוּא עוֹבֵד וְאֵלַי מְיַחֵל.   10
וּכְשֶׁאִישׁ בִּי נוֹגֵעַ וּמַגִּיר בִּי זַרְעוֹ
אֲנִי מְשֻׁיֶּכֶת לְמִישֶׁהוּ אַחֵר
שֶׁבְּתוֹךְ הַדְּמָמָה חוֹפֵר מְחִלּוֹת
וְאֵלַי הוּא מִתַּחַת חוֹתֵר.
כִּי הַזֶּרַע הַפּוֹעֵם בִּי אֵינֶנּוּ שֶׁל אִישׁ   15
שְׁחַרְחַר וּמְתֻלְתָּל וְגָבוֹהַּ
רַק מִתּוֹךְ הֶעָפָר אוֹתוֹ לְקַחְתִּיו
וּמֵאָז הוּא מַמְשִׁיךְ בִּי לִנְבֹּעַ
שֶׁאֲנִי אֱלֹהָיו וְהוּא אֱלֹהַי
הַגָּדוֹל הַגִּבּוֹר הַנּוֹרָא   20
אֲנִי קוֹרְאָה לוֹ בְּשֵׁמוֹת רַבִּים
וְהוּא בְּשֵׁמוֹת רַבִּים לִי יִקְרָא.

My God the soul You placed in me
pours within me as sand in an hourglass
and the earth at my heights will touch the dust at my depths.
Sometimes, at night, I remember
5   that in the ground is hidden the shadow
from where He invokes me with many names
from where He prays to me
that I am His great and awesome God
that I created Him and Him I kill
10   and it is I He worships and for me He yearns.
And when a man touches me and pours into me his seed
I am linked to Someone Else
who in the silence digs tunnels
and to me He burrows from below.
15   For the seed throbbing in me is not of a man

> dark and curly and tall
> but from the dust I took it
> and since then it continues to flow in me
> for I am His God and He is my God
> 20 great and mighty and awesome
> I invoke Him with many names
> and He with many names invokes me.[25]

The first line of this poem is taken from the beginning of one of the introductory prayers of the traditional morning service:

> My God the soul You placed in me is pure. You created it, You formed it, You blew it into me, and You preserve it within me, and in the future You will take it from me and return it at the end of days. As long as my soul is within me I acknowledge You, Lord my God and God of my ancestors, Master of all deeds, Lord of all souls. Blessed are You, Lord, who restores souls to dead bodies.

This prayer is based on the post-biblical Jewish notion of the soul as a separate eternal entity housed in the human body. The biblical divine "breath of life" (*nishmat hayyim*) that entered Adam at the time of his creation (Genesis 2:7) was eventually transformed in Jewish thought into the eternal soul (*neshamah*) that God places into human beings upon their birth and maintains even after death. The prayer praises God for endowing humanity with a soul and preserving that soul, and it expresses the faith that, at the end of days, in messianic times, God will resurrect the dead by reuniting the eternal soul with the body of each person who has died.

The poem begins with an exact quote of the first phrase of the traditional prayer, "My God the soul You placed in me" (1), but then shifts from the second person address in the prayer to third person references to God. Feeling unsure of her relationship with God, the speaker merely describes that relationship, without addressing Him directly.

One cannot imagine a more striking contrast between the prayer's metaphor of the soul as a breath of air and the poem's metaphors of the soul as sand and dust (1–3). The prayer's metaphor is ethereal, while the poem's metaphors are material. The soul (*neshamah*) related to the breath of life (*nishmat hayyim*) of the biblical account of creation has been reduced to the lifeless dust (*afar*) out of which God formed Adam (Genesis 2:7). In the prayer, the soul breathed by God into humans is preserved intact within the body; in the poem, its presence within the speaker is like sand that gradually falls in an hourglass over a fixed period of time, all the while losing the original energy with which it was endowed. The image of the earth at the speaker's heights represents strength and self-affirmation, but, like the slowly falling sand of the hourglass, that earth too descends and touches the dust at the depths of the speaker, suggesting the depletion of her psychological, emotional, and spiritual resources (3). While the eternal indestructible nature of the soul is clear in the prayer, the sand and earth imagery raises serious questions about how the soul within the speaker will regain its strength. The speaker suggests doubts as to who, figuratively speaking, would turn the hourglass upside down to start the sand pouring again, and who would restore the earth to the heights within her.

If the speaker were to remain conscious only of her mortality and depleting inner resources, she would be put into a rather depressed state. Yet sometimes during that darkest time, the night, she remembers that there is a hidden realm ("the shadow," 5) from where her deity calls to her, presumably to raise her spirits (4–10). It is significant that, initially, this deity is not identified as "God," nor is it given any name; it is simply identified with forms of the third person masculine singular pronoun. Later in the poem, it is referred to in a similarly anonymous manner as "Someone Else" (12). The relationship between this deity and the speaker is described at first as the reverse of the traditional divine–human relationship. He prays to her; she is "His great and awesome God" (7–8), and she has the power of life and death over Him (9).

The speaker then describes a process in which she can begin to interact more directly with this deity. The deity makes every effort to dig His way out of His hiding place and reach the speaker (12–14). Having described the initial attempt of the deity to reach her, the speaker shifts metaphorical realms and portrays her eventual union with the deity by means of sexual imagery (15–18). The deity enters her as a male lover's semen would penetrate her body. Yet, although her union with the deity resembles the experience of being inseminated by a lover, the speaker emphatically disassociates it from the human sexual realm: "And when a man touches me and pours into me his seed . . . / the seed throbbing in me is not of a man / dark and curly and tall (11, 15–16). Furthermore, she insists that it is she who has taken the semen from "the dust" (*afar*, 17), which is associated with the underground realm of the deity. "Dust" is also associated with the depleted resources within the speaker, as mentioned earlier in the poem, and thus this religious experience provides an opportunity to refresh those resources and experience a psychological and spiritual renewal.

The speaker connects the soul within her, to which she referred at the beginning of the poem, with the divine element that enters her in the course of the poem by using words with the same root to refer to their metaphorical representations: the sand of the hourglass and the semen. The soul "pours [*niggeret*] . . . as sand in an hourglass" (2) and the lover "pours [*maggir*] into [her] his seed" (11). The connection is one of contrast, indicating that at first her soul has lost strength, but, once the divine element enters her, her soul is revived.

By this point, the speaker and her deity have a mutual relationship of equal status which allows them to engage in a process described by the speaker as a series of invocations: "I invoke Him with many names / and He with many names invokes me" [*ani qorah lo beshemot rabbim / vehu beshemot rabbim li yiqra*] (21–22). This passage derives from an expression, *qara beshem Adonay*, found in several biblical passages in which a character invokes the Tetragammaton. In the poem's portrayal of the mutual worship of God and humanity, there are two significant deviations from the original biblical expression. Instead of *qara beshem* ("invoke the name"), the expressions are *ani qorah lo* and *vehu . . . li yiqra* (literally "I call to Him" and "He to me calls"), suggesting that there is still some distance between the two entities over which they call out to each other. In addition, rather than the invocation of one particular name of God (the Tetragammaton), "many names" are invoked by both the human being and her God, suggesting the need for a more fluid and complex set of terminologies for each entity to use in their attempts to understand each other. The chiastic arrangement of these final two lines of the poem places the first person of the speaker at the beginning and the end of the passage and the third person of God in the middle. This emphasizes the all-encompassing role of the speaker's perspective and calls attention to the personal, individualistic, and subjective nature of the religious experience portrayed in the poem.

אֱלֹהֵי הָאֲגָּסִים

אֱלֹהֵי הָאֲגָּסִים בָּלַע אֶת אַגָּסָיו
וּבְהִבָּלְעָם רָאוּ שֶׁהֵם בְּצַלְמוֹ כִּדְמוּתוֹ
שֶׁתָּמִיד לֹא הָיָה לָהֶם גּוּף
רַק נִדְמוּ לִהְיוֹת אַגָּסִים
זְהֻבִּים שֶׁקְּרוּמָם רָקוּעַ.   5
אֱלֹהֵי הָאֲגָּסִים בָּלַע אֶת אַגָּסָיו
וּבְהִבָּלְעָם חָשׁ בְּאַגָּסִיּוּתוֹ הַמִּתְגַּלֶּמֶת
בִּקְלִפָּה מְחֻסְפֶּסֶת שֶׁאוֹתוֹ תּוֹחֶמֶת
וְעוֹשָׂה לוֹ גְּבוּלִין.

The God of Pears

When the God of pears swallowed His pears
they saw they were in His image after His likeness
and they never had a body
they just seemed to be pears
5   with golden skin stretched thin.
When the God of pears swallowed His pears

He felt his emerging form as a pear
with a rough peel limiting Him
and bounding Him.[26]

The relationship between the spiritual and the material, as well as that be-
tween divinity and humanity, is presented here with the unconventional an-
thropomorphic image of God eating pears. These are "His pears" (1). When
swallowed, the pears recognize that they are "in [God's] image after His like-
ness" (2), just as God declared before creating humanity, "Let us make Man
in our image, after our likeness" (Genesis 1:26). In contrast to the tendency of
traditional Jewish texts to portray verbal dialogue as the primary means for hu-
manity and divinity to relate, here the deity physically takes the human into
Himself, making humanity one with God. In this process, both humanity and
God learn something of which they had not been aware. When God ingests
the pears, they realize that their sense of being embodied was an illusion, that
they were always pure spirit, like God (1–5), and God in turn realizes that He
actually has a body that limits Him (6–9). This paradox of the pears and their
God discovering that they are the opposite of what they thought they were is
a means for the poet to convey the intricate relationship between the physical
and the spiritual in human experience. The spiritual (God) swallows the physi-
cal (the pears), and thereby they become one. However, the essence of each
changes; the pears become spirit and God is embodied. A curious feature of
the imagery in this poem is the contrast between the pears' imagined view of
their physical state (that they had "golden skin stretched thin," 5) and the
physical state that God discovers He has ("a rough peel limiting Him," 8). The
pears' imagined state suggests a physical form which, although it is reaching
its limits, has a beauty of its own, while God's physical existence lacks beauty
and is very confining. Humanity seems to get the better deal. It can transcend
the limitations of physical existence once it is infused with the spiritual; but in
the process, God, the spiritual entity who is ideally free and limitless, must
sacrifice Himself in order to enter into a relationship with humanity.

In comparing this poem with the previous poem, "My God the soul You
placed in me . . . ," one is struck by the physical nature of the metaphors used in
both poems to portray human–divine relations. In the previous poem, God's
presence within the speaker is portrayed as semen penetrating and flowing
within her; in this poem, the human being enters God as food would enter a
human being. In both cases, one element enriches the other: God "insemi-
nates" the human and God "eats" the human. In both metaphors, humanity has,
at least in part, a passive role: as a woman receiving semen or as food devoured
by a body. Nevertheless, both poems suggest a certain degree of mutuality. In

the previous poem, God and humanity worship each other and call each other by name; in this poem, both God and humanity learn more about themselves by interacting, for they need each other. In other words, humanity needs God to discover its true spiritual essence, and God needs humanity in some sense to sustain Himself, even if it is at the expense of limiting His pure spiritual nature.

סֻכּוֹת

חוּפָה הָאַרְעִי עַל רָאשֵׁינוּ.
הָאַרְעִי הוּא יָרֹק. צָהֹב וְחוּם וְאָפֹר הוּא הַקֶּבַע.
חוּפָה הָאַרְעִי עַל רָאשֵׁינוּ. הָבָה נִתְיַפֶּה בְּעֵינָיו.
נַשְׁאִירֵנוּ פֹּה. מִן הַחַמָּה הוּא יָצֵל. מִן הַצִּנָּה יְכַנֵּס.
נַשְׁאִירֵנוּ עִמָּנוּ. הוּא עֹגֶן יַטִּיל.   5
מִי לָנוּ אָב כָּמוֹהוּ.
חוּפָה הָאַרְעִי עַל רָאשֵׁינוּ.
יַצִּיבוּתֵנוּ לֹא תִּירָא אוֹתוֹ. נַהֲפוֹךְ הוּא
שִׁבְעָה נְבִיא לוֹ מִזִּקְנֵי עֲדָתֵנוּ
אוֹתָם שְׁחוּט שֶׁל מֶשֶׁךְ עֲלֵיהֶם מָשׁוּחַ.   10
יוֹם אַחַר יוֹם יַעַבְרוּ לְפָנָיו, בִּגְלִימוֹת, בִּצְנִיפִים.
שֵׁב עִמָּנוּ, אַרְעִי, שֵׁב.
מְקוֹמְךָ עִמָּנוּ.
אָנוּ צֶאֱצָאֵי הַחֶרֶב הַמִּתְהַפֶּכֶת.
וּמִי לָנוּ אָב כָּמוֹךָ.   15

BOOTHS

The Ephemeral protects our heads.
The Ephemeral is green. Yellow and brown and gray is permanence.
The Ephemeral protects our heads. Let's beautify ourselves for Him.
Let's leave Him here. He will shade us from the sun. He will gather
  us from the cold.
5 Let's leave Him among us. He will cast an anchor.
Who's a better father than Him?
The Ephemeral protects our heads.
Our stability will not frighten Him. On the contrary
we'll bring seven elders of our tribe
10 anointed with an expression of duration.
Day after day they will pass before Him, in robes, in turbans.
Dwell with us, Ephemeral, dwell.
Your place is with us.
We are descendants of the ever-turning sword.
15 And who's a better father than You?[27]

The booth (sukkah) in which Jews traditionally dwell for the fall holiday of Sukkot is the central metaphor of human–divine relations in this poem. It is paradoxical that divinity, which is traditionally seen as eternal, is here given the name *ha'aray* (translated here as "the Ephemeral") and is concretely represented by the cut green branches that serve as the roof of the sukkah, which can only last a limited period of time. One can expect more from the Ephemeral than one might imagine, the speaker suggests; it can provide shelter and protection, and even a stabilizing anchor (1–7). The Ephemeral, like the God of Jewish tradition, is the most reliable father figure one can have ("Who's a better father than Him?" 6).

In line 2, the speaker calls attention to a significant contrast between the divine and the human. The color of divinity is green, exuding life and natural vitality, like the color of the branched sukkah roof. The colors of the human realm, which here is presented as more permanent than the divine realm, are the death-related colors of yellow, brown, and gray, resembling the human-made material of the walls of the sukkah. The speaker believes that, if we beautify ourselves in the same way that Jews traditionally decorate the drab walls of a sukkah, we can overcome our yellow, brown, and gray, and be more like the green of divinity (3). Thus, the vitality that comes naturally to the deity will be achieved by humans if they consciously set out to imitate God.

In line 8, the speaker raises the possibility that "our stability" might frighten the more ephemeral divinity. However, she declares, we humans can bridge the gap between us and divinity in this realm as well by providing seven elders to walk before divinity. These elders are analogous to the seven biblical patriarchal guests symbolically invited to the sukkah meals in Jewish tradition, called by the Aramaic term *ushpizin* (8–11). These "elders of our tribe" (9), dressed "in robes [and] in turbans" (11), display a dynamism that is rooted in the past, which will appeal to the deity, who Himself combines qualities of movement and protective stability. The Hebrew for the expression "anointed with an expression of duration" (*ḥut shel meshekh aleihem mashuaḥ*, 10) derives from a talmudic aggadic discussion of why the biblical Queen Esther was also called by the name Hadassah: "Ben Azzai said: Esther was not tall and not short, but of medium height, like a myrtle (*hadassah*). Rabbi Yehoshua ben Korhah said: Esther was greenish and an expression (literally "thread") of grace was spread over her (*ḥut shel ḥesed mashukh aleha*)" (Megillah 13a). The speaker changes the word *ḥesed* (grace) in the original expression to *meshekh* (duration), a word with the same root as *mashukh* (spread). She also changes the word *mashukh* (spread) in the original expression to *mashuaḥ* (anointed). The choice of this allusion and its transformation fit well with the imagery of the poem. The myrtle (*hadassah* or *hadas*) is one of the three plant species that are combined for the *lulav* ritual of Sukkot, and, just as the waving of the *lulav* represents in part an attempt to connect with God, so the pleasant expression of Esther that was so appealing is related to the role of the elders in bringing us close to God. However, what attracts God is not the grace expressed by the beautiful Esther who appealed to King Ahasuerus in the Purim story, but rather the continuity of commitment to tradition that the elders express. Like the Messiah (*mashiah*, literally "anointed one"), they are anointed with the authority to serve as an intermediary between humanity and the divine.

Only after the appearance of the seven elders does the speaker feel prepared to turn to the deity directly and beg Him to dwell with humanity: "Dwell with us, Ephemeral, dwell. / Your place is with us" (12–13). The original Hebrew suggests, through the choice of words, the melding of the divine and human realms. The request of God to dwell (*shev*) has the same root as the word for dwell in the blessing recited upon fulfilling the ritual obligation "to dwell in the sukkah" (*leishev basukkah*). And the expression "your place is with us" makes use of the Hebrew word for "place" (*maqom*), which is a rabbinic epithet for God. Thus, God dwells as we dwell, and our place is also His place.

In the final lines of the poem, it becomes clear why the speaker thinks that the Ephemeral is the best father humanity could have. Her reference to "the ever-turning sword" (14) that God established to block the way of Adam and Eve to paradise (Genesis 3:24) evokes a post-Holocaust sense of having been expelled from the relative innocence of the pre-Holocaust world. Like Adam and Eve, who had to accept the consequences of eating the forbidden fruit, after the Holocaust humanity must struggle with the upheaval in the moral order caused by the evil brought forth in World War II. The speaker refers to herself and her fellow humanity as "descendants of the ever-turning sword" (14). They are not victims of the sword, nor are they Adam and Eve expelled from paradise. They are connected most directly to the sword itself. Its ever-turning nature signifies that the current post-Holocaust generation has difficulty finding the path to trust in existence and therefore must turn to God for guidance. The Ephemeral is the divinity best suited for this generation so full of religious doubts. He is not overly stable and, thus, can share in the human uncertainties of today's post-Holocaust era, even as He provides us with some degree of security.

Sensing the Presence and Absence of God

אֵלֵךְ לְהַפִּיל תְּחִנָּתִי

אֵלֵךְ לְהַפִּיל תְּחִנָּתִי
שֶׁאֵין אֲנִי יְכוֹלָה לְשֵׂאתָהּ עוֹד.
אַיֵּה אַפִּילֶנָּה?
תְּחִנָּתִי נִגְעֶצֶת בִּי בְּאֵימָה.
תְּחִנָּתִי מִפַּחַד נֶאֱלֶמֶת.   5
שָׁנִים הַרְבֵּה נִצְמְדָה אֵלַי.
אַיֵּה אַפִּילֶנָּה?
אֲנִי לוֹחֶשֶׁת אֵלֶיהָ דְּבַר-סוֹד.
הִיא מִפַּחַד נִסְתֶּמֶת.
שָׁנִים הַרְבֵּה תְּחִנָּתִי נָשָׂאתִי–   10
אֵיךְ אַפִּילֶנָּה?

I'll Go to Submit My Plea

I'll go to submit my plea
which I can no longer bear.
Where shall I submit it?
My plea fastened to me in terror.
5   My plea mute from fear.
So many years attached to me.
Where shall I submit it?
I whisper to it a secret matter.
By fear it is blocked.
10   So many years I bore my plea—
How shall I submit it?[28]

The Hebrew term *tehinnah* in the title of the poem, translated here as "plea" (1), is used in traditional Jewish liturgy to signify a prayer of petition before God. The term sometimes refers more specifically to a genre of petitionary prayer traditionally recited by women. This association with women's prayers fits well with the imagery of motherhood throughout the poem. The plea is portrayed metaphorically in the poem as the speaker's baby; she bears the plea (2, 10), just as a mother first carries a fetus in pregnancy and later carries a baby before it can walk and a child when it is tired. The plea clings to its mother like a scared child so terrified it cannot speak ("My plea fastened to me in terror. / My plea mute from fear. / So many years attached to me" 4–6), and she in turn mothers the plea by speaking to it in a soft and reassuring manner ("I whisper to it a se-cret matter," 8).

It would seem that the speaker has reached the limits of her ability to bear the plea. It is too burdensome to keep it inside herself; she has carried it within her-self for too long, and she will only find relief if she can finally express it. Thus, she cries out in her desperation: "Where shall I submit it?" (3, 7) and "How shall I submit it?" (11). Furthermore, when the speaker declares that her plea is "fas-tened" to her (4), the original Hebrew for "fastened," *ninetset*, carries the con-notation of stuck in as a sharp thumbtack would be pushed into a hard object. The plea, thus, has a palpable independent existence of its own and embeds itself in the speaker, causing much pain to her soul.

The expression *lehappil tehinnati*, translated here as "to submit my plea" (1), can be understood idiomatically in its original biblical context as "to present my plea" (see, for example, *mappil ani tehinnati lifnei hamelekh*, "I present my plea to the king," Jeremiah 38:26). The Hebrew verb *lehappil*, however, can literally mean to throw down. It is also used in contemporary Hebrew to signify the action of aborting or miscarrying a fetus. Thus, perhaps the speaker suggests here her desire to cast the plea to the ground or to destroy the plea as if it were an un-wanted child. This interpretation would fit well with the desperate sense of frus-tration that the speaker feels in her inability to locate a place to present her plea.

Although the speaker cannot discover a God to whom to present her plea, the poem is permeated with the language of religious experience. In addition to the word *tehinnah*, the speaker refers to the plea's fear with the language of God-fearing awe: *eimah* ("terror," 4) and *pahad* ("fear," 9). In addition, the speaker conveys to the plea "a secret matter" (*devar sod*, 8), an expression with mystical associations. Nevertheless, the experience conveyed is more along the lines of the horror at not having another to address than the religious fulfillment of pouring out one's soul to God. The plea represents in a metonymic way the speaker who is terrified that there does not appear to be any divinity to whom she can appeal. When she refers to the plea as "mute" (*ne'elemet*, 5) and "blocked" (*nistemet*, 9), she suggests that the possibility of self expression has been forcefully denied. The plea must stay imprisoned within the person, who thereby experiences the frustration of being unable to enter into a meaningful relationship with the divine.

אֱלֹהַי נוֹשֵׁם לְצִדִּי
בַּל יֶחְדַּל מִלִּנְשֹׁם.
כְּשֶׁהַכֹּל נִבְלָם שׁוֹמְעִים בַּשֶּׁקֶט
אֶת מְצוּקָתָם הֶחָשָׁאִית שֶׁל הַסְּלָעִים
וְאֶת רַחַשׁ הַטַּל הָרַב הַנִּגָּר עֲלֵיהֶם   5
מֵאָז הִכָּה בָּם מֹשֶׁה.

My God breathes next to me
let Him not stop breathing.
When all is restrained one hears in the silence
the secret distress of the rocks
5   and the whisper of much dew pouring on them
ever since they were hit by Moses.²⁹

In the Bible, God breathes the breath of life into Adam (Genesis 2:7), but one never encounters in biblical or later traditional Jewish literature references like the one in this poem to God breathing in the way that a human being does (1). As reassuring as the metaphorical image of someone who is breathing next to you can be, it suggests that God is as vulnerable as a human being whose breath of life will stop some day when he dies. God's main role would seem to be to stay alive beside the speaker, and the speaker does not appear to expect any further intervention in her life by God. All she asks is that He "not stop breathing" (2). Furthermore, one senses that the reassurance conveyed in the first line could easily be undermined: just as we fear that someone close to us would cease breathing and die, the speaker is concerned that God too could fail her.

In lines 3 to 6, it is as if God really has stopped breathing, and there is only the silence that engulfs the speaker when the experience of God's reassuring presence is lost. Yet, within that silence, one can hear that which under normal circumstances is not heard, namely "the secret distress of the rocks" (4), an image which suggests human suffering that is usually well hidden by the solid barriers that people erect between each other. Now people can feel empathy for each other's suffering, and, by listening carefully, they can also discern a hidden source of comfort that might compensate for the absence of God in our lives: "the whisper of much dew pouring on [the rocks]" (5). The image of dew is reassuring, because dew is used in the Bible to represent nurturing and caring, as when the prophet Hosea declares in a vision of future redemption that God will be "to Israel like dew" (Hosea 14:6).

The biblical allusion in line 6 to Moses hitting the rock (Exodus 17:1–7; Numbers 20:1–13), however, is more puzzling. What is the significance of introducing an act of violence in a poem in which the speaker seeks to reveal that which is potentially comforting in existence? It seems even more inappropriate to the spirit of the poem that the speaker uses the word *sela* for "rock" which appears in the version of the story in Numbers 20 when God gets angry at Moses for hitting rather than speaking to the rock, instead of *tsur*, which is used in the version of the story in Exodus 17 in which God sanctions Moses' hitting of the rock. Perhaps the image serves here to focus attention on human agency. The dew that falls on the rocks is related to the water that flowed out of them, and that water flowed only after a human being took the initiative to hit the rock. In another sense, however, no human agency is needed in the present, according to the poem, because the dew that provides comfort actually comes from the heavens, and it operates on its own, continuously pouring since biblical times. Its regularity and long-standing existence make it a more reliable source of existential reassurance than the image of God in the beginning of the poem as a being who may some day stop breathing.

בְּרֵאשִׁית בָּרָא אֱלֹהִים
אֶת הַשָּׁמַיִם שֶׁבְּעֶצֶם אֵינָם
וְאֶת הָאֲדָמָה שֶׁרוֹצָה בָּם לָגַעַת.
בְּרֵאשִׁית בָּרָא אֱלֹהִים
חוּטִים מְתוּחִים בֵּינֵיהֶם   5
בֵּין הַשָּׁמַיִם שֶׁבְּעֶצֶם אֵינָם
וּבֵין הָאֲדָמָה הַמְשַׁוַּעַת.
וְאֶת הָאָדָם הוּא יָצַר
שֶׁהָאִישׁ הוּא תְּפִלָּה וְהוּא חוּט
נוֹגֵעַ בְּמַה שֶׁאֵינֶנּוּ   10
בְּמַגָּע שֶׁל רַךְ וְדַקּוּת.

In the beginning God created
the heavens that actually are not
and the earth that wants to touch them.
In the beginning God created
5   threads stretched between them
between the heavens that actually are not
and the earth that cries for help.
And He created Man,
for a person is a prayer and a thread
10   touching what is not
with a soft and delicate touch.[30]

Although this poem begins with the first three words of the Hebrew Bible, *bereshit bara Elohim* ("In the beginning God created," Genesis 1:1), the biblical creation story is undermined by the second line of the poem. This technique is reminiscent of the way that the speaker in "My God the soul You placed in me . . ." undermines the original meaning of the prayer that begins "My God the soul you placed in me" by quoting the traditional text in the first line and then proceeding in a radically different direction of meaning. There is a twist

to the creation story the speaker is telling here, because while the earth (re-
ferred to here not as *erets*, as it is in the original biblical text, but rather as *ada-
mah*) is real, the heavens are not. Nevertheless, despite the supposed nonexist-
ence of the heavens, the earth wants to have contact with them.

The earth is portrayed as wanting to touch the heavens (3) and as crying out
for help from the heavens (7). "Man" (*ha'adam*) is linked etymologically to
"earth" (*ha'adamah*), and therefore God created "Man" as the entity best
equipped to express the earth's cry for heavenly assistance (8). It is not that a
person would have to pray in order to connect the two realms; it is that, in his
or her very being, "a person is a prayer and a thread" (9) that can put earth and
the heavens in touch with each other.

This prayer of human origin is different from the expression of the earth's de-
sire for physical closeness to the heavens or the earth's cry to the heavens for
help. It is by means of this prayer that humanity enters into a loving relationship
with the heavens. The heavens still may not exist ("touching what is not," 10),
but prayer reaches out anyway "with a soft and delicate touch" (11). Thus, despite
the contemporary sense that a divine dimension does not exist, the world longs
for God, and it is the prayers of human beings that express that longing. Prayer
is a necessary part of human experience and an essential component for the con-
tinued existence of the world, whether or not traditional belief is affirmed.

The notion that humanity delicately reaches out to touch a nonexistent en-
tity, however, is disturbing for what it tells us about the possibility of a divine–
human encounter. Humanity appears here to be well meaning, but also self-
deceiving, as it undertakes an attempt to reach out for contact with the divine
that is doomed to fail. Despite the underlying questions about the possibility
of human–divine interaction, in the world of the poem, God is real and hu-
manity is real, and perhaps the imagined encounter between heaven and
earth in the poem has a reality of its own, if only in the human mind.

מִי יְקַחֵנוּ

מִי יְקַחֵנוּ אֶל חֵיקוֹ עִם עֶרֶב–
הָאֵל הַגָּדוֹל עָיֵף כָּל כָּךְ
וְאֵין בְּכֹחוֹ לְשֵׂאתֵנוּ עוֹד.
עֲצַמְנוּ מִמֶּנּוּ.
לוּ פְּרָחִים אָנוּ–עוֹד תְּקֹפוֹ נִיחוֹחֵנוּ   5
לוּ מַיִם–וְאֲדֵינוּ נָגְעוּ בְּשׁוּלָיו.

מִי יְקַחֵנוּ לְחֵיקוֹ עִם עֶרֶב–
הָאֵל הַגָּדוֹל עָיֵף כָּל כָּךְ
וּתְפִלּוֹתֵינוּ אֵינָן מַגִּיעוֹת עָדָיו
כְּבֵדִים מִשְּׁקִיעָה הַיָּמָּה נָגַלְנוּ–   10
כְּאֶל חֵיק רָחָב.

מִי יְחַלֵּץ הַתְּפִלּוֹת מִתַּחְתֵּנוּ
שׁוּרוֹתֵיהֶן הַכְּבֵדוֹת יִפְרֹף לְאַט,
כְּמוֹ בְּסַבְיוֹן יִנְשֹׁף בָּהֶן רוּחַ–
שֶׁיִּקְחוּ תְּפִלּוֹתֵינוּ כְּמֶשִׁי פָּרִיךְ   15
אֶת הָאֵל הַגָּדוֹל הֶעָיֵף אֶל חֵיקָן
עַד יֵרָדֵם וְיָנוּחַ.

WHO WILL TAKE US

Who will take us to his chest in the evening—
The great God is so tired,
He has no strength to bear us anymore.
We're too much for Him.
5   If we were flowers—our pleasant aroma would overwhelm Him
if we were water—our mist would touch His hem.

Who will take us to his chest in the evening—
The great God is so tired
and our prayers do not reach Him
10   heavier than sunset we've rolled to the sea—
as to a broad chest.

Who will release our prayers from beneath us
slowly combining their heavy lines,
a wind will blow them as it blows a weed—
15   so that our prayers like fragile silk will take
the great and tired God to their chests
till He falls asleep and rests.[31]

Humanity's desire to find comfort in God is conveyed in this poem by means of the metaphor of being taken to the chest of a male figure, perhaps a father, perhaps a lover (1, 7). Assurance can come, it would appear, only from a strong figure who can wrap his arms around people and pull them tightly to his chest. This divine figure, however, is too tired to comfort them (2–4, 8). If only there were another way to relate to God, declares the speaker. If we were like flowers, our "pleasant aroma" (niḥoaḥ, reminiscent of the incense offered by the priests in ancient Israel) would rise up to "overwhelm Him" (5). If we were like water, our mist would ascend to "touch His hem" (6). This kind of contact is ephemeral—aromas and mist quickly disperse in the air—and in the process only a part of humanity, represented by the aroma of the flower and the mist of the water, actually makes contact with God.

However, this contact through aroma and mist is only hypothetical, for humanity's "prayers do not reach [God]" (9). Unable to rise up and be comforted by a divine "chest" (1, 7), and burdened down by its unreleased prayers, humanity sinks down and is immersed in the "broad chest" of the sea (10–11). This sinking of humanity is more emphatic in manner than the sun when it sets ("heavier than sunset," 10). The sea, however, does not provide the reassurance that is expressed in a human embrace, but rather the oblivion of drowning.

Just as humanity sought some being to provide divine assurance, it now seeks some being to unburden itself from its prayers and send them up to God. This process is described in an ever changing set of metaphorical images. At first, the lines of prayer that are so heavily weighing down humanity must be released and combined together (12–13). Although this act of combination is portrayed as a slow process, it eventually gives way to a different metaphorical image of the prayers as the light parts of a weed being blown up to heaven (14). This metaphorical image is then transformed into the image of the prayers as fragile silk providing comfort to God (15–17). Here the ephemeral images of the pleasant smell and mist as a means to contact God in the first stanza are replaced by the somewhat more concrete images of weed fragments and silk. By the end of the poem, it is not God who comforts humanity with His chest, but rather human prayers that comfort God, with silk-like chests on which He can find the rest that He really needs.

Adaptations of Prayer Imagery

אֶחָד

דַּרְכֵּנוּ הוֹפֵךְ הָאֱלוֹהַ אֶחָד.
הוּא, שֶׁבְּכָל מָקוֹם
הוּא, הַמְפֻזָּר וּמְפֹרָד,
הִנֵּה לִקְרָאתֵנוּ נִרְעָשׁ וְנִפְחָד–
הִנֵּה כָּאן   5
אֶצְלֵנוּ
הָיָה לְאֶחָד.

ONE

Through us God becomes one.
He, who is everywhere,
He, so scattered and dispersed,
here He's before us agitated and fearful—
5   look here
by us
He became one.[32]

קָדוֹשׁ

אַל תִּכְלֶה כִּכְלוֹת שָׁמֶיךָ,
כִּכְלוֹת אַרְצְךָ, כִּכְלוֹת אֲבַק צְבָאָם.
בִּבְלִימָתְךָ אֶתְקַדֵּשׁ.

SANCTIFICATION

Don't perish when Your heavens perish,
when Your earth perishes, when the dust of their hosts perishes.
In Your nothingness I am sanctified.[33]

הַגֵּף

אַל תִּפְתַּח לָנוּ שַׁעַר. הֲכֵינוּ פְּתִיחָה
וְכָשְׁלוּ מְזוּזוֹת וּמַשְׁקוֹף.
הַגֵּף סְפָרֵינוּ. עֲפָרֵנוּ הַגֵּף. הַגֵּף טַל וּמָטָר. וּבְרָכָה.
הַגֵּף הַשַּׁעֲשׁוּעַ. הַגַּחְלִילִית הַקּוֹרֶצֶת. הַלַּחְלוּחִית שֶׁלְּקְרַאת.
הָרְוָחָה.   5
הַגֵּף פִּתְחֵי הַגּוּף וְהַדֶּרֶךְ.
הַגֵּף דְּמוּת צַלְמֶךָ וְחֶמְדַּת מַבָּטְךָ.

SHUT

Don't open the gate. We've been smitten by openings,
and doorposts and lintels have failed.
Shut our books. Shut our dust. Shut the dew and the rain. And
    blessing.
Shut enjoyment. The glittering firefly. The vitality in preparation.
5   The relief.
Shut the openings of the body and the way.
Shut Your likeness and image and the delight of Your look.[34]

The "Aleinu" prayer, recited in the "Musaf" service of the Days of Awe and
at the end of each of the three traditional daily prayers, concludes with the
biblical prophetic quote, "On that day the Lord will be one and His name
one" (Zechariah 14:9). In the biblical text and the liturgical context in which
it is placed, the image of God's lack of oneness conveys the fact that not all of
humanity accepts God's ultimate sovereignty, and His becoming one means
that all of humanity will one day unite in recognition of God. In the first
poem, "One," God's lack of unity is presented more literally as His being
"scattered and dispersed" (3). The traditional notion of God's omnipresence,
"He, who is everywhere" (2), is undermined by the suggestion that parts of
Him are found in various places in the cosmos. The Hebrew original for "scat-
tered and dispersed," *mefuzar umeforad,* appears in the book of Esther when
the villain Haman justifies his desire to wipe out the Jews of Persia by telling
King Ahasueres that they are "scattered and dispersed" throughout the king-
dom, yet they insist on observing their own laws rather than the laws of the
king (Esther 3:8). This allusion suggests that, like the Jewish people following
the destruction of the Temple, God Himself is in a state of exile (in keeping
with traditional Jewish imagery), His energy is dissipated, and thus He is

unable to function in the way He should. He must approach humanity in a way described with words used to express the humility of the prayer leader of the "Musaf" service for the Days of Awe in the "Hineni" prayer: "agitated and fearful" (*nirash venifḥad*, 4). Having drawn close to human beings, God can rely on them to pull all of His disparate elements together and make Him "one" (7), for, as line 1 states, "Through us God becomes one."

While the Hebrew title of the second poem "Qiddush" can simply mean "sanctification," it is most readily associated with Kiddush, the traditional ritual text recited over wine at the beginning of Sabbath and holiday meals. The language of the poem plays on the first paragraph of the Friday evening Sabbath Kiddush, *vayekhullu hashamayim veha'arets vekhol tseva'am* ("And the heavens and all of their host were completed," Genesis 2:1). In the poet's Kiddush, the root *k-l-y* of the biblical term *vayekhullu* is used not in its meaning of "complete," but rather in its alternative meaning of "destroy" (*al tikhleh kikhlot shamekha*, "Don't perish when Your heavens perish," 1). This Kiddush is not a celebration of God's completion of creation, but rather the expression of fear that the world could be destroyed. In lines 1 and 2, the speaker begs God not to allow Himself to be destroyed along with creation. In line 3, the speaker goes beyond that prayer and declares that, even if God ceases to exist, she will be able to discover the realm of sanctity on her own ("In Your nothingness I am sanctified").

Taking off on the liturgical poem "Petaḥ lanu sha'ar" ("Open For Us the Gate") of the Yom Kippur "Ne'ilah" service, the speaker in the third poem "Shut" asks the opposite of God: "Don't open the gate" (1). In the original liturgical context, the gate that people want to be open is the gate of heaven through which their prayers of repentance will enter. In this poem, gates represent more generally openings, or new possibilities. Such hopeful expectations, however, can be very painful, for when doors that have been opened end up leading to nowhere or are shut in one's face, one is more hurt than if hope for a positive change had not been held out in the first place ("We've been smitten by openings," 1) These openings, suggests the speaker, are in fact not very promising; having been opened and closed so often, their "doorposts and lintels have failed" (2).

The openings the speaker asks God to shut belong to a number of realms: travel ("dust," 3; "the way," 6), the intellect ("our books," 3), nature ("the dew and the rain," 3; "glittering firefly," 4), sexual relations ("the vitality in preparation" [*halaḥluḥit sheliqrat*, literally "the moisture toward"], 4; "openings of the body," 6), and general well being ("blessing," 3; "relief," 5). The speaker saves the most painful opening that disappoints for last: that of "the likeness and image" of God (7), with whom we expect to have a relationship, for we were, according to Genesis, created in His image and likeness (Genesis 1:26). That image, with its expression of God's "delight" (7) in us, raises the most promising prospect of all: full acceptance by God. Nevertheless, the speaker wants that closed off, too, because it stands in a troubling contrast to the actual sorry state of the world, about which God does not seem to care. The hope of being greeted warmly by God may be too much to expect in a world that at times He seems to have abandoned.

CHAPTER FIVE

Hava Pinhas-Cohen
"To the place where love has a manifest name."

Hava Pinhas-Cohen (1955–) was born in Jaffa and raised in Tel Aviv and Ramat Aviv.[1] Her parents, of Sephardic Bulgarian origin, immigrated to Israel after World War II. The family's political orientation ranged from Socialist Zionist to Communist (her uncles were founders of the Israeli Communist Party). She recalls her father, who died prematurely in a work accident, taking her as a child, dressed in a white shirt, for a walk on Jerusalem Boulevard in Jaffa on May 1, the international labor solidarity day. Her family raised her with a strong anti-religious bias, yet she developed a curiosity about the traditional religiosity that had been central to her family three generations before she was born. A concrete manifestation of that religiosity was a set of traditional Jewish prayer books that had once belonged to her great grandfather. Over time, she was driven to discover the rejected faith of her family's past. "It took me many years," she writes, "until I had the courage to locate within me the language of prayer and to accept it as a part of my most intimate world. In order to accept the inheritance of my great grandfather, I had to internalize the rebellion of my father and his generation against the exile [*galut*] and the exilic Jew, the God who keeps the Jew from placing the 'working class,' universal humanism, national normality at the top of his social hierarchy. Only later, in an archeological manner, was I able to dig into the language and to arrive at a different time that tells something about me and to state, 'Lord, open my lips and my mouth will speak Your praise' [Psalms 51:17]."[2]

At the age of sixteen, Pinhas-Cohen became involved in Gesher, an organization that seeks to develop ties between religious and secular Israeli Jews. As she began to be exposed to traditional Jewish culture, it bothered her that her secular education had cut her off from knowledge about traditional Judaism. Eventually she became more religiously observant, and, after her army service, she studied Hebrew literature and art history at the Hebrew University in Jerusalem. She also studied at Kerem, a humanistic Jewish institution for teachers, where she continued her exploration of Judaism.

She married a man raised in a traditionally observant Moroccan-Jewish family, who died an untimely death due to illness. They had four daughters together. For a period of time, they lived in Anatot, a West Bank settlement, primarily, she told me in an interview I conducted with her, because housing was relatively inexpensive there. She currently lives in Jerusalem. In discussing her ideological transition from a secular to a religious worldview, she has stated, "It has been an ongoing and painful search that has unceasingly connected and created conflicts between my intimately personal self and my family, between the knowledge of selfhood and a clarification of my relationship to Israel, to a national entity."[3] She explains the complexity of this process by declaring, "I could not allow myself (from the point of view of my spiritual life) to enter into an unequivocal and sweeping [self-] definition by turning my back on my parents' home and becoming traditionally observant on one particular day in a particular year, but rather I placed myself in a long process that has not yet ended and is replete with doubts . . . and it has a very painful aspect, because it is difficult for me to arrive at any kind of inner wholeness."[4] She does not characterize herself as strictly Orthodox. When asked in a recent interview to describe the nature of her religious observance and her relationship to prayer, Pinhas-Cohen replied, "I am a believer, I fulfill some of the commandments, I observe the Sabbath and the dietary laws . . . . I live my life prayerfully, as a believer . . . . To be in nature, in a field, on a mountain, in scenery—[these experiences are] part of my need to be prayerful. To maintain an intimate emotional household with my daughters is to be prayerful. To conduct an honest conversation to the end with a person to whom I am close . . . is to be prayerful . . . ."[5] In my interview with her, she expressed to me a strong dislike for having to submit to external authority, which clearly has put her in tension with the norms of traditional Jewish observance.

Natural settings in the Land of Israel provide her with an experience of God's presence that carries with it a physical dimension. She explains that her poetry "reveals that [her] private way to arrive at an awareness of the divine is by means of the sensual world of the Holy One Blessed be He . . . by means of recognizing [her] mutual relationship with the nature of Israel. . . ."[6] She goes on to say, "My attraction to Israel and to its nature, mainly to the desert, is an erotic attraction to the divine. There in the desert in general and in the Judean desert in particular, He reveals Himself in a way that is special to this place.

So, it is wonderful to me that in Hebrew one of the names of God is 'the place [*hamaqom*].'"[7]

Hebrew is for Pinhas-Cohen an important source that connects her with the worlds of faith in Israel's ancient biblical past. "The Hebrew language that I write and speak today," she observes, "constitutes my personal connection as an individual to the historical continuity . . . of the Hebrew language. Sometimes, perhaps, it weighs on me, but I feel that it mainly obligates me. It ties me as a woman to Hannah's prayer, to Rachel's anger at Jacob, to Naomi's feeling of alienation when she returned to Bethlehem . . . . It ties me to the realm of the sublime, to Moses' great poem which he composed before he died . . . , the same Moses who knew how to choose with great succinctness a few words when he turned to God with the plea that his sister Miriam be cured of skin disease."[8]

She also feels connected to Jewish texts in other languages such as Aramaic, Yiddish, and Ladino, which reflect the history of Jewish life in the Diaspora. As a child, Pinhas-Cohen experienced the typical polarity of an immigrant household caught between the parents' native tongue from the old country and the language of the new country adopted by the children. "My parents and my friends' parents," she writes, "spoke in the language of the old homeland [Ladino], mixed with Hebrew words."[9] With her grandmother she could only speak in Ladino, while her grandfather could converse with her in Hebrew to some extent, drawing on what he had learned in his traditional Jewish upbringing and in Zionist activities in Sophia. In keeping with the positive re-evaluation of the Diaspora's past in recent generations of Israeli writers, Pinhas-Cohen has occasionally incorporated Ladino into her Hebrew poems. In particular, she sees in the folk heritage of the Jews a key to reconnecting with past religiosity. "Our world in the twentieth century," she declares, "sanctified rationalism and forced psychology on the unbridled and creative aspects of the soul of humanity. This world forced on us a negation and the tendency to ignore folk expressions that are sometimes pre-verbal, although formulated in folk languages and mainly in oral culture."[10]

In comparing her interest in the visual arts with her literary creativity, she speaks of art as a form of religious revelation: "I think that the arts grow from the same root—[art] is a way to contemplate the world. It is also an intuitive way to join with existence beyond surface reality."[11] Having been connected to both the secular and religious worlds of Israel, Pinhas-Cohen is conscious of the important role she can play in breaking down the cultural barriers between those worlds by means of artistic creativity. Writers like her who in some sense live in both worlds, she observes, "carry within them two cultures, two identities struggling to unify content with form into one integrated work that will meet the criteria of the literary community."[12] Since its inception in 1990, she has been the editor of the literary journal *Dimui*. Originally published under the auspices of Ma'ale, a cultural organization associated with religious Zionism, since 2005 it has been published by Beit Morasha of Jerusalem, an academic center founded by religious Zionists with the stated purpose of "enhanc[ing] the Jewish and Zionist character of the State of Israel."[13] One of the central missions of the journal is to stimulate the creative talents of all writers attempting to create art that integrates the secular and the religious. As Pinhas-Cohen puts it, the journal is designed to allow for the artistic expression of religiously observant Jews, while at the same time being "open to the dialectical and experiential worlds of works that combine within them two cultures seeking the right expression. . . ."[14]

As far as Pinhas-Cohen is concerned, there is no inherent contradiction between Hebrew literature and religion. "The question is not . . ." she states, "[between] artistic creativity and religious faith, because with almost no difficulty one can find in the infrastructure of every Hebrew work a relationship to faith, sometimes in the manner of 'a cry or a question to the God who is not present [haElohim she'einenu]' ([in the words of Israeli writer] Yitzhak Orpaz), the stand of the individual against the herd, a consciousness of one's existence within the collective memory of Jewish experience, sometimes in a dialectical manner of tension between the human being and eternity, or in a third manner of unity between humanity and the cosmos."[15]

Pinhas-Cohen began publishing poetry in the early 1980s in the literary journal *Itton 77* and in the newspaper *Maariv*. In her poetry on religious themes, she regularly expands the horizons of the language of tradition as she expresses her own spiritual vision. "Language calls things by name," she has stated. "The poet is not satisfied with the world of names he has inherited from his predecessors. He seeks the way to expand the world of names, symbols, and signs."[16] The first set of poems I will consider portray idiosyncratic, individualistic spiritual paths. In some of the poems ("Communion," "Photosynthesis," "A Manifest Name," and "This is the Time"), the speaker is a woman who approaches religious experience in a manner that significantly differs from that of the male-dominated prayer service in a traditional synagogue. Two poems, "Communion" and "Photosynthesis," are written from the perspective of a woman on the other side of the ritual divider (*mehitsah*) between men and women in the synagogue. In "A Manifest Name," we are presented with the image of an ancient Israelite woman who stays home while the rest of her people participate in the revelation at Mount Sinai. In "This Is the Time," the speaker invents a new female-oriented ritual practice as an alternative to that dominated by male Jews. While one of the poems, "Before His Gates," does not present an explicitly feminine alternative to male religiosity, it does express the difficulty of the speaker who seeks spiritual fulfillment in the established traditional framework. In the second set of poems, the focus is on what the speaker would like to communicate directly to God. In these poems, God is seen as mysteriously distant, but also as a potential source of peace and inspiration. Two of the poems, "Plea" and "A Mother's Prayer Before Dawn," are written from a mother's perspective.

The other two, "What Is His Intention" and "A Woman's Mourner's Kaddish," focus on the speaker's disappointment in God for having allowed the existence of suffering in the world.

The Individual Spiritual Path

הִתְיַחֲדוּת

אֲנָשִׁים גְּבוֹהִים בְּטַלִּיתוֹת
כְּמוֹ צִפֳּרִים לְבָנוֹת
עַל הָרֵי יְרוּשָׁלַיִם.
מַה נִּסְתָּר תַּחַת הַגְּלִימָה–
מַלְכוּת לְשָׁעָה,   5
אוּלַי. וַאֲנִי בְּמַחֲשָׁבָה
זָרָה מַה כָּמַהְתִּי אוֹ, מַה
לְהִתְכַּנֵּס בְּרַגְלַיִם יְחֵפוֹת וְלַחֲסוֹת
תַּחַת טַלִּית הַכֹּהֵן הַגָּדוֹל שֶׁלִּי
וּבְתִפְלַּת כֹּהֲנִים, שְׁתַּיִם, שְׁתַּיִם   10
יָדֶיךָ לְפָנַי. רָצִיתִי שֶׁתִּמָּשֵׁךְ הַתְּפִלָּה
וְיִהְיֶה גַּג עַל הָרֹאשׁ, וְקִירוֹת לְפָנִים.
כָּל הַקָּהָל לְפָנִים
יָנִיד גַּם לִי רֹאשׁוֹ הַמַּלְבִּין
וְאוּלַי אָז, גַּם כָּל הַנִּסְתָּרוֹת   15
יִהְיוּ גְּלוּיוֹת
כְּמוֹ מַשְׁמָעוּת
הֶהָרִים סָבִיב–
לִירוּשָׁלַיִם

COMMUNION

Tall men in prayer shawls
like white birds
on Jerusalem's hills.
What's hidden under the robe?
5   A momentary kingdom,
perhaps. And I, a forbidden
thought, oh how I longed
to enter barefoot and take refuge
under the prayer shawl of my high priest
10   and in the priestly prayer, two by two

your hands before you. I wished the prayer would last
and be a roof above my head, and white walls.
The whole congregation before me
would nod its whitened head
15   and perhaps then all that's hidden
would be revealed
like the meaning
of the hills around
Jerusalem.[17]

From the other side of the divider between men and women in a traditional
synagogue, the speaker observes "[t]all men in prayer shawls" (1), the male de-
scendants of the priestly caste of ancient Israel blessing the congregation with
the three-part blessing prescribed by God in the Bible (Numbers 6:22–27). Dur-
ing this ceremony, the priests stand facing the congregation with prayer shawls
over their heads, for it is forbidden for the worshippers to see their faces while
they offer the blessing. As the priests bless the people, the speaker imagines re-
alities beyond that of the scene she sees: the outside world of nature and the
inner world of holiness. She makes an immediate association between her view
of the priests covered by white prayer shawls with black stripes and a nature
image which lies outside the confines of the synagogue: "white birds / on Jerusa-
lem's hills" (2–3). She also associates the priests with elements of religious mys-
tery and divine power: "What's hidden under the robe? / A momentary king-
dom" (4–5). The word for "hidden," *nistar*, evokes the mystical dimension of
existence; the word for "robe," *gelimah*, connotes a long flowing garment worn
by an official; and the word for "kingdom," *malkhut*, suggests not only the glory
of human power, but more importantly, God's role as sovereign of the universe.
    Inspired by these images of nature and religiosity in her imagination, the
speaker experiences a very strong longing (*kamahti*, a word that can connote
yearning for the divine) to transgress the boundary of the divider between the
men's and women's sections; to enter into that mysterious world under the
prayer shawl of her husband, (her "high priest," 9); and to share his priestly
role as he stretches his two hands out to bless the congregation (6–11). She
imagines this experience as lasting for a long time, the prayer shawl serving as
a roof and walls that protect her, while the congregation responds by nodding
their heads toward her (11–14). The association between religiosity and nature
with which the speaker begins the poem returns at the end of the poem. The
speaker speculates that, if she can fulfill her fantasy of entering under her hus-
band's prayer shawl when he blesses the congregation, she can arrive at an un-
derstanding of the mysteries of existence: "and perhaps then all that's hidden

[*kol hanistarot*] / would be revealed / like the meaning / of the hills around / Jerusalem" (15–19).

The speaker's fantasy of entering the men's section of the synagogue consists of a significant blend of the traditional and the subversive. When she enters "barefoot" (8), she is following the traditional practice of priests, who remove their shoes before blessing the congregation. Even though her entrance under her husband's prayer shawl is inappropriate because women are not traditionally granted the position of priest, she does so in an attempt to "take refuge" (8), and in so doing her action is no different from that of children in a traditional synagogue, who customarily seek their father's protection under his prayer shawl during the priestly benediction. At the same time, when the speaker walks barefoot, she can be seen as casting off the civilizing constraints of shoes that create a barrier between herself and the world. This fantasy is, in many ways, a challenge to religious norms, "a forbidden / thought" (*mahshavah / zarah*, 6–7), as she puts it, a term associated with the forbidden fire (*esh zarah*) for which Aaron the priest's sons Nadab and Abihu were put to death by God (Leviticus 10:1–3). The term is also used in later traditional Jewish literature to refer to thoughts that interfere with one's concentration in prayer.

The title of the poem, "Hityahadut," has an ambiguous meaning. In Jewish sources, the verb *hityahed* can connote being connected to others or being alone.[18] In modern Hebrew, the root *y-h-d* operates on these same two levels: the word *beyahad* means together, while the word *yahid* means an individual. This term, which operates on seemingly opposite levels of meaning, serves well to express the paradoxical nature of the speaker's fantasy. In one sense, the imagined experience is one of communion with God's holiness, with the priests, and with the community of worshippers. In another sense, this is a very personal, individual vision which challenges communal norms.

פּוֹטוֹסִינְתֶּזָה

חָשַׁבְתִּי לִהְיוֹת עָלֶה אֶ־חָד
בֵּין עֲלֵי הַדֶּשֶׁא
אוֹ מַחַט–
בֵּין עַנְפֵי הָאֹרֶן
יְחִידָה בֵּין קְהָל מְרַשְׁרֵשׁ   5
קוֹל בִּקְהִלָּה שֶׁל מַטָּה
מֵעֵבֶר לַפָּרְגּוֹד, רַחַשׁ נָשִׁים
מְמֻלְלוֹת בְּשִׂפְתוֹתֵיהֶן תְּפִלַּת יְחִידָה
מִטְפַּחַת צִבְעוֹנִית וּבְשֶׂם שׁוֹשַׁנִּים תָּפֵל
עֲנֵנוּ אָבִינוּ, עֲנֵנוּ,   10
וְנִמְצְאוּ וַדַּאי דִּבְרֵיהֶן מְכֻוָּנִים
וּבַקָּשָׁתָן עַל חוֹלָה אוֹ עֲקָרָה
פַּרְנָסָה אוֹ בְּתוּלָה שֶׁעָבַר זְמַנָּהּ.

אֲנִי–מֶחֱצָה עָשִׂיתִי–
חַלּוֹן בֵּרַרְתִּי בְּתוֹךְ מִסְגֶּרֶת עֵץ   15
וּפָנָיו מִזְרָחָה לְבֵית קְבָרוֹת מַלְבִּין
לְיַד פַּרְדֵּס.

אֵיךְ הַצֶּמַח אֶת הָאוֹר סוֹפֵג
וְיוֹדֵעַ לְהַטְמִיעַ וּלְהוֹצִיא–
פְּרִי וִיהֵא גַּם–   20
זֶרַע. אֵיךְ.
עֲנֵנִי אָבִי, עֲנֵנִי.

PHOTOSYNTHESIS

I thought I'd be one leaf
among the leaves of grass
or a needle—
among the pine branches
5   individual in a murmuring congregation
a voice in a community on earth
beyond the curtain, the whispering of women
mumbling with their lips an individual prayer
a colorful kerchief and stale rose-scented perfume:
10 Answer us, Father, answer us,
and for sure their words are focused,

their petition for the sick or barren,
livelihood or a virgin past her prime.

I—a divider made—
15   a window I set within a wooden frame
facing east to a whitened cemetery
by an orchard.

How does the plant absorb the light
knowing how to hide and put forth—
20   fruit that will also become—
a seed? How?
Answer me, Father, answer me.[19]

As in "Communion," this poem is told from the point of view of a speaker located in the women's section of a traditional synagogue. The similarity in perspective is not surprising, since the poet indicates they were written on the same day in the year 5750 of the Hebrew calendar (1989). There is a sharp contrast between the speaker's desire to feel at one with her fellow worshippers and the actual atmosphere among the women in which she finds herself. She would be happy to be a small, insignificant part of the larger whole, like a blade of grass or a pine needle (1–4), an "individual in a murmuring congregation / a voice in a community on earth" (5–6). Her fellow women worshippers, however, are oblivious to any sense of the transcendence of their individuality in an entity that encompasses them. Their prayers are devoted only to asking God to aid them. The help they ask for is most valid, help for "the sick or barren / livelihood or a virgin past her prime" (12–13). Yet each is capable only of whispering and mumbling her prayers as an individual (7–8). When the speaker declares, "and for sure their words are focused" (11), she indicates her respect for, but perhaps also her criticism of, the nature of these women's prayers. The Hebrew original for "focused" (*mekhuvvanim*) connotes the special attention (*kavvanah*) one is expected to pay to one's prayer as one directs one's heart to God. Yet, if that is the extent of their special attention, their religious imagination is surely impoverished for being narrowly focused on personal needs. The women's spiritual limitations are indicated by the expression the speaker uses to refer to the divider that sets off the women from the men in the synagogue: *me'ever lapargod* ("beyond the curtain," 7). This expression alludes to the rabbinic term *me'ahorei hapargod,* which refers to a divider between the divine presence and the angels in heaven. To hear something *me'ahorei hapargod* signifies in rabbinic literature that one has gained knowledge of that which takes place in the divine realm. In their location on the other side of the divider between men and women in the synagogue, however, the women are actually very far from any connection with that transcendent realm. The external appearance of the women also indicates their lack of spiritual vitality. They each try to appear attractive by means of "a colorful kerchief and stale rose-scented perfume" (9), yet their attention to the external devices of clothing and of personal aroma (with not very pleasing cosmetics at that) deflect them from a more profound encounter with the divine.

The speaker, therefore, must look beyond the gender-segregated synagogue prayer for spiritual fulfillment. She imagines herself replacing the divider between men and women, which she has called *pargod*, with an alternative divider, which she calls *meḥitsah*, the term usually used to refer to the divider in the synagogue (14). Paradoxically, this divider is actually a window that allows her to open up to the world outside the synagogue (15). The window is "facing east" (16), as Jews do in prayer, and it looks out at a scene that combines an image of death ("a whitened cemetery," 16) with an image of life ("an orchard," 17). What makes this scene preferable to that which she experiences in the women's section of the synagogue? Perhaps it is the contact with the opposing primordial forces of life and death that attracts the speaker as an alternative to the self-absorbed petitionary prayers of the women.

In the final stanza, the speaker abruptly shifts her point of view and turns directly to God. Having left the confines of the synagogue, at least in her imagination, she is now ready to address her own prayer to the divine. Unlike that of the other women in the synagogue, who pray in the more traditional form of first person plural ("Answer us, Father, answer us," 10), the speaker prays in the first person singular ("Answer me, Father, answer me," 22). Her petition for God's response does not involve the kind of request for divine assistance in repairing a distressful situation that was characteristic of the other women's prayer, but rather a question about photosynthesis, one of the wonders of nature: "How does the plant absorb the light / knowing how to hide and put forth — / fruit that will also become — / a seed?" (18–21). Earlier in the poem, the speaker had expressed the desire to be part of a community by comparing herself to a blade of grass or a pine needle. Now she returns to plant imagery to express her desire to interact with God. Photosynthesis serves here as a metaphor for spiritual wholeness. Plants have a marvelous way of interacting with their environment. They effortlessly receive their energy from the light of the sun and transform that energy into fruit that contains seeds that fall to the ground and bring forth new plants. In an analogous fashion, the speaker yearns to transcend the petty concerns of the hour and focus on receiving an infusion of divinity which will give her the spiritual energy to contribute creatively to the world.

An unusual representation of a word in the original Hebrew of the poem could not be easily translated. Because in Hebrew the number "one," *eḥad*, appears after the noun it is modifying, the first line of the poem, "I thought I

would be one leaf," ends with *eḥad*. The poet divides the word into its two syl-
lables, with a hypen between them: *e-ḥad*. This would appear to follow the tra-
ditional practice of drawing out the pronunciation of the word *eḥad* in the first
verse of the collection of biblical passages known as the "Shema" when it is re-
cited in the context of prayer: "Hear O Israel, the Lord our God, the Lord is
one" (*Shema Yisra'el, Adonay Eloheinu, Adonay e-ḥad*, Deuteronomy 6:4). This
drawn out pronunciation emphasizes the central idea of this verse, that the Jew
is committed to belief in God's unity. In the poem, by alluding to this practice,
the poet connects herself with one of the most intense moments of prayer in
traditional Judaism, thereby raising the spiritual significance of her religious ex-
perience to the highest level.

שֵׁם מְפֹרָשׁ

כֻּלָּם כְּבָר הָלְכוּ אֶל הָהָר וּמְחַכִּים
מְחַכִּים לִרְאוֹת, בְּשֶׁקֶט רַב מְחַכִּים,
שֶׁלֹּא כְּמִנְהָגָם גַּם הַחֲמוֹרִים, גַּם הַגְּמַלִּים
בַּשֶּׁקֶט הַזֶּה צִפּוֹר לֹא צִיְּצָה
גַּם יְלָדִים עַל כִּתְפֵי אֲבוֹתֵיהֶם,   5
וְהַשֶּׁקֶט רַב מִנְּשׂוֹא כְּמוֹ לִפְנֵי דָּבָר
נוֹרָא וְגָדוֹל וַאֲנִי עוֹד רָצִיתִי
לְהַסְפִּיק וְלִתְלוֹת אֶת הַכְּבָסִים
לַעֲשׂוֹת זְמַן לְעַצְמִי לְתַקֵּן רֵיחוֹתַי
וְחִמַּמְתִּי אֶת הֶחָלָב לַתִּינוֹק, שֶׁלֹּא יִרְעַב   10
שֶׁלֹּא יִבְכֶּה חָלִילָה, בָּרֶגַע הַלֹּא
מַתְאִים, כַּמָּה זְמַן עַד כְּלוֹת. הַצִּפִּיָּה
שֶׁתִּתְיַבֵּשׁ הַכְּבִיסָה וְהַתִּינוֹק מָה.
אִישׁ לֹא יָדַע
וַאֲנִי רָאִיתִי שָׁרוּחַ קַלָּה, כְּמוֹ נְשִׁימָתוֹ שֶׁל אִישׁ יָשֵׁן, עָבְרָה   15
בַּכְּבָסִים וְנִפְחָה כֶּרֶסָה
שֶׁל כֻּתָּנְתִּי וּמַפַּת הַשַּׁבָּת
הָיְתָה מְפֹרָשׂ לָבָן בְּאֶמְצַע הַמִּדְבָּר
וְיָצְאוּ מִשָּׁם עַל הַתְּכֵלֶת
הַרְחֵק לַמָּקוֹם בּוֹ   20

נִפְרֹט רִמּוֹנִים וְנֹאכַל עֲסִיסָם
לַמָּקוֹם בּוֹ
לְאַהֲבָה
שֵׁם מְפֹרָשׁ.

A Manifest Name

They've all gone to the mountain to wait
to wait and see, most quietly they wait,
against their nature even donkeys, even camels
in this quiet a bird did not chirp
5 even children on their fathers' shoulders,
the quiet too much to bear as if before a matter
so awesome and great but I still wished
to finish hanging the laundry
to make time for myself, to refresh my aroma
10 and I warmed the baby's milk, lest he be hungry,
lest he cry, perish the thought, at an improper
moment, how much longer till it ends. The expectation
that the laundry will dry and the baby, what.
No one knew
15 but I saw a light wind, like the breath of a person asleep, pass
through the laundry and inflate the middle
of my shirt and the Sabbath tablecloth
was a white sail in the middle of the wilderness
and we went from there on azure
20 far to the place where

we'll open pomegranates and devour their juice
to the place where
love has
a manifest name.[20]

Set in biblical times, this poem imagines an Israelite woman in the encamp-
ment at the foot of Mount Sinai as the people anticipate the revelation of the
Ten Commandments (Exodus 19–20). While the other Israelites, and even
their animals, await the awesome revelation from God, the speaker insists on
fulfilling her domestic obligations: "but I still wished / to finish hanging the
laundry / to make time for myself, to refresh my aroma / and I warmed the
baby's milk" (7–10). Although she states that she insists on feeding her baby to
prevent him from crying in hunger and thus ruining the theophany at Sinai
(10–12), it is clear that more important to her is the need not to lose sight of the
everyday needs and pleasures of life, even at a time of high religious drama. In-
deed, when she adds the expression "perish the thought" (*halilah*, 11) to her ref-
erence to the baby crying, one senses a somewhat sarcastic critique of the pre-
occupation of the others with spiritual matters to the exclusions of matters of

equal or perhaps superior importance, like feeding babies. Her instinct to keep house, as opposed to attending the revelation, comes across in the poem as reflecting basic gender differences in ancient as well as in contemporary Israel. The men attend to the public spiritual experiences, and it is in the context of those experiences that they relate to their children ("children on their fathers' shoulders," 5), whereas the women remain more firmly committed than the men to the domestic realm.

The speaker makes use of a rabbinic midrashic text about the story of the revelation at Sinai in a way that raises questions about the traditional understanding of that event:

> When the Holy One Blessed be He gave the Torah no bird chirped [*tsavah*, rather than *tsiyytsah* as in line 4 of the poem], no fowl flew, no ox lowed, Ophanim did not fly, Seraphim did not say "Holy, holy," the sea did not move, people did not speak. The world was completely quiet and still and the voice of God, "I am the Lord your God" went out. . . . [God] quieted the whole world so that all creatures would know that no one but Him said, "I am the Lord your God." (Shemot Rabbah 29:9)

This unnatural phenomenon of complete quiet in the world was, according to the midrashic text, engineered by God so that the Israelites would know that He alone was revealing His will to them. In the poem, the reference to absolute silence serves to emphasize how undesirably unnatural the experience of the revelation is as the people and even the animals wait quietly "against their nature" (*shelo keminhagam*, literally "not like their custom," 3).

As she undergoes the more natural experience of tending to her domestic responsibilities, the speaker receives her own revelation, which is very different from the one received by her fellow Israelites at Sinai. A wind blows through her laundry, creating in her a vision in which, unlike the Israelites as a whole who will be doomed to travel for forty years by land through the wilderness, she will set sail by sea for the Promised Land (14–24). This wind resembles the breath of a person asleep, who, like her, has stayed at home to take care of his or her needs. In contrast to the focus on the divine dictates in the Ten Commandments that were granted to the entire people at Sinai, her revelation is of the sensual pleasures of Canaan, where the Israelites will "open pomegranates and devour their juice" (21).

One can interpret the last three lines of the poem, "to the place where / love has / a manifest name" (*lamaqom bo / la'ahavah / shem meforash*, 22–24), as describing Canaan as a place where the concept of love is clearly recognized and understood, and where love between human beings is greatly valued, perhaps in contrast to the atmosphere of the revelation at Sinai, with its focus on the human obligations to God. However, there may be another significance to these lines. The word *maqom* can mean "place," but in rabbinic Hebrew it is also a term for God, while the term *shem hameforash* is a rabbinic euphemism for the Tetragrammaton, the sacred four-letter biblical name of God, which was pronounced in ancient Israel only by the High Priest on Yom Kippur. We could therefore read the lines to mean: to God (*lamaqom*) within whom (*bo*) / "for love" (*la'ahavah*) is the sacred divine name (*shem meforash*). According to this interpretation, the speaker is expressing the belief that, once the people enter the land, they will discover that in love one finds the true divine revelation, for that is the most sacred name of God. The female speaker who refrained from attending the divine revelation at Sinai has, by means of her affectionate caring for her home and child, demonstrated that she has known this truth all along.

מוּל שְׁעָרָיו

וְאֵין בִּי אוֹתָהּ נְמִיכוּת קוֹמָה
לִשְׁאֹף כְּמוֹ עֶבֶד לְיַד אֲדוֹנוֹ
וְאֵין בִּי אוֹתָהּ נְמִיכוּת רוּחַ לְיַשֵּׁר
לְבָבִי הַתּוֹעֶה כְּמוֹ בַּד כֻּתְנָה
מְתַחַת כְּבֵדוֹ שֶׁל מַגְהֵץ   5

כִּי מַה שֶּׁרוֹאוֹת עֵינַי וּמַה שֶּׁבָּא
בִּשְׂפָתַי אֵין חוּט קוֹשֵׁר
רַק שָׂפָה זָרָה
וּמֶרְחָק שֶׁכָּל הָאֹפֶק
מְקֻפָּל תַּחְתָּיו   10

וַאֲנִי דּוֹפֶקֶת עַל דַּלְתוֹת
זְכוּכִית סוֹבְבוֹת עַל צִיר
לִמְסֹר גּוּפִי וְנַפְשִׁי
בַּכְּנִיסָה לַלּוֹבִּי שֶׁבּוֹ שׁוֹעֵר
לָבוּשׁ מַדִּים שׁוֹמֵר   15
לִשְׁעָרָיו שֶׁל עוֹלָם מֻזְהָב
שֶׁאֵין לוֹ חֵלֶק בִּי
יָדַי דּוֹחֲפוֹת אֶת הַזְּכוּכִית הַנָּעָה
וְקוֹלוֹת רַבִּים אַחֲרַי אוֹמְרִים
"פְּתַח לָהּ שַׁעַר"   20

וּלְעַצְמָם הֵם מִתְכַּוְּנִים.

BEFORE HIS GATES

I have not that meagerness of stature
like a servant yearning beside his master,
I have not that meagerness of spirit to straighten
my straying heart like cotton cloth
5   under the weight of an iron

for what my eyes see and what comes
to my lips no thread connects
only a foreign tongue
and a distance under which
10   is folded the whole horizon

I knock on glass
revolving doors
to deliver my body and soul
at the entrance of the lobby in which a uniformed
15   guard keeps watch
over the gates of a golden world
which has no part in me
my hands push the moving glass
and many voices behind me say
20   "Open for her the gate"

but it's to themselves they refer.[21]

The expression "Open for her the gate" (20) in the penultimate line of this poem alludes to the *piyyut* in the final "Ne'ilah" prayer of Yom Kippur, which declares, "Open for us the gate." The gate referred to in the *piyyut* is the gate of heaven, which those who pray hope will be opened by God to receive their entreaties for forgiveness from sin. The speaker in this poem longs to experience the oneness with God that is the ideal outcome of Yom Kippur, but the traditional ways of uniting with God are impossible for her to follow. As she stands "before His gates," in the words of the title, the speaker is incapable of assuming the stance of humility before God ("that meagerness of stature," 1; "that meagerness of spirit," 3) that, according to tradition, is a necessary prerequisite for the human being seeking to approach the divine. The speaker makes use of two similes to convey this humility of which she is incapable. One is from the realm of tradition: "like a servant yearning beside his master" (*lishof kemo eved leyad adono*, 2, which echoes the biblical expression *ke'eved yishaf tsel*, "like a servant who longs for shadow," Job 7:2). The image of people as God's servants also appears in the *piyyutim* of the Days of Awe. The other is a more modern, mundane simile in which her "straying heart" is straightened out as an iron smooths out the wrinkles in a piece of cotton cloth (3–5). The speaker's spiritual failings thus appear to be on two levels: 1) she cannot submit her will to God and wait expectantly for God to grant her what she wants or needs, like a servant before his master; and 2) she has a drive to pursue her passions in ways that do not conform to divine expectations, like a wrinkled cotton shirt before it has been given a good ironing.

In an ideal world, prayer helps us to express our religious response to life. In the case of the speaker, however, there is no connection between the words of prayer she is called on to utter and how she actually experiences the world: "for what my eyes see and what comes / to my lips no thread connects" (6–7). The words of prayer are "only a foreign tongue" (8) which cannot truly express her response to life. The alienation between language and self is emphasized in the original Hebrew. Although the word for "my lips" (*sefatay*), which represents the self, is the same as the word for "language" (*safah*), they are in essence very different from each other. All she can feel is how far away she is from God; beyond her is "a distance under which / is folded the whole horizon" (9–10).

Having despaired of the power of the words of prayer, the speaker imagines a more intimate involvement with God, and she knocks on the gates that separate humanity from divinity with an offer to submit her "body and soul" to God (11–13). The gates, however, take the form of a modern phenomenon: a glass revolving door (11–12). This image would appear to be problematic because, in such a door, one can easily exit as soon as one has entered, thereby suggesting that the attempt to submit to God will have a temporary existence at best. On the one hand, the divine realm into which she enters is an enticing "golden world" (16). On the other hand, it is not all that inviting, like a hotel lobby presided over by a uniformed guard (14–16). In a passage in Mishnah Avot 3:11, there appears a list of actions that disqualify a person from being assured of a place in the world to come, in other words, eternal reward in the afterlife (*ein lo ḥeleq la'olam haba*). In the poem, the speaker reverses the expression and says that the golden world "has no part in me" (*she'ein lo ḥeleq bi*, 17). Thus, for the speaker, the concern is not eternal reward through acceptance into the world to come, but rather, the ability to internalize the divine eternal realm within her soul.

As the speaker pushes the doors, she hears from behind her what appear at first to be words of encouragement as many people call out to God to open the gates for her (19–20). But this sense that the community within which she prays is really seeking her entrance into the divine realm proves to be only an illusion. In the final line of the poem, she expresses the realization that the others actually do not care whether she finds the spiritual fulfillment she seeks, and it's rather "to themselves they refer" (21).

זֶה הַזְּמַן

וּבַחֲמִשָּׁה עָשָׂר לְחֹדֶשׁ שְׁבָט זֶה הַזְּמַן בּוֹ אֲנִי
מִתְקַנֶּנֶת לְיוֹם כִּפּוּרִים, לְיוֹם צוֹם וְלַעֲשׂוֹת
תְּשׁוּבָה מְלֵאָה וּפְגִישָׁה בֵּינִי לְבֵינֶךָ.
זֶה הַזְּמַן לִפְתֹּחַ אֶת הַחַלּוֹנוֹת וּלְחַפֵּשׂ אֶת הַשָּׁמַיִם
לְאַחַר שֶׁיָּרַד הַגֶּשֶׁם בְּעִתּוֹ   5
וּבְחֶבְיוֹן הָעֵצִים מִתְרַחֵשׁ דָּבָר נִסְתָּר מֵהָעַיִן
זֶה הַזְּמַן שֶׁל הַדְּבָרִים לְהַגִּידָם וּבְסָמוּךְ, לַעֲשׂוֹתָם.
נַפְשִׁי פְּנוּיָה לְךָ וְאֵין אִישׁ
תּוֹבֵעַ זְמַנְּךָ בִּתְקִיפוּת שֶׁל חֲכָמִים
וְיֵשׁ אֵיזֶה קֶשֶׁב בָּעוֹלָם לְבַת קוֹל מְצֻפֶּנֶת   10
מֵעַיִן שֶׁתֵּצֵא בְּעִתָּהּ וְאָדָר יָבִיא גְשָׁמָיו
וּפִתְחֵי בָתִּים יִפָּנוּ זֶה לִקְרַאת זֶה בְּקַעֲרוֹת סֹלֶת בְּלוּלָה
בְּשֶׁמֶן וְרֵיחַ נִיחוֹחַ יַעֲלֶה וְאִם וּבִתָּהּ שֶׁרָאוּ אֶת הַחֹדֶשׁ תֵּצֶאנָה
לַשָּׂדֶה. זֶה הַלַּיְלָה בּוֹ הַיָּרֵחַ מֵעַל הַפַּרְדֵּסִים מָלֵא
וְהָאֲדָמָה מִתְעַבֶּרֶת וַאֲנִי גוֹזֶרֶת עַל עַצְמִי קֶשֶׁב   15
לְגֶרֶשׁ מֵהָאֹפֶק פְּגוּמֵי כְּעוּר וָעִיר
וּלְחַפֵּשׂ לִי גַּג לְהִשְׁתַּטֵּחַ עָלָיו בְּבִגְדֵי אוֹר רַכִּים
וְאֶמְבַּט שֶׁל מֵי גְשָׁמִים לִטְבֹּל בְּתוֹכוֹ שֶׁבַע פְּעָמִים
לִפְשֹׁט צוּרַת אִשָּׁה וְאִם וְלִלְבֹּשׁ הַלַּיְלָה מַרְאֵה כַּלָּה רַכָּה לִקְרָאתְךָ
(שֶׁאֵינָהּ מִבְּנֵי שֵׁם) מִימִינִי מִדְבָּר וְלִשְׂמֹאלִי יֵשׁ יָם   20
וַאֲנַחְנוּ מִכֹּחַ הַיּוֹם וְהַקָּרְבָּן
מֵעַל הַדְּבָרִים.

שֶׁאִם לֹא כֵן אֵלֵךְ בַּעֲשָׂרָה בְּתִשְׁרֵי
בְּתוֹךְ קָהָל לָבָן, בִּפְנֵי עֲיֵפוּת וּמֶרִי וּבְגָדִים
חֲמוּצִים מִדָּמִים וְאֶתֵּן עֵדוּת בִּפְנֵי בֵּית־   25
דִּין שֶׁל מַטָּה.

THIS IS THE TIME

The fifteenth of the month of Shevat is the time I'm
prepared for Yom Kippur, for a day of fasting
complete repentance and a meeting between me and You.
This is the time to open the windows and to search the sky
5   after rain fell in its season
and deep within the trees something hidden from sight comes to
        pass
this is the time to tell things and immediately to do them.
My soul is available for You and no one
demands Your time with the forcefulness of sages

10   and in the world there's a kind of attentiveness to a heavenly voice
                concealed
        from sight that emerges in its season while Adar brings its rains
        and doors of houses turn to each other with bowls of finest flour
                mixed
        with oil and a pleasant aroma rises and a woman and her daughter,
                who saw the month, go out
        to the field. This is the night the moon is full above the orchards
15   and the earth becomes pregnant and I force myself to be attentive
        to expel from the horizon ugly urban blemishes
        and seek a roof to lie on in soft clothes of light
        and a rainwater bath to dip in seven times
        to strip off the form of wife and mother and wear tonight the look of
                a soft bride before You
20   (I being not a Semite) to my right the desert, to my left the sea
        and we by the power of the day and offering
                                                    are beyond all matter.
        For if not I'll go on the tenth of Tishrei
        in a white congregation, with an expression of fatigue and rebellion
                and clothes
25   red from blood and I'll testify before
                                            an earthly court.[22]

The fifteenth day of the Hebrew month of Shevat, known in Jewish tradition as Tu Bishevat, falls in late January or February, at the time of year when trees first begin to blossom in Israel. In ancient Israel, it was celebrated as the New Year of the trees for purposes of calculating the ritual obligations of the fruit offerings to God in the Temple. In modern times, the Zionist movement transformed Tu Bishevat into a day to celebrate the reforestation efforts of the Jewish settlers in the Land of Israel, and, after the founding of the State, it became a fixed date on the civil calendar, marked by groups of school children planting trees.

For the speaker, this New Year of the trees provides an opportunity to create a religious practice that would serve as an alternative to the period of repentance that is marked during the ten days in autumn that begin with Rosh Hashanah, the traditional Jewish New Year on the first day of the Hebrew month of Tishrei, and culminate on the tenth day of Tishrei, Yom Kippur. As is traditional practice on Yom Kippur, the speaker will transform Tu Bishevat into a day of fasting, repentance, and encounter with God (1–3). Unlike the traditional Yom Kippur observance, however, she does not spend the day in syna-

gogue. Instead, in the spirit of the Tu Bishevat season, she goes out into na-
ture, sensitive to the clear skies of the emerging spring that follows the rainy
winter season (4–5). It is in nature that she will discern the presence of God:
"deep within the trees something hidden [*nistar*, a word that connotes a mys-
tical dimension] from sight comes to pass" (6); "and in the world there's a kind
of attentiveness to a heavenly voice concealed [*mutspenet*]" (10). As she cele-
brates this personal holiday, she feels driven to self expression through speech
and action ("this is the time to tell things and immediately to do them," 7). In
contrast to the traditional Yom Kippur synagogue service conducted by men
in a serious ascetic atmosphere, she imagines a scene pervaded by the femi-
nine and by images of nature: "a woman and her daughter . . . go out / to the
field" (13–14), "the earth becomes pregnant" (15), "bowls of finest flour [are]
mixed / with oil and a pleasant aroma" (12–13), and "the moon is full above the
orchards" (14).

Because Tu Bishevat is a minor holiday with no prescribed ritual obligations
in present times, both the speaker and God will have the time for a special re-
lationship that might not be available on the Days of Awe, when she would be
occupied with holiday observances and God would be busy attending to the
ritual practices of Jews ("My soul is available for You and no one / demands
Your time with the forcefulness of sages," 8–9). This interaction with God is
sensuously charged, allowing the speaker to transcend the limitation of her every-
day identity as a member of a family and even as a Jewish descendant of Noah's
son Shem ("to strip off the form of wife and mother . . . / (I being not a
Semite)," 19–20). Her sense of being distanced from Jewish identity and ritual
practice is reinforced by her statement, "to my right the desert, to my left the
sea" (20), which alludes to the passage in the traditional Jewish bedtime prayer
that evokes the protection of God's angels: "In the name of the God of Israel, to
my right Michael, to my left Gabriel, before me Uriel, behind me Raphael, and
above my head God's presence." The speaker, thus, has transformed the tradi-
tional Jewish notion of supernatural protection by angels into a more humanis-
tic experience of feeling at home in nature.

The speaker immerses herself in a ritual bath of rainwater seven times, in
preparation for becoming the "soft bride" of God Himself (17–19). She is the of-
fering (*qorban*) to God to which she refers in line 21, accompanied, like the
offerings in the ancient Temple, by the "finest flower mixed / with oil" (*solet
belulah / beshemen*, 12–13) and the pleasant aroma (*reah nihoah*, 13) of incense.
In this natural setting between the vast expanses that mark the borders of Israel
to the east and the west ("to my right the desert, to my left the sea," 20) and with
the power of the holiness of the day, the speaker will be able to transcend the
material world of civilization ("to expel from the horizon ugly urban blemishes,"
16) and actually rise to a level *beyond all matter* (22).

By calling her Tu Bishevat "Yom Kippur" (2) and by referring to the traditional Yom Kippur merely by its date, "the tenth of Tishrei" (23), the speaker places her day of atonement on a higher plane than that of the traditional one. Furthermore, at the end of the poem, she makes clear that she will have great difficulty with the observance of the traditional Yom Kippur if she does not have the opportunity to celebrate Tu Bishevat in the manner that she proposes (23–26). Unsure that she will be granted the opportunity to celebrate her own early springtime Yom Kippur, the speaker feels the need to warn the male-dominated traditional community in which she lives that, if it does not want her to disrupt the religious structures that it holds dear, it had better allow her to seek the spiritual outlet on Tu Bishevat that she so desperately needs. She actually threatens that, if she is not allowed to celebrate it, she will come to the traditional Yom Kippur observance in the synagogue spiritually drained and driven to rebel against the male-dominated holy day ("with an expression of fatigue and rebellion," 24), wearing not the customary white clothing that signifies purity, but "clothes / red from blood" (24–25), the substance that, when associated with menstruation, makes a woman ritually impure according to Jewish tradition. On Yom Kippur, Jews are judged by the heavenly court (*beit din shel malah*), but her testimony will be before an earthly court (*beit din shel matah*, 25–26), the community of men whose insensitivity to her spiritual needs, she fears, will continue to cause her much anguish.

Communicating with God

בַּקָּשָׁה

כַּאֲשֶׁר תִּינוֹק בְּיָדִי
וְחָלָב אֱנוֹשִׁי רוֹקֵם אֶת חַיָּיו,
בָּאִים בַּלֵּילוֹת פְּעִימוֹת וְקוֹלוֹת קְצוּבִים
רַכָּבוֹת–

בְּתַחֲנָה מְסֻיֶּמֶת עַל הָאָרֶץ הַזֹּאת,   5
בְּרַגְלַיִם יְחֵפוֹת בְּקֹצֶר־יָד
פָּשַׁטְתִּי זְרוֹעוֹת
כְּמוֹ קַרְנֵי אַיִל מִתּוֹךְ סְבַךְ
לְחִישַׁת הָאָרֶץ לַשָּׁמַיִם
שְׁמַע, וַעֲשֵׂה סֻכַּת רַחֲמֶיךָ   10
כְּמוֹ צֵל הַגֶּפֶן וְהַתְּאֵנָה
אַל תְּנַסֵּנִי, נָא.

יֵשׁ עֵצִים וְיֵשׁ סְבַךְ, רֵיחַ שֶׁל אֵשׁ
וּמַרְאֵה עָשָׁן. עִם אִמָּהוֹת לֹא מְשַׂחֲקִים
מַחֲבוֹאִים–   15

בְּקֹצֶר יָדִי מְכַסָּה עַל עֵינַי
קוֹלִי אוֹבֵד בִּצְעָקָה
אַל־קוֹלִית

אַיֶּכָּה

PLEA

With a baby in my hand,
human milk weaving his life,
at night come rhythmic beats and sounds
trains—

5   At a certain station on this earth,
barefoot and with limited strength,
I stretched forth my arms
like the horns of a ram from a thicket
a whisper of earth to heaven
10   listen, and make the tabernacle of Your mercy

like the shade of a vine and a fig tree
don't test me, please.

There is wood and a thicket and the smell of fire
and the sight of smoke. With mothers one doesn't play
15   hide and seek—

With my limited strength I cover my eyes
my voice is lost in a cry
beyond sound

Where are You?[23]

There is a tension in the beginning of this poem between the speaker's power to nourish her baby ("With a baby in my hand, / human milk weaving his life," 1–2) and the speaker's feeling of vulnerability as she hears frightening sounds at night ("rhythmic beats and sounds, / trains," 3–4), which raises the question of the extent to which she will really be able to protect her child from danger. What is the significance of the one-word line "trains" (4)? Perhaps the image of trains may evoke in the reader an association with the Holocaust, in which trains were the main vehicle used to transport the victims to the concentration camps, or perhaps in a more general way trains signify here the inevitable periods of transition that people experience in life. This latter interpretation is strengthened by the speaker's use of the metaphor of life as a train journey in the line "At a certain station on this earth" (5). It is possible that, at least in part, the speaker's anxiety reflects the ongoing preoccupation that Israeli parents have with the future of their children in a country that has been in a state of war for its entire existence.

The Hebrew title of the poem, "Baqqashah," is a term traditionally used to refer to a prayer of petition. It is in the second stanza that the speaker presents her plea to God. She does so fully aware of how weak and vulnerable she is ("barefoot and with limited strength," 6). In expressing her desperate desire for God's protection for herself and her child, she resorts to traditional biblical and liturgical imagery. "[M]ake the tabernacle of Your mercy / like the shade of a vine and a fig tree" (10–11), she pleads, thereby alluding to the image in the traditional evening prayer of God spreading His tabernacle of peace upon humanity and to the biblical image of security and tranquility in the account of King Solomon's rule (I Kings 5:5) and in the prophetic vision of the end of days (Micah 4:4): "each person under his vine and under his fig tree." Yet, her way of expressing this plea is not in articulate, forcefully argued language. Rather, it is expressed as "a whisper of earth to heaven" (9) and, later, as her "voice . . . lost in a cry / beyond sound" (17–18). Due to the difficulty of engaging in verbal prayer, the speaker turns to physical gestures, stretching forth her arms (7) and covering her eyes (16), both expressions of intense prayer that evoke the hand motions that traditional Jewish women make upon lighting the Sabbath candles. These gestures reflect how she can only act with "limited strength" (*beqo-tser yadi*, 16, literally "with the shortness of my hand").

The poem is replete with references to the binding of Isaac story (Genesis 22): the ram caught in the thicket (8, 13), the test (12), the wood (13), and the fire (13). However, unlike Abraham, who willingly submitted to the command to sacrifice his son Isaac, the speaker does not wish to be tested. Indeed, she admonishes God not to withdraw from her; if He thinks this is a game, He is wrong, because as a mother she deservers better treatment ("With mothers one doesn't play / hide and seek," 14–15). Indeed, she suggests, just as Adam hid from God after sinning and God sought him with the question *Ayyekah?* ("Where are you?" Genesis 3:9), now it is her turn to call to the hidden God and seek His presence (19). The reversal of both the binding of Isaac and Garden of Eden stories constitutes a very strong condemnation of God. The speaker is not prepared to undertake the sacrifice of her children's security just because God asks this of her. Indeed, as far as she is concerned, because her child is so vulnerable and God's protection does not seem assured, it is God, not humanity, who must be considered the guilty party.

תְּפִלָּה לְאֵם בְּטֶרֶם שַׁחֲרִית

בְּשָׁעָה שֶׁאֲנִי עוֹמֶדֶת לְבַשֵּׁל דַּיְסַת סֹלֶת
הָסֵר מִמֶּנִּי כָּל מִינֵי מַחֲשָׁבוֹת זָרוֹת
וּכְשֶׁאֲנִי נוֹגַעַת בְּגֵו הַתִּינוֹק וּמַדָּה חֻמּוֹ
שֶׁיֵּלְכוּ מִמֶּנִּי כָּל מִינֵי טְרָדוֹת
שֶׁלֹּא יְבַלְבְּלוּ מַחְשְׁבוֹתַי.   5
וְתֵן לִי אֹמֶץ לְזַכֵּךְ פָּנַי
שֶׁיּוּכַל כָּל אֶחָד מִילָדַי
לִרְאוֹת פָּנָיו בְּתוֹךְ פָּנַי
כְּמוֹ בְּמַרְאָה רְחוּצָה לִקְרַאת חַג

וְאֶת הַחֹשֶׁךְ הַמֻּשְׁקָע מִפְּנִים   10
פָּנַי–כַּסֵּה בְּאוֹר.
שֶׁלֹּא תִּפְקַע סַבְלָנוּתִי וְלֹא יֵחַר גְּרוֹנִי
מִצְּעָקָה מִתְחַבֶּטֶת וּמִתְעַבָּה
שֶׁלֹּא יִהְיֶה לִי רִפְיוֹן יָדַיִם
מוּל הַבִּלְתִּי נוֹדָע   15
וְשֶׁלֹּא יִפְסַק אַף לֹא לְרֶגַע
מַגָּע בָּשָׂר בְּבָשָׂר בֵּינִי לְבֵין יְלָדַי

תֵּן בִּי אַהֲבָתְךָ שֶׁיְּהֵא בִּי דַּי לַעֲמֹד בְּפֶתַח הַבַּיִת וּלְחַלְּקָהּ
בִּפְשַׁטוּת בָּהּ פּוֹרְסִים לֶחֶם וּמוֹרְחִים חֶמְאָה כָּל בֹּקֶר
מְחַדֵּשׁ נִיחוֹחַ חָלָב רוֹתֵחַ וְגוֹלֵשׁ וְרֵיחַ הַקָּפֶה מְכַסִּים   20
עַל קָרְבַּן תּוֹדָה וְקָרְבַּן תָּמִיד
שֶׁאֵינִי יוֹדַעַת אֵיךְ נוֹתְנִים.

A Mother's Prayer Before Dawn

As I stand cooking fine-grained cereal
remove from me all manner of forbidden thoughts
and as I touch my baby's body to measure his fever
may all manner of cares leave me
5 and not trouble my thoughts.
   And give me the courage to purify my face
   so that all my children
   can see their faces in my face
   as a face washed for the holiday in a mirror.

10   And the darkness deep within
      my face—cover with light.
      So that I don't lose patience and my throat is never hoarse
      from a struggling and thickening cry
      so that I'm not helpless
15   before the unknown
      and so that nothing will prevent even for a moment
      the contact of flesh between me and my children.

      Instill in me Your love so that I can stand at the entrance of my home
          and distribute it
      as simply as one slices bread and spreads the butter each morning
20   anew, the aroma of boiling, flowing milk and the smell of coffee
          covering over
      the thanksgiving and daily sacrifices
      that I know not how to offer.[24]

The Hebrew term translated in the title as "Dawn," *shaharit*, is the name of the traditional daily morning prayer service. The title of the poem, "A Mother's Prayer Before Dawn," thus, could more literally be translated, "A Mother's Prayer Before the Morning Prayer." Outdoing her husband and the other men in the commmunity in spiritual commitment, she begins to pray before the official synagogue morning service attended by the men begins. In her prayer, the speaker asks God for help in two areas that are interrelated: her inner being and her relationship with her children. She cannot be the kind of mother she wishes to be if she is troubled by "forbidden thoughts" (2) or "all manner of cares" (4). The "forbidden thoughts" (*mahshavot zarot*) that concern her are not necessarily those thoughts that, according to Jewish tradition, interfere with one's concentration in prayer. They are more related to the anxiety of not knowing what the future will bring ("so that I'm not helpless / before the unknown," 14–15), which can create a sense of despair within her ("the darkness deep within," 10).

Along with her desire to avoid inner anguish, she wishes to be as positive a presence as she can in the lives of her children, so that her face will reflect back to her children a true knowledge of who they are at their best ("And give me the courage to purify my face / so that all my children / can see their faces in my face / as a face washed for the holiday in a mirror," 6–9), so that she is always calm and never shouts at them ("So that I don't lose patience and my throat is never hoarse / from a struggling and thickening cry," 12–13), and so that there is always a physical closeness between her children and herself ("as I touch my baby's body to measure his fever," 3; "the contact of flesh," 17).

Most importantly, the speaker yearns for the capacity to love her children. The ability to love is expressed in the final stanza by means of an image that recalls the opening image of the poem in which the mother rises early in the morning to cook cereal for her family (1). Here, the mother stands at the entrance to her home distributing to the members of her family the breakfast she has prepared ("as simply as one slices bread and spreads the butter each morning / anew, the aroma of boiling, flowing milk and the smell of coffee," 18–20). The speaker's preparation of the breakfast is analogous to the priest in ancient Israel presiding over a sacrifice. She prepares cereal from "fine grains" (*solet*, 1) like the meal offerings of the Temple, the aromas of milk and coffee (*nihoah halav . . . vereah haqafeh,* 20) serve here as the incense (*nihoah*) whose smell (*reah*) overpowers that of the sacrifice, and her breakfast is a thanksgiving sacrifice (*qorban todah*) and a daily sacrifice (*qorban tamid*) (21). As a woman who could never have been a priest in ancient Israel and as a person living generations after the abolition of sacrifices, she does not know how to offer the biblically ordained sacrifices (22). However, as a mother, she does know how to care for her family, and it is that caring that will be her offering to God. In a sense, the speaker presents the mother as an alternative priest who perhaps can be the bearer of divine blessing to those for whom she cares, just like the priests who presided over the sacrifices in ancient times and their descendants who continue to bless the people to this day.

לְמַה כַּוָּנָתוֹ

מָחָר שַׁבָּת שִׁירָה וְהֶחְלַטְתִּי לָלֶכֶת וּלְדַבֵּר
עִם הַכֹּל־יָכוֹל.
מֻכְרָחָה לְדַבֵּר אִתּוֹ
מַשֶּׁהוּ הִשְׁתַּבֵּשׁ בְּתַכְלִית
אֲדַבֵּר אִתּוֹ בְּגֹבַהּ הָעֵינַיִם   5
וְאֶשְׁאַל אוֹתוֹ לְמַה כַּוָּנָתוֹ
כְּשֶׁהוּא שׁוֹלֵחַ אֵשׁ בְּפִנּוֹת הַבַּיִת.
מִישֶׁהוּ טוֹבֵעַ
וּמִישֶׁהוּ אַחֵר שָׁר.
וּמִישֶׁהוּ נִזְכָּר לְחַלֵּק פֵּרוּרִים   10
לַצִּפֳּרִים לְמַעַן
הַשֵּׁם הָרַחֲמִים וְהַמָּחָר.
עוֹד מְעַט שַׁבָּת וּבִגְרוֹנִי
עוֹלָה וְיוֹרֶדֶת דִּמְעַת דָּם
עוֹד מְעַט כָּלָה וְאֵין מוֹצָא.   15
וְאֵין מִי יוֹצִיא מִתּוֹךְ גְּרוֹנִי
בְּאֶצְבַּע עֲדִינָה דִימְעָדָמָה
וְהוִי בָּעֵת הַזֹּאת יָדָהּ
שֶׁל אִמָּא שְׁבוּרָה.
מָחָר שַׁבָּת שִׁירָה אֵלֵךְ לְדַבֵּר   20
כְּמוֹ אֵלִיָּהוּ עַל הַיַּרְדֵּן
אוּלַי יִשְׁמַע
אוּלַי יָבוֹא
אוּלַי יוֹצִיא קוֹל מֵהַקָּנֶה.

WHAT IS HIS INTENTION

Tomorrow is the Sabbath of Song and I've decided to go and speak
with the Almighty.
I must speak with Him
something's gone fundamentally wrong
         I'll speak to Him eye to eye

5   and I'll ask what His intention is
             when He sets a fire to the corners of a house.
Someone drowns
and someone else sings.

10   And someone remembers to give crumbs
to birds for the sake of
God's name mercy and tomorrow.

It'll soon be Sabbath and in my throat
a tear of blood rises and descends
15   soon it will end with no way out.
And no one takes from my throat
the tearblood with a delicate finger
and oh at this time
Mommy's hand is broken.
20   Tomorrow is the Sabbath of Song I will go and speak
like Elijah by the Jordan
        perhaps He'll hear
                perhaps He'll come
                        perhaps He'll sound a reed.[25]

On the Sabbath of Song (*shabbat shirah*), the biblical passage relating the successful crossing of the Sea of Reeds by the Israelites and their triumphant victory song (Exodus 14–15) is read in the synagogue. In this poem, there is an obvious tension between the puzzled attitude of the speaker who cannot understand why God acts or does not act in the world (1–4) and the experience of redemption conveyed in the Sea of Reeds story, in which God's motivation to save the Israelites from the Egyptians is very clear. The issue the speaker wishes to discuss with God is that "something's gone fundamentally wrong" (4), for there is evil in the world, and she cannot understand how God, the ruler of the universe, can cause people to suffer, as in the tragedy of a house that catches on fire (7).

The world is troubling also because some suffer ("someone drowns," 8), like the Egyptians at the Sea of Reeds, and others celebrate ("someone else sings," 9), like the Israelites after they were saved at the Sea of Reeds. This may refer to the lack of rhyme and reason for some people suffering and others thriving, or it may refer to people who celebrate the downfall of their enemies. The act of kindness of feeding the birds to which the speaker refers in lines 10 and 11 is in fact a custom practiced in some Jewish communities on the Sabbath of Song, in appreciation for the songs birds provide humanity. This human act "for the sake of / God's name mercy and tomorrow" (11–12) stands in marked contrast to the role that God plays in not sufficiently opposing evil in the world; even if God does not act mercifully, at least some people are capable of doing so.

It will not be easy for the speaker to address God. All the sorrow and suffering of the world is captured in the tear mixed with blood (conveyed by the neologisms *dimat dam*, "a tear of blood," 14) and *dimadamah* ("tearblood," 17) that chokes her throat. She yearns for someone to comfort her by removing that tear, but there is no one to help, as if she were a child whose mother's hand is broken (16–19).

The speaker hopes for a response from God like that received by the prophet Elijah in I Kings 17:1–7 (21). In this story, at God's bidding, Elijah dwells for a period of time near the Jordan River, where he drinks water from a nearby riverbed and eats food provided him by ravens. Eventually, God withholds rain to the extent that the riverbed dries up. Elijah's experience, meant to convey to the wicked King Ahab God's power to control nature, serves here as a powerful antidote to the impression the speaker has had that God has withdrawn from active involvement in the world.

There is a significant interplay between the image of people feeding birds on the Sabbath of Song and that of ravens feeding Elijah, and another significant interplay between the image of God demonstrating His involvement in the world by drowning the Egyptians in water and the image of God drying up the riverbed in Elijah's time. One image, that of people feeding birds, alludes to a possible way for people to involve themselves in repairing that which is deficient in the world. Three out of these four images, however, emphasize God's role in the world, which is the central unresolved issue of the poem. One can discern a certain degree of closure in the speaker's speculation about God at the end of the poem, which pulls together the imagery of involvement in the world that has pervaded the poem: "perhaps He'll hear / perhaps He'll come / perhaps He'll sound a reed" (22–24). The Hebrew word for reed, *qaneh*, actually refers to the leafy top of the reed, while the Hebrew word in the expression Sea of Reeds is *suf*, a reference to the reed plant. Thus, the speaker suggests, out of the victory at the Sea of Reeds comes an image of making music with a reed, an image well in keeping with the Song of the Sea and the music of the birds customarily fed on the Sabbath of Song.

קַדִּישׁ יְתוֹמָה

יִתְגַּדַּל וְיִתְקַדַּשׁ	לֹא תִהְיֶה מְנוּחָתְךָ וְלֹא יֵצְאוּ לִי בָּנִים מִזַּרְעֶךָ
	לֹא אַצְדִּיק אֶת הַדִּין וְאֹמַר וְאֹמַר וְאֹמַר יִתְבָּרַךְ
	יִתְגַּדַּל וְיִתְקַדַּשׁ שְׁמֵהּ רַבָּא בְּעָלְמָא דִּי בְרָא
וְיִשְׁתַּבַּח וְיִתְפָּאַר	כִּרְעוּתֵהּ וּרְצוֹנִי כּוֹאֵב וּמַכְאִיב וּמֵטִיל צֵל
	וְגַם אוֹר וְאָנוּ רוֹקְדִים עַל הַקְצֶה בְּקֶצֶב 5
וְיִתְרוֹמַם	כְּפוּל צְעָדִים בֵּין הָאוֹר הַשּׂוֹרֵף לַצֵּל הָרוֹטֵט
	נָעִים בִּתְנוּעָה לַמּוֹשֵׁךְ בַּחוּטִים
וְיִתְנַשֵּׂא	יְהֵא שְׁמֵהּ רַבָּא מְבָרַךְ לְעוֹלָם וּלְעָלְמֵי עָלְמַיָּא
	הִנֵּה גַּם אֲנִי מַכְנִיסָה רֹאשׁ וּפָנִים
וְיִתְהַדָּר וְיִתְעַלֶּה	לַמָּקוֹם בּוֹ בִּקַּשְׁתָּ "אָמֵן" וְ"אָמֵן" כְּמוֹ לְפָנִים 10
וְיִתְהַלָּל	שֶׁיִּמְשֹׁךְ וְיוֹלִיךְ וְיוֹבִיל וְיִסְחַב וִיטַלְטֵל נִשְׁמָתִי
	עַל אוֹתוֹ סֻלָּם שֶׁאֵין לוֹ קֵץ
הַלְלוּיָהּ	יְבִיאֵנִי אֵלֶיךָ וְיַעֲשֶׂה לִי דְּמוּתְךָ

יִרְאֶה עָנְיִי וְיִשְׁמַע רִיבִי וְיַעֲשֶׂה לְךָ שָׁלוֹם בַּמְּרוֹמִים
לְעֵלָּא וּלְעֵלָּא מִן כָּל שִׁירָתָא שֶׁיָּדַעְתִּי 15

A Woman's Mourner's Kaddish

Your rest will not be and no sons will
    come to me from your seed   Magnified and sanctified
I won't justify the judgment and say and
    say and say blessed
Magnified and sanctified be His great
    name in the world He has created
according to His will and my desire hurts
    and causes hurt and casts a shadow   and praised and glorified
5   and also light and we dance on the edge
    in double
time between the burning light and the
    trembling shadow   and exalted
complying with the One who pulls the
    strings
may His great name be blessed forever
    and ever   and extolled
look I too insert my head and face
10 into the place you pleaded "Amen" and
    "Amen" as before   and honored and adored

so it will pull and direct and guide and
    drag and carry my soul   and lauded
on that same ladder that has no end
may it bring me to you and make for me
    your image   Halleluyah

May He see my affliction and hear my
    claim and make peace for you on high
15   far beyond all hymns I know[26]

This is the final poem in the collection *Shirei Orfe'a*, which Pinhas-Cohen published after the illness and untimely death of her husband. The poem is, in effect, her own version of the Mourner's Kaddish traditionally recited by Jews. The Mourner's Kaddish is an affirmation of faith in God's will recited at the very time when someone who has lost a loved one would most likely question God. The Kaddish in this poem is an unconventional one. It does not bear the traditional title of the Mourner's Kaddish, *qaddish yatom*, in the masculine, but rather *qaddish yetomah*, in the feminine. This is not the Kaddish that mainly men recite in traditional practice, but rather the utterance of a woman. Perhaps there is some significance to the use of *yetomah*, which literally means "orphan." It is true that, although the Mourner's Kaddish is recited not only by those who lost a parent, but also by those who lost a spouse, a child, or a sibling, it is generally referred to as *qaddish yatom*, literally the Orphan's Kaddish. Yet one wonders if, having lost her father when she was relatively young, the poet is making associations here between that experience and the loss of her husband when he was in his prime.

The speaker cannot simply repeat the words of the Kaddish one after the other. The traditional words of the prayer are constantly interrupted by her own thoughts. It is as if every time she tries to say the prayer she becomes distracted by her personal response to her husband's death. Her desperate effort to return to the traditional words of prayer is conveyed by the repetition in line 2 of "and say and say and say." Her overt rejection of the Kaddish as a statement of faith is expressed when she declares her unwillingness to affirm the traditional concept of the justification of God's judgment (*tsidduq hadin*) that is expected at the time of a death: "I won't justify the judgment" (2). She also challenges God when she follows the Kaddish's declaration that the world was "created / according to [God's] will" with an expression of her own "desire," which "hurts and causes hurt and casts a shadow" (3–4). The poem is structured graphically to place words of praise from the Kaddish, along with the word "Halleluyah," which appears frequently in Psalms, in a separate column physically detached from the rest of the poem. It is as if the poet seeks to distinguish between statements of pure faith in the traditional liturgy and her broken up Kaddish in the main body of the poem.

At the beginning of the poem, the speaker's mind jumps from one troubled thought to another. She is concerned about the eternal rest of her husband, and she mourns the fact that they never had male offspring (1). In the middle of the poem, her thoughts shift to a vision of dancing with her husband. There is an unstable intensity to this dance: "and we dance on the edge in double / time stepping between the burning light and the trembling shadow" (5–6). It is as if, from her perspective, after the death of her husband, the speaker realizes how precarious their life together had been, since that life had been overshadowed by his impending death.

At this point in the poem, however, the speaker begins to submit herself to God's will. At first, this submission takes on a harsh ironic tone as she speaks of God as "the One who pulls the strings" (7), as if people are merely marionettes in God's hands. Then, in an act of will, she attempts to enter into a more direct relationship with God in the way that her husband did in his prayer ("look I too insert my head and face / into the place you pleaded 'Amen' and 'Amen' as before," 9–10), with the hope that God will help her to reunite with her deceased husband ("so it will pull and direct and guide and drag and carry my soul / on that same ladder that has no end / may it bring me to you and make for me your image," 11–13). She is not necessarily expressing here a death wish, but rather a way to find relief from the great depths of loneliness she feels after her husband's passing.

In the final two lines of the poem, the speaker is ready to pray, to issue her own sincere plea to God that He comfort her in her suffering and that He bring peace to her late husband's eternal soul. She no longer needs to fight the words of the Kaddish; she can even incorporate some of these words into her personal prayer. The final line of the traditional Kaddish, "May He who makes peace on high make peace for us . . . ," becomes "May He . . . make peace for you [her husband] on high" (14). Just as the version of the Kaddish recited during the period from Rosh Hashanah to Yom Kippur declares that God greatly transcends any prayers uttered by human beings (le'ella ule'ella min kol birkhata veshirata ["far beyond all blessings and hymns"]), so the speaker prays that the peace brought to her husband will transcend her own poetic entreaties on his behalf (le'ella ule'ella min kol shirata sheyadati ["far beyond all hymns I know"], 15). By the end of the poem, the speaker is no longer disappointed with God for having cruelly taken her husband from her. Instead, she is ready to let go of the sense of loss she has experienced in response to her husband's death. Now she sees God as a potential source of comfort for herself ("May He see my affliction and hear my claim," 14) and of care for the spirit of her husband ("and make peace for you on high," 14). With that return of faith, she now draws near to the religious worldview that her husband affirmed in life, thereby achieving a measure of unity with him.

CHAPTER SIX

Admiel Kosman
"Creator, aren't You listening?"

ADMIEL KOSMAN (1957–) was born in Haifa and raised in a modern Orthodox home. His father, a European-born textile worker, had fled the Nazis during World War II before immigrating to Israel.[1] After graduating from high school, Kosman participated in the *yeshivat hesder* program, which allowed him to combine compulsory army service with yeshiva training in traditional Jewish texts. He then attended the Bezalel art academy in Jerusalem for a year. After a period of further yeshiva study, he pursued the academic study of Talmud at the undergraduate and graduate levels at Bar Ilan University, which is under Orthodox Jewish auspices, and subsequently became a member of its Department of Talmud. After teaching for several years at Bar Ilan University, he left to accept appointments as a faculty member in the School of Jewish Studies at the University of Potsdam (Germany) and as Academic Director at Abraham Geiger College, a reform rabbinical seminary in Potsdam.

Although his family was traditionally observant when he was growing up, his parents encouraged him to explore elements of general culture as well. One example of this was their support for his interest in taking art lessons even before he enrolled to study at Bezalel. Kosman characterizes his family as not having been intensely religious. "I grew up in a home in which [the males] wore a *kippah* [skullcap]," he relates. "But beyond that I don't think that I was taught the true elements of faith. From the point of view of my social framework, I was not far from being secular."[2]

Kosman has refused to accept any political, religious, or national label for himself. "I am not a 'rightist' or a 'leftist,'" he has declared. "I am not tied to a party, I am not an 'Israeli,' and I don't even feel myself to be a 'Jew.'"[3] He has resisted being pulled in the direction of either of the cultural extremes of orthodoxy and secularism that sometimes threaten to tear apart Israeli society. In a review of a Hebrew translation of the French Jewish thinker Emmanuel Levinas's *Nine Talmudic Readings*, Kosman writes of his envy of Levinas's ability to develop an approach to Judaism in France distant from the Israeli realities of "the halakhic Judaism that was sucked further and further into the vortex of obsessiveness over niggling details and the unpleasant business of imposing them on itself and others" and "that new 'Israeli-sabra' experience that developed in Israel, an experience whose very essence is no more than a brazen act . . . of denying the past."[4]

As Neri Livneh notes, in addition to his research in Talmud, Kosman "has studied [the works] of psychoanalytical expert Jacques Lacan, [and the religious teachings of] Christianity, Islam, and Buddhism,"[5] incorporating the psychological and religious insights of these sources into his understanding of Jewish spirituality. Although, as Kosman has stated, he observes traditional Jewish rituals as an obligation to the Jewish people and as a means to transmit certain values to his children, to be religious for Kosman is not to have any certitude about metaphysical realities. "I have great difficulty seeing myself, and certainly I don't see God or the angels,"[6] he has declared. The value of any religion for him is the insights it conveys about how to transcend the egotistical drive for power and fully appreciate the everyday pleasures of interpersonal relationships and of nature. "Religiosity," he writes, "means for me a constant struggle to leave the enforced framework in which I grew up, a framework of impressing others, power struggles, wars of passion, and a world in which the 'ego' is the speaker at all times. I want to seek an inner world, a world in which there is love and kindness, quiet, and an alternative insight into the flow of life."[7] The ideal state of holiness, according to Kosman, is "when . . . you don't immediately notice who is first and who is second, who is more successful than you and who is falling behind you; when you live in this quiet your actions will flow only from love, from freedom."[8]

Kosman's search for a religiosity that transcends the ego came about in part as a reaction to the models of masculinity to which he was exposed during the formative years of his studies in the all-male settings of a yeshiva high school and an army combat unit. During that period, he was driven to reject what he observed as the kind of "phallic pattern of thinking [which] is responsible, among other things, for a person's inability to make room in his being for others, a situation that gives rise to lies, wars, religious hypocrisy, and a sense of emptiness and misery."[9] Such masculinity drives people to treat others as objects in an attempt, as he puts it, "to conquer the whole world and to be the most beloved, the most admired, the best in one's profession."[10] Kosman's religious search has reflected his desire to be liberated from this self-defeating gender identity. "To search for

God," he explains, "[is] to search for a place where there is a kind of happiness that comes from recognition of the other."[11] This, as Livneh paraphrases it, is "true love [which] is the moment in which a person recognizes the other and sees the other not as an object whose sole purpose is to look up to him and provide for his needs, but as a subject with qualities all his own."[12]

Kosman rejects what he calls "the 'police' God"[13] of Orthodox Judaism, because he finds Him to be too overwhelming a figure to be compatible with the religiosity he seeks. "I have a problem with the Orthodox God and with Orthodox Judaism," he states. "As soon as God is perceived as something threatening who cares whether you read the Torah with this pronunciation or that . . . to me, this isn't a God, but the same kind of centralist phallic construct, because God is in the center and all the rest are nothing but . . . objects."[14] He is particularly drawn to the dialogic theology of Martin Buber. "God is always present between two people . . . ," he states, "holiness is always present in the opening of one heart to another. . . . What Buber says is don't ever look at others and wish to be like them. Instead, open your heart and listen."[15]

In an interview I conducted with Kosman, his discussion of the religious values he holds dear was punctuated by a number of central ideal concepts: trustworthiness (ne'emanut), covenant (berit), love (ahavah), compassion (ḥemlah), faith (emunah), lovingkindness (ḥesed), dialogue (di'alog), and open-heartedness (petiḥat halev). For Kosman, all of these concepts are characteristic of the kinds of relationships with God, nature, and his fellow human beings to which he aspires. In its purest form, he observes, the traditional Jewish Sabbath embodies these ideals: "[D]uring one day of the week a people meditates and does not control nature and frees its heart to sense the world, the other, its children, and the trees that move in the wind."[16] When you reach this religious ideal "and make room within yourself to include something other than yourself, then you live a type of joy . . . , [for] to live with God is simply to be happy."[17]

Orthodox Judaism, Kosman declared to me in the interview, is too heavily committed to drawing a clear distinction between natural urges, which it rejects, and the religious experience of holiness embodied in its culture, which it affirms. For Kosman, true religiosity must involve a dialogue between what we call nature and what we call the holy, so that they can be experienced as fully integrated in the human psyche. He also sees this tension between nature and holiness being played out in the area of traditional Jewish religious language. As is typical of established religions, he said to me, Judaism calls on its adherents to perform speech acts based on texts written by other people in other eras. The language of traditional Judaism serves the purpose of repressing the volcano within us, of convincing us that we are monolithic and not connected to the drives within us, and that we should "put the mess in order [lesadder et ha-balagan]," as he put it. It is therefore necessary for new language to emerge that will "take apart [established] expressions [lefareq bittuyyim]" with the purpose of revitalizing religious language. When he writes poetry, Kosman explained to me, he does not consciously set out to deconstruct the language of traditional Jewish texts, but somehow this is what happens.

In an article on the relationship between art and religion, Kosman declares that "art is an expression of repressed parts in the private personality of the individual and in the society that aspire to find a means of expression, because the pressing needs of daily life cover and hide these 'irrelevant' parts and cast them to the margins of life."[18] There is no question for him that the process of artistic creation has a religious dimension. "[A]rtistic experience for me," he states, "has always been a mystical experience (in various levels of intensity, of course). And for this purpose I must define here the mystical experience as a unifying experience, an experience that uproots the creator from the plane on which his daily life is conducted from a center of 'self,' the center to which and from which go all of our activities. The mystical experience is the experience of merging with existence."[19] He then goes on to write that this religious experience of artistic creation "is therefore an experience of the pushing down of barriers between the private I and all of existence outside of it, which in regular consciousness is seen as separate."[20]

Despite his harsh criticism of the language of Jewish tradition, Kosman has sought to discover in rabbinic and hasidic texts traditional roots for the religiosity in which he believes. For several years he has published a column titled "Otsar qatan" ("A Small Treasure") in the Israeli newspaper *Haaretz*, in which he explores aspects of classical Jewish narratives that are not typically discussed in traditional circles. As in his poetry on religious themes, so in this column he pushes the limits of a conventional religious worldview. In the introduction to a collection of revised versions of these columns, Kosman makes clear how difficult it can be to straddle the two worlds of Orthodoxy on the one hand and free intellectual inquiry on the other when he thanks two professors who were colleagues of his at Bar Ilan during the time he wrote the columns: "Thanks to their struggle for the possibility to create out of inner freedom, I was given the possibility to write in the framework of the Talmud Department at Bar Ilan University unacceptable thoughts such as those presented here to the reader."[21]

Kosman began writing poetry at the age of eighteen, toward the end of his high school studies. His early training as a writer included a poetry workshop led by three prominent Israeli poets of the time, Yehuda Amichai, T. Carmi, and Amir Gilboa. While Kosman was still in high school, Gilboa had one of Kosman's poems published in the literary journal *Moznayim*, and during the period of Kosman's army service, Gilboa arranged for the publication of Kosman's first collection of poetry.

The need to integrate the sensual and the holy, which is so central to Kosman's theology, is evident in his poems on religious themes. In "A Poem," it is the role of the poet to bridge the gap between the sensuality of nature and the divine law that seeks to limit sensuality. In *"Piyyut,"* among those elements of human existence for which the speaker blesses God as Creator are "all kinds of sexual / intimacies . . . all kinds of positions."

Another prevalent theme in Kosman's poetry is his preoccupation with how God and humanity actually interact. The speaker in "When That Man Was Killed" refers to prayer as a way to establish contact with "the hidden strings that make us dance / like puppets in a theatre / on this earth." God and humanity search for each other and eventually meet by accident in "We've Reached God." In *"Piyyut,"* God is praised as the creator of everything, that which is desirable and that which humans would like to avoid. In "Something Hurts" and "A Note in the Western Wall," the speaker begs God to intervene and repair all that is wrong in human affairs. Some speakers in his poetry question God's method of ruling the world, at times with an angry, sarcastic tone, as when the speaker in "A Note in the Western Wall" calls out to God, "What happened to You?"

The relative weakness of humanity in comparison with God plays out in different ways in Kosman's poetry. In "A Psalm," the speaker calls on God to make humanity small, in keeping with the poet's conviction that a central element of religious experience is the realization of the importance of overcoming our power-hungry egotistical relationship with the world. In "A Poem," on the other hand, the poet exploits his smallness to challenge God by playing the alternative creator right under God's nose.

Kosman seeks in a number of poems to establish his relationship to traditional notions of prayer and faith. In two poems, "And As One Prays" and "I Don't Move When I Pray," the speaker delves into the experience of traditional Jewish prayer in terms of the inner consciousness of the person who is praying. These two poems draw on Kosman's own experiences praying in an Orthodox Jewish setting as a child and as an adult. The other poets I am considering in this study do not reflect in such a deeply penetrating manner on the traditional prayer experience. In the cases of Amichai and Reich, this may be because they left the framework of Orthodox practice relatively early in life; in the cases of Zelda, Rivka Miriam, and Pinhas-Cohen, it may be due to the fact that the practice of regular traditional prayer, particularly in public settings, has not been as central to women's experience as it has been to men's. In two poems, "Oh, the Active Intellect, the First Cause" and "Psalm of the Day," Kosman expresses a yearning for a simple faith that transcends rational conceptions and language in general. In both poems, one senses the possibility of a reconciliation with the God with whom the poet mainly struggles.

The Human and the Divine

כְּשֶׁנֶּהֱרַג הָאִישׁ הַהוּא

כְּשֶׁנֶּהֱרַג הָאִישׁ הַהוּא, שָׁרוּעַ בְּצַד הַכְּבִישׁ
וְרֹאשׁוֹ הַבָּקוּעַ שׁוֹתֵת דָּם,
הָיְתָה לִי הַזְּדַמְּנוּת נְדִירָה
לְהַסְבִּיר לְךָ כַּמָּה מִסּוֹדוֹת הַתְּפִלָּה.

גַּלִּים שֶׁל חֲרָדָה נָשְׁבוּ עִם הָאֲוִיר הַקַּר 5
מְכֻוָּן הַיָּם לַחֲלֹף מֵעַל לְחִי
הֶהָרוּג הַחֲלָקָה לְמִשְׁעִי, לִנְגֹּעַ
בְּנִתְזֵי הַדָּם. כְּשֶׁיָּרַד
הַלַּיְלָה שָׁמַעְנוּ
כָּל הַזְּמַן שַׁיָּרוֹת שֶׁל פַּחַד נָעוֹת 10
מֵעָלֵינוּ כְּמוֹ עֲנָנִים מְאַיְּמִים.

הַתְּפִלָּה–אָמַרְתִּי לְךָ אָז בְּצִדֵּי הַכְּבִישׁ הָרֵיק–הִיא
נְגִיעָה חֲרִישִׁית וַעֲדִינָה בַּחוּטִים הַסְּמוּיִים הַמַּרְקִידִים
אוֹתָנוּ כְּבֻבּוֹת תֵּאַטְרוֹן עַל הָאֲדָמָה
הַזֹּאת. 15

WHEN THAT MAN WAS KILLED

When that man was killed, stretched out by the side of the road,
his head split open profusely bleeding,
I had a rare opportunity
to explain to you something of the mysteries of prayer.

5 Waves of anxiety blew with the cold air
from the direction of the sea to pass upon the cheek
of the victim smooth to perfection, to touch
the spurts of blood. When night
fell we kept hearing
10 caravans of fear moving
above us like threatening clouds.

Prayer—I said to you then by the side of the empty road—is
a silent and delicate contact with the hidden strings that make us
dance
like puppets in a theatre
15 on this earth.[22]

It is significant that the event which provided the speaker with the "rare opportunity" (3) to explain the nature of prayer to another (perhaps his son or pupil) was a fatal road accident which they had witnessed (1–4). It is paradoxical that witnessing horrifying violence, which one would expect would call into question the nature of God's relationship to the world, allows for an understanding of prayer not yielded by other, more benign experiences. The speaker tells how he set out to discuss "something of the mysteries [*kammah misodot*, with its mystical connotation] of prayer" (4), that is, spiritual insights into the nature of prayer that are partial in nature, but deeper than those held by the average person.

The speaker recalls graphic details related to the physical condition of the victim: "his head split open profusely bleeding" (2) and "the spurts of blood" (8). Those details are contrasted by the image of "the cheek / of the victim smooth to perfection" (6–7), expressed in Hebrew as *lehi / heharug hahalaqah lemishi*, which calls to mind the Hebrew expression for "clean shaven," *megullah lemishi*. It would appear that the speaker is particularly disturbed by the notion that uncontrollable violence was perpetrated on a man whose beardless face attests to the civilized orderliness of his life.

This horrible contrast between senseless violence and the meaningful order of ordinary life evokes an atmosphere of anxious fear. "Waves of anxiety" pass by in the form of a cold wind from the sea (5–6), and, as night falls, "caravans of fear" constantly travel overhead "like threatening [rain] clouds" (8–11). The images that convey this anxiety and fear—waves, wind, caravans, and clouds—suggest strong, dynamic, overwhelming forces that threaten humanity with death and destruction. It is this deeply felt dread of death that allows the speaker and the person he addresses to be open to understanding the way that prayer can establish a connection between human beings and God.

The speaker makes his explanation of prayer "by the side of the empty road" (12). No longer does he focus on the dead man, but rather on the sense of a void evoked by his death. Contrary to what we might expect, the speaker's explanation of prayer does not refer directly to God. Instead, he merely states that prayer is "a silent and delicate contact with the hidden strings that make us dance / like puppets in a theatre / on this earth" (13–15). The fact that puppets do not control even the most basic movements of their bodies does not necessarily mean that the speaker is espousing a belief in determinism. What he appears to be suggesting is that our realization that ultimately we do not determine when we will die, evoked by witnessing scenes like the car accident, makes us feel like puppets on a string controlled by God. For the speaker, prayer is not a direct challenge to the control God has over our lives, but rather an almost affectionate reconciliation with the knowledge that we do not control our ultimate fate, "a silent and delicate contact with the hidden strings that make us dance" (13). Because of grammatical differences between Hebrew and English, the translation does not capture the impact of the fact that in the original Hebrew the word "this" in "this earth" (15) stands alone as the last word in the last line of the poem. That last line, containing only the short word for "this," *hazot*, which ends with the emphatic sound "t," powerfully expresses the finality of death which the speaker and the person he addresses were forced to confront at the scene of that accident.

וְעִם הַתְּפִלָּה הָאֲנִי

וְעִם הַתְּפִלָּה
הָאֲנִי מְחַשֵּׁב לְהֵחָלֵץ כְּמוֹ פְּקָק. שֶׁעַם נִטְרָף
עַל מַיִם רַבִּים. אַדִּירִים.

לְהַתִּיךְ אֶת רִגְשַׁת הַנְּחִיתוּת לְצָרְפָהּ לְהָפְכָהּ
לְשַׁרְשֶׁרֶת־כֶּסֶף־עֲדִינָה.   5

AND AS ONE PRAYS

And as one prays
the "I" is about to be freed like a bottle cap. A cork pulled off
on great and mighty waters.

To melt the feeling of inferiority to purify it and transform it
5   into a delicate silver necklace.[23]

In the previous poem, "When That Man Was Killed," prayer was presented as a process of coming to terms with a divine force beyond us. In this poem, prayer has the very different purpose of effecting internal psychological transformation. According to the speaker, prayer allows one to overcome the power of the ego ("the 'I'") and repress the natural drives of the id, a process that the speaker compares with the removal of a tightly fitting cap, which results in the liquid contents of a bottle bursting out (1–3). The speaker would appear to be asserting that the conscious identity we hold, the one we present to the world, is a partial and rather superficial element of our being, as the cap is a small object that merely covers the bottle. Prayer, however, affords us the opportunity to get in touch with our deeper selves and to express all that we hide: our emotions and longings, and our libidinous and other sensual drives. This release of that which is hidden within us, the speaker believes, is an essential element of spiritual fulfillment that we can gain in the act of prayer.

In lines 4 and 5, the speaker then uses a different metaphor to describe prayer. Here, the image of the transformation of the raw material of silver into the beautiful form of a piece of jewelry ("a delicate silver necklace," 5) portrays the

process in which prayer allows one to act upon one's "feeling of inferiority" (4).
In prayer, the conviction we hold deeply that we are less than worthy, unaccept-
able to ourselves and to others, loses the power it has over us, and the internal
energy so invested in feeling inferior becomes completely transformed into a
feeling of delight in who we are.

What is the relationship between the two central metaphorical images in this
poem? In both cases, a transformation takes place: in the first, that which is con-
tained is released, and in the second, raw material is transformed into an object
of value. Both stanzas deal with self-images that are psychologically and spiritually
damaging: one is based on self-repression, and the other is based on self-denigration.
Prayer allows one to overcome both distorted views of the self, making possible
a great potential for creativity and happiness. As in the previous poem, "When
That Man Was Killed," God is not mentioned directly as an element in the
realm of prayer. The speaker, however, implies that a reaching up to God in
prayer allows one to transcend the self. One may discern a possible allusion to
God in line 3. The original Hebrew for the words "great and might waters,"
mayim rabbim addirim, appears in Psalms 93:4 in the phrase *miqolot mayim rab-
bim addirim mishberei yam addir bamarom Adonay* ("More than the sounds of
mighty waters, greater than the waves of the sea is the great Lord on high"). The
poet may have chosen this allusion to convey the notion that prayer connects
us with a God who is portrayed in Psalms as more powerful than the greatest
natural forces, and it is that God who can help us to release our inner drives and
lift us from our lack of self worth.

אֵינֶנִּי מִתְנוֹעֵעַ בִּשְׁעַת הַתְּפִלָּה

אֵינֶנִּי מִתְנוֹעֵעַ בִּשְׁעַת הַתְּפִלָּה. אֲנִי עוֹמֵד קַר וְקָפוּא. דָּרוּךְ
לַבָּאוֹת. הַמַּחֲשָׁבוֹת מְטַפְּסוֹת עָלַי חֶרֶשׁ כְּמוֹ צְבָא־מְסְתַּנְּנִים,
נִתְפְּסוֹת לָהֶן זְרִיזוֹת בְּחַדֵּי־הָאֲבָנִים, וּמַעְפִּילוֹת הָלְאָה.

אֵינֶנִּי מִתְנוֹעֵעַ בִּשְׁעַת הַתְּפִלָּה. אֲנִי עוֹמֵד קַר וְקָפוּא. בְּתוֹכִי זְרוּעַ זֶה
מִכְּבָר הַהֶרֶס, הַחֻרְבָּן, וְאִם אָמַרְתִּי כִּי אֵינֶנִּי מִתְנוֹעֵעַ   5
בִּשְׁעַת הַתְּפִלָּה, אַךְ בִּפְנִים הָאֲדָמָה הַקָּשָׁה כְּצוּר לִי נִבְקַעַת
בְּשֶׁבֶר וִילָלָה כְּלִסְעָרַת פֻּרְעָנוּת מְמַשְׁמֶשֶׁת.

אֵינֶנִּי מִתְנוֹעֵעַ בִּשְׁעַת הַתְּפִלָּה. אֲנִי מַשְׁלִיךְ אֶת צְרוֹר
מַפְתְּחוֹתַי אֶל־עַל וּמַעֲמִיד פְּנֵי מֵת. קַר וְקָפוּא.

I Don't Move When I Pray

I don't move when I pray. I stand cold and frozen. Prepared
for what's to come. Thoughts climb up on me secretly like an army
    of infiltrators,
adroitly grabbing onto protruding rocks, and climbing onward.

I don't move when I pray. I stand cold and frozen. In me has been
    planted
5   for a long time the ruin, the destruction, but although I say I don't
        move
    when I pray, within me earth as hard as flint splits open
    with a despairing wail as if before a storm of calamity about to come.

I don't move when I pray. I cast my ring
of keys on high and pretend that I am dead. Cold and frozen.[24]

In contrast to the traditional Jewish custom of moving one's body back and forth or side to side as one prays, when the speaker prays, he stands still. The expression "when I pray" (1) in Hebrew is literally "at the hour of the prayer" (*beshe'at hatefillah*). The term *tefillah* is sometimes used in rabbinic texts to refer to the central prayer of the traditional Jewish service, the silent standing prayer also known as the "Amidah." It is the most important set of traditional Jewish prayers, in which basic human needs are the subject of petition and praise presented to God, and Jews typically engage in bodily movements in a particularly intense manner while reciting it. Yet, when he recites the "Amidah," the speaker affects an almost death-like position, standing "cold and frozen" (1). He does not ask God for anything, nor does he offer praises to God. He simply waits expectantly, "[p]repared / for what's to come" (1–2). The word for "prepared," *darukh*, is also used to connote a bow with a taut string or a gun that is cocked and ready to shoot. Thus, although he is not moving, the speaker has much internal potential energy that is waiting to be released.

As he prays standing still, the speaker is aware of thoughts inside him that are interfering with his concentration. Jewish tradition recognizes that such "foreign thoughts" (*maḥshavot zarot*) frequently arise in the minds of those who engage in traditional Jewish prayer, for the recitation of the same words on a daily basis easily degenerates into a rote exercise during which one's mind may tend to wander. The speaker portrays these thoughts with an image that derives directly from the Israeli historical experience: "an army of infiltrators" (*tseva mistanenim*, 2), that is, enemy Arabs who infiltrate the Israeli border in order to commit acts of sabotage and terror. The image of the thoughts "climbing onward"

(3) is expressed in Hebrew as *mapilot halah*, a biblical allusion to the Israelites who defied God by climbing up a mountain (*vayapilu la'alot el rosh hahar*) to attack their enemies when God did not approve (Numbers 14:44). The root for *mapilot* was also used to refer to the illegal Jewish immigrants to Palestine (*mapilim*) at the time of the British Mandate in the 1940s. Just as the Israelites defied God's authority, and just as the illegal Jewish immigrants and the Arab infiltrators challenged those who ruled the Land, so the speaker sees these thoughts as an outside alien force that threatens his spiritual and psychological integrity.

The second stanza begins exactly like the first stanza with a declaration that, rather than moving during prayer, the speaker stands "cold and frozen" (4). This time, however, the speaker's description of what goes on within himself is more ominous than it was in the first stanza. Now the potential energy that was hinted at in the first stanza is released in a process of internal "ruin" and "destruction" (5) in which "earth as hard as flint splits open / with a despairing wail as if before a storm of calamity about to come" (6–7). With this he has degenerated from a state of disturbing thoughts as he waits for what will be to a complete inner break down in the face of an imagined future of horror.

The first two stanzas portray the inner workings of the speaker at prayer as a process of increasing anxiety and fear. The speaker once again begins the third and final stanza with the statement that he does not move when he prays (8), but then, rather than immediately move on to describe his "cold and frozen" stance as he experiences an ever deteriorating emotional state, he accompanies his reference to being "[c]old and frozen" (9) with the statement that he pretends to be dead as he casts his "ring / of keys on high" (8–9). Keys represent the control we have over that which is most precious to us, such as a home, a car, or a safe, which we keep locked and only we have the means to open. It would appear that this symbolic act represents the complete submission of the speaker's drive to control his fate to the will of God. He is now free of disturbing thoughts and of the pain of past suffering, a creature of God in full acceptance of whatever is to come, even his mortality.

The image of casting keys up to heaven alludes to a Talmudic legend on the destruction of the First Temple in Jerusalem:

> When the First Temple was destroyed young priests gathered together group by group with the keys of the Temple in their hands, and they ascended to the roof of the Temple and declared to God: "Master of the universe! Since we have not been privileged to be trustworthy custodians, let the keys be submitted to You," and they threw them on high, and a kind of portion of a hand emerged and received them, and they jumped and fell into the fire." (Taanit 29a)

Just as the young priests took responsibility for the destruction of the Temple, so by imitating their action in the legend, the speaker declares that he too is responsible for the emotional ruin and destruction within him. By throwing the keys up to heaven, the speaker admits that he has not been "a trustworthy custodian" of his own soul. The priests recognize that there is a transcendent dimension to which they can send the keys for safekeeping until the Temple is restored. Similarly, the speaker, unable to restore himself spiritually, submits control of himself to a transcendent deity that he hopes will save him from his internal deterioration. The "kind of portion of a hand" that emerged from heaven to receive the keys in the talmudic text, however, is absent in the poem; apparently it is not as clear today to what transcendent deity one could turn in a time of failure.

The poem concludes with the words "Cold and frozen" (9), which had appeared in lines 1 and 4. Here the meaning is different from what it was at the beginning and in the middle of the poem. It is not so much a cover for the agitation within his soul that it was in the first two instances, but rather a stance of complete subjugation to a power that will heal him of all his emotional troubles. In an apparent imitation of the priests' mass suicide in the Talmudic passage, the speaker declares that he pretends to be dead (9), suggesting that he has allowed himself a final descent into the emotional paralysis of despair. In the end, perhaps, he will ascend back to a life-affirming existence.

הִגַּעְנוּ לֵאלֹהִים

הִגַּעְנוּ לֵאלֹהִים.

לְגַמְרֵי בְּמִקְרֶה. לְמַעֲשֶׂה, נִתְקַלְנוּ בּוֹ.
הָיִינוּ בַּחֲצִי הַדֶּרֶךְ, בְּמוֹרַד הָהָר,
עִם כָּל מִטְעַן הַחֲמוֹרִים הָרַב,
וּלְפֶתַע, בְּעִקּוּל הַדֶּרֶךְ, כְּשֶׁהִטִּינוּ לְהַבִּיט,   5
נִתְקַלְנוּ בּוֹ.

גַּם הוּא חִפֵּשׂ אוֹתָנוּ,
כְּמוֹ אֶבֶן יְקָרָה, אָמַר, כְּמוֹ מַרְגָּלִית,
מַמָּשׁ כְּמוֹ אֲבֵדָה.
כְּשֶׁכָּכָה, בְּמִקְרֶה לְגַמְרֵי,   10
בְּאַקְרַאי גָּמוּר, הָיִינוּ בַּחֲצִי הַדֶּרֶךְ, וְהִגַּעְנוּ
אֶל הָאָרֶץ הַיְעוּדָה.
כְּלוֹמַר, הִגַּעְנוּ לֵאלֹהִים.
וּמָצָאנוּ מְנוּחָה גְמוּרָה מִן הַחַיִּים.
הָיָה זֶה לְגַמְרֵי בְּמִקְרֶה, דְּהַיְנוּ,   15
בַּחֲצִי הַדֶּרֶךְ. כְּשֶׁיָּרַדְנוּ מִן הָהָר,
הַחֲמוֹרִים וְהַשַּׂקִּים עָמְדוּ לְבַד,
שְׁמוּטִים וּכְפוּפֵי-בֶּרֶךְ, בְּעִקּוּל הַצַּד.
הַחֹם הָיָה כָּבֵד מִנְּשֹׂא.

בִּקְצֵה הַשְּׁבִיל נִתְקַלְנוּ בּוֹ. הוֹלֵךְ וּבָא. מַמָּשׁ בָּאֶמְצַע הוּא עָמַד.   20
הוֹלֵךְ וּבָא. לְאֵין שִׁעוּר גָּבוֹהַּ, דַּק כְּמוֹ שַׂעֲרָה, בְּקֶרֶן הַזָּוִית,
בִּקְצֵה הַשְּׁבִיל, נִתְקַלְנוּ בּוֹ, בְּחִפּוּשָׂיו הַנּוֹאָשִׁים,
אַחַר הָאֶבֶן הַיְקָרָה. אַחַר הַמַּרְגָּלִית.

אֲנַחְנוּ מִצִּדֵּנוּ כְּבָר הָיִינוּ בַּחֲצִי הַדֶּרֶךְ וְהִטִּינוּ לַחֲזֹר.
אוּלַי רָאִינוּ בּוֹר. אוּלַי רָאִינוּ בּוֹר שֶׁל מַיִם,   25
וְהִטִּינוּ אֶת עַצְמֵנוּ מִן הַשְּׁבִיל לְרֶגַע קָט.

אֲבָל הַחֹם הָיָה כָּבֵד מִנְּשֹׂא, וְהָעוֹלָם בָּעַר כְּמוֹ כִּבְשָׁן.
וְאָז, כְּמוֹ נִפְתְּחוּ כָּל הַשָּׁמַיִם לְפָנֵינוּ בִּמְשִׁיכַת רוֹכְסָן.
וְזֶנּוּ אֶת עֵינֵינוּ הַשְּׂרוּפוֹת

בְּמַה שֶׁלֹּא רָאָה אֱנוֹשׁ וּבֶן תְּמוּתָה מֵאָז   30
בָּרָא הָאֱלֹהִים אָדָם לִשְׁלֹט
עַל פְּנֵי הָאֲדָמָה הַיַּבֶּשָׁה הַזֹּאת.

We've Reached God

We've reached God.
Completely by chance. Actually, we came upon Him.
We were half way down the mountain,
a heavy load was on the donkeys,
5 and suddenly, at a bend in the road, when we turned to look,
we came upon Him.

He too sought us,
like a precious stone, He said, like a pearl,
just like something lost.
10 When completely by chance,
absolutely by accident, we were half way, and we reached
the designated land.
That is, we reached God.
And we found absolute rest from life.
15 It was completely by chance, that is,
half way, going down the mountain,
the donkeys with their sacks stood alone,
turned aside with knees bent, at the narrow bend.
The heat was more than we could bear.

20 At the edge of the path we came upon Him. Coming and going.
     Precisely in the middle He stood.
Coming and going. Tall beyond measure, thin as a hair, right in the
     corner,
at the edge of the path, we came upon Him, in His desperate search,
for the precious stone. For the pearl.

We, in turn, were already half way and we started to return.
25 Perhaps we saw a cistern. Perhaps we saw a cistern of water,
and we turned aside from the path for just a moment.

But the heat was more than we could bear, and the world burned
     like a furnace.
And then, it was as if the heavens opened before us with the pull of
     a zipper.
And we feasted our burnt eyes

30 on that which no mortal has seen since
God created Man to rule
upon this dry land.[25]

   This poem reworks a number of biblical images associated with accounts of divine revelation to redefine traditional notions of the human–divine relationship.[26] The juxtaposition of the images of the mountain and the donkeys (3–4) evokes the story of the binding of Isaac (Genesis 22), in which God tells Abraham to sacrifice Isaac on a mountain, and the father and son travel to that mountain by donkey. The mountain image also suggests Mount Sinai, site of the revelation of God (Exodus 19–20). The "designated land" (12) alludes to Canaan, the land which God promised Abraham He would grant to his descendants (e.g., Genesis 12:7). The expression "we turned aside from the path" (26) can be associated with Moses' turning aside to see the burning bush (Exodus 3:3), as well as with Balaam's ass turning aside when she perceives the angel of God standing in the road (Numbers 22:23). It is true that the words used in the poem to allude to these instances of divine revelation do not always appear in the original biblical stories. Canaan is never referred to in the Bible as "the designated land" (ha'arets haye'udah), and Moses says asurah when he prepares to turn to see the burning bush, while in the poem the people's act of turning aside is expressed with a word with a different root, vehittinu. The word vehittinu, however, does have the same root as the Hebrew term in the original story of Balaam's ass: vatet ha'aton min haderekh ("the ass turned from the path"). The speaker uses the term ḥamor ("donkey," 4, 17) from the binding of Isaac story and not the term aton (ass) from the Balaam story. It would seem that the tendency of the speaker to play with biblical language makes the point that he wishes to reconceive the notion of revelation on his own terms, rather than on those of the Bible.
   When God reveals Himself to His people in this poem, it is not like the call to Abraham first to sacrifice then not to sacrifice his son on Mount Moriah, nor the call to Moses from the burning bush to return to Egypt and lead the Israelites to freedom, nor the revelation of the Ten Commandments accompanied by thunder and lightning on Mount Sinai, nor the angel of God holding a sword that appeared to Balaam's ass. All of these biblical events consist of dramatic and overwhelming acts on the part of God as He attempts to communicate with human beings. In this poem, the people reach God by accident. The chance nature of this encounter is emphasized by repeated references in the first half of the poem to this fact: "Completely by chance. Actually, we came upon Him" (2); "we came upon Him" (6); "completely by chance, / absolutely by accident." (10–11); and "It was completely by chance" (15). When the speaker states, "He too sought us" (7), we are given the impression that the people were in search of God and God was in search of the people. Perhaps the significance of "half way down the mountain" (3) is that the people had ascended the mountain to find God and, having failed to do so, were in the process of leaving the mountain when God appeared to them. The people's search for God is only suggested here, while God's search for the people is described directly as if He

had been searching for a lost gem (7–9). It would thus appear that God had a more single-minded commitment to this search for connection than did the people.

The image of God searching for the people as if they were "a precious stone" (*even yeqarah*, 8) or "a pearl" (*margalit*, 8) recalls God's reference to the Israelites as *segullah* ("a treasure," Exodus 19:5; Deuteronomy 7:6, 14:2, 26:18). The image may have been borrowed from a midrashic text which explains why the book of Genesis tends to relate relatively few details about the life of characters less important to God and more details about characters who are more important to Him:

> This is to be compared to a pearl [*margalit*] that fell in sand. A person feels around in the sand and sifts it through a sieve until he finds the pearl. And when he finds it he casts away the grains from his hand and takes the pearl. (Tanḥuma Vayeshev 1, quoted by the medieval commentator Rashi in reference to Genesis 37:1)

If God's discovery of the people is seen as His recovery of a lost precious object, the people's discovery of God is presented as an end to their wanderings. The trip through great heat with laden donkeys is finally completed when the people find God. Now they have arrived at a place which will provide them relief from their travels ("absolute rest from life," 14). In referring to the discovery of God with the words "we reached / the designated land" (11–12), the speaker may be challenging the notion of the centrality of the Land of Israel, shared by secular and religious Israelis alike, and asserting that the spiritual home of closeness to God may be more important than the physical home Jews have found in Israel.

It is significant that the people find God at a time when they and their beasts of burden have turned away from the path of their wanderings: "the donkeys . . . / turned aside" (17–18); "at the edge of the path" (20, 22); and "we turned aside from the path" (26). As long as the people were purposely moving forward, it was not possible for them to discover God, but when they paused from their forward-moving direction of seeking mastery and control over their fate, they were open to being found by God.

The speaker portrays the actual divine revelation vouchsafed to the people in two ways. The first is a more anthropomorphic description of a human-like figure in the middle of their path: "Tall beyond measure, thin as a hair" (21). As Dror Eydar has observed,[27] this expression may allude to an aggadic passage in the Talmud:

> At the end of days, the Holy One Blessed be He will bring the evil inclination and slaughter it before the righteous and before the wicked. To the righteous it will seem like a tall mountain and to the wicked it will seem like a thin hair. One group will weep and the other group will weep. The righteous will weep,

saying, "How could we have conquered such a tall mountain, and the wicked
will weep, saying, "How could we have not conquered this thin hair?" And
even God will be amazed together with them. (Sukkah 52a)

Thus, just as according to the talmudic passage the evil inclination can assume
opposing forms based on the spiritual qualities of the individual who views it,
so can God. Even the same person under different circumstances can perceive
God differently from the way he or she did previously. There may be some
significance to the fact that the speaker has made use of imagery traditionally
associated with the evil inclination to refer to God. This would be in keeping
with the poet's tendency to break down the barriers between the holy and the
profane in his writing.[28]

The second way the divine revelation is portrayed resembles more the tradi-
tional notion of a vision of God in the heavens (28–32). The expression "the
heavens opened [*niftehu kol hashamayim*]" (28), for example, alludes directly
to the description of a divine revelation to the prophet Ezekiel: "the heavens
opened [*niftehu hashamayim*]" (Ezekiel 1:1). This heavenly revelation, accom-
plished as easily as if someone pulled open a zipper, brings relief to the "burnt
eyes" (29) of the people who have been traveling for so long. The speaker states
that this is a sight never revealed "since / God created Man to rule / upon this
dry land" (30–32). The choice of the word "rule" (*lishlot*) may suggest that ever
since human beings have undertaken their role of ruling the world they have
been more distant from God. Thus, just as one may be more likely to find God
when one is not looking for Him, so when people are willing to cease trying to
control the world they have a better chance of transcending the suffering of
human existence, as represented by the hot, burdensome journey in the poem,
and finally reach God.

שִׁיר

הִנֵּה הַשֶּׁקֶט מִתְמַסְמֵס בֵּין הַשָּׁדַיִם שֶׁל הָעֶרֶב
הָעוֹלֶה עָלָיו בַּעֲנָנִים גְּדוֹלִים, רַכִּים, מֵעַל סְדִין
הָאֹפֶק. קְצָת מִתַּחַת לוֹ, לְמַטָּה, כְּמוֹ חוֹצֶה
אֶת הָעוֹלָם, בְּקַו אָדֹם, בּוֹעֵר, הַפַּס הָעַז
שֶׁל תַּחְתּוֹנֵי הַיּוֹם הַמְּפֻשָּׁלִים.   5

עַל הַשָּׁמַיִם כְּבָר כְּתוּבִים בִּדְיוֹ סְתָרִים הָאִסּוּרִים.
עֲשֶׂרֶת הַדְּבָרִים הַחֲקוּקִים אֲשֶׁר נִתְּנוּ לָעָם בְּמַתָּנָה.
מְפֹרָשִׁים. מְפֹרָשִׁים וַחֲמוּרִים מֵאֵין כְּמוֹתָם. אִישׁ
כְּבָר לֹא יָכוֹל יוֹתֵר לִתְעוֹת בִּתְחוּם הַסַּכָּנָה!

אֲבָל מִתַּחַת, שְׁמַע, מַמָּשׁ מִתַּחַת וּמֵעֵבֶר לַגְּדֵרוֹת, מִתַּחַת   10
לְאַפּוֹ שֶׁל אֱלֹהִים, יֵשׁ מְשׁוֹרֵר. רוֹעֵד. רָזֶה. חִוֵּר.
זוֹחֵל–כְּמוֹ לְטָאָה קְטַנָּה–מִתַּחַת לַגָּדֵר,

אֶל תּוֹךְ־הָאֹפֶל הַמַּחֲלִיף מִינֵי צְבָעִים. הוּא מְטַפֵּס, לְאַט–
כִּי הוּא עִוֵּר–מֵעַל הַקִּיר. רוֹשֵׁם בִּגְרָפִיטִי עֲנָק, מַדְהִים,
מִלָּה־מִלָּה, אֶת כָּל הַשִּׁיר. מִתַּחַת לְאַפּוֹ שֶׁל אֱלֹהִים–   15

אַתָּה שׁוֹמֵעַ? מִתַּחַת לְאַפּוֹ–יָבוֹאוּ הַשּׁוּרוֹת הָאֲרוּרוֹת הַלָּלוּ!

A Poem

See how silence melts between the breasts of evening
rising upon it in big, soft clouds above the sheet
of the horizon. A little under it, below, as if crossing
the world, in a red, burning line, the brazen stripe
5   of the day's underpants rolled back.

On the heavens the prohibitions already written in secret ink.
The Ten Commandments, engraved, granted to the people as a gift.
Clearly stated. Clearly stated, strict like nothing else. No one
can now go astray in the realm of danger!

10   But, beneath, listen, just beneath and beyond the fences, under
God's nose, there's a poet. Trembling. Thin. Pale.
Crawling—like a little lizard—under the fence,

into the darkness changing colors. He climbs, slowly—
for he is blind—over the wall. He writes in gigantic, amazing graffiti,
15   word by word, the whole poem. Under God's nose—

Do you hear? Under His nose—these accursed lines arrive![29]

The speaker begins with a highly eroticized view of an evening skyline. Images of clouds resembling breasts, and the red sunset on the horizon as a bright burning red line drawn across the day's rolled-back underpants evoke for the poet the enticing sight of a woman relaxing in bed preparing for sexual relations (1–5). This initial set of images is sharply contrasted by the speaker's perception of the words of the Ten Commandments as engraved in "secret ink" on the evening sky (6–9). The speaker refers to the commandments as being very explicit and strict, preventing anyone from getting into moral or ritual danger. The strictness of the law, thus, appears to come to prevent the fulfillment of the appreciation of nature associated with the fantasy of erotic bliss evoked in the first stanza. The Hebrew term for "secret," *setarim*, is, appropriately, associated with spiritual mysteries. However, the Hebrew term for "secret ink," *deyo setarim*, calls to mind the Hebrew term for "coded writing," *ketav setarim*; perhaps the speaker is suggesting that the words of divine revelation are not fully comprehensible to the people to whom they were transmitted, for they are written in a heavenly code which is not easy for human beings to decipher.

The tension between these two visions of natural beauty and unrestrained sexuality on the one hand and obedience to the law on the other is broken by the image developed in the rest of the poem of a poet who defies divine authority. At the time of the revelation of the Ten Commandments, God told Moses to keep the people from even touching Mount Sinai (Exodus 19:12–13). In the poem, a poet challenges divine limits, albeit in a less than open manner: he goes "beyond the fences, under / God's nose" (10–11), "[c]rawling . . . under the fence" (12). His defiance of God is described with words reflecting his weakness: "Trembling. Thin. Pale" (11), "like a little lizard" (12), and "blind" (14). He is insignificant, yet he takes advantage of the fact that he does not stand out in order to compete with God by writing a poem.

The poet's challenge to God's authority by composing a poem is portrayed here as an act of writing "gigantic, amazing graffiti" without God noticing what he is doing (14–15). Just as graffiti often expresses thoughts not generally acceptable to the mainstream of society, such as radical political views or erotic fantasies, so the poet's words, in some sense, transgress the integrity of the divine order. Furthermore, just as graffiti tends to be written in a messy manner and is seen as defacing human structures, so the "accursed lines" (16) that the poet writes cannot adequately compete with the beauty of nature ("the darkness changing colors," 13) nor with the security that the divine law provides to human beings. Nevertheless, the poet is driven to develop his own vision that transcends the tension between nature and sensuality on the one hand and divine law on the other. The final line of the poem, "Do you hear? Under His nose—these accursed words arrive!" (16), indicates that the poet is both defiant and insecure in his challenge to divine authority. He is amazed and perhaps a bit disconcerted that he can get away with his presumptuous attempt to cut through the tension that tradition has maintained between the spiritual and the physical. Nevertheless, he does not shy away from making use of his art to assert an alternative vision that will bring together these two seemingly opposed realms.

שִׁיר שֶׁל יוֹם

לְיוֹם שְׁלִישִׁי בַּשַּׁבָּת

עַכְשָׁו נִגְמְרוֹת כָּל הַמִּלִּים, וּמַתְחִילָה, סוֹף־סוֹף. מְעַט מְעַט וּבִמְהִירוּת.
כָּל הַצְּרִיחִים מְטֹהָרִים מֵהִרְהוּרִים רָעִים. מֵהַגַּסּוּת, מֵהַיְּהִירוּת.
מֵעַל רָאשֵׁי הַמִּגְדָּלִים עוֹלָה הָאַהֲבָה. שְׁקוּפָה מְאֹד, בִּזְהִירוּת.
כִּי מִי רוֹצֶה בְּיוֹם שְׁלִישִׁי כָּזֶה לְהִשָּׁבֵר?

עַכְשָׁו נִגְמְרוֹת כָּל הַמִּלִּים, וּמַתְחִילָה, סוֹף־סוֹף. מְעַט מְעַט וּבִמְהִירוּת.   5
יֵשׁ אֱלֹהִים, וּמַלְאָכִים, כָּל צְבָא הַשָּׁמַיִם. הַכֹּל שִׁכּוֹר מִבְּהִירוּת.
מֵעַל רָאשֵׁי הַמִּגְדָּלִים עוֹלָה הָאַהֲבָה. שְׁקוּפָה מְאֹד, בִּזְהִירוּת.
כִּי מִי רוֹצֶה בְּיוֹם שְׁלִישִׁי כָּזֶה לְהִשָּׁבֵר?

PSALM OF THE DAY

For the Third Day of the Week
Now all the words are finished, and there's a beginning, finally.
    Little by little and fast.
All the turrets are purified of evil thoughts. Of coarseness, of
    pretentiousness.
Above the tops of the towers rises love. Most transparent and with
    caution.
For who would wish on a third day like this to be broken?

5   Now all the words are finished, and there's a beginning, finally.
    Little by little and fast.
There is a God, and angels, the whole heavenly host. All is
    intoxicated from clarity.
Above the tops of the towers rises love. Most transparent and with
    caution.
For who would wish on a third day like this to be broken?[30]

The meaning of the title of this poem, "Psalm of the Day" (*shir shel yom*), is ambiguous. In one sense, it is the term used to refer to the psalm assigned by Jewish tradition to be recited on a particular day of the week at the end of the morning prayer service. In another sense, it may suggest that this is a psalm celebrating the day and all that it offers. The poet emphasizes the first meaning by providing a subtitle, in Rashi script, which is traditionally used for commentaries to the Bible and Talmud, as well as for instructions to the worshipper in older traditional Jewish prayer books. The subtitle refers to the introductory formula for the psalm recited on Tuesday, the third day of the week: "This is the third day of the week on which the Levites would recite [the following psalm] in the Temple." The central theme of the psalm traditionally assigned to Tuesday, Psalm 82, is an anguished call to God to bring justice to the world. This poem has a very different purpose. It does not express the desire for a yet-to-be-revealed justice, but rather the satisfaction of arriving at a state of tranquility and fulfillment. Justice and the rule of law are not the speaker's central concerns here; instead, what he seeks is the ability to arrive at an experience of love by overcoming negative personal qualities that serve to undermine one's peace of mind.

According to Jewish tradition, Tuesday is considered a good day to begin a task, because, in chapter one of Genesis, it is only on the third day of creation that it is stated twice that God saw His creation as good (Genesis 1:10, 12). The celebratory nature of the poem would fit well with this traditional notion that Tuesday is a lucky day. The experiences conveyed in the poem begin where words end: "Now all the words are finished, and there's a beginning, finally" (1, 5). Perhaps in reference to the fact that the traditional psalm of the day is the concluding prayer of the traditional daily morning service, the speaker is saying that, now that the recitation of the fixed words of prayer have been completed, we can have a *real* religious experience that transcends the overused texts of the traditional prayer book.

The love that rises in lines 3 and 7 emerges only when humanity can liberate itself from "evil thoughts," "coarseness," and "pretentiousness" (2). This liberation is seen as a process of purification or as a triumph over elements associated with medieval castles, such as "turrets" (2) and "towers" (3, 7). The castle imagery may represent the ways that we fortify ourselves from true human contact by creating tension with others. Once love emerges, the speaker can declare with overwhelming certainty ("intoxicated from clarity," 6) that, indeed, God and the angels do exist (6). This is a transparent world, free of lies and deceit. The refrain at the end of each stanza, "For who would wish on a third day like this to be broken?" (4, 8) indicates that it is self-evident to the speaker that anyone who can see the world as he does would easily transcend any tendency to break down on a psychological or spiritual level.

A grammatical oddity appears in the first line of each stanza: that which is translated somewhat freely as "and there's a beginning" is simply the feminine singular verbal form "and begins" (*umathilah*) with no subject. In the context of the poem, the most likely subject for this verb is the feminine singular noun *ahavah* ("love," 3, 7). Thus, in lines 1 and 5, which represent the early stages of the transformation celebrated in the poem, we are told that something has begun, but it is only at a later stage that we learn that it is love. Another significant feature of the poem is that both stanzas are identical, except for each of their second lines. This calls attention to a link between the humanistically oriented second line of the first stanza, which refers to the removal of negative qualities of one's personality ("purified of evil thoughts," 2) and the more theologically oriented second line of the second stanza, which speaks of the existence of divinity ("There is a God," 6). The order of these two variable lines suggests that the human moral self-cleansing of the first stanza is a necessary prerequisite for the theological revelation in the second stanza. Furthermore, the high degree of repetition of words at the ends of lines and the regular rhyming pattern in the Hebrew (a-a-a-b, a-a-a-b) gives the poem a formal celebratory quality, echoing the regularized features of traditional liturgical poetry. The words that are linked by the "a" rhyme (which is *ut* in Hebrew)—*uvimehirut* ("and fast," 1, 5), *mehayehirut* ("of pretentiousness," 2), *bizehirut* ("with caution," 3, 7), and *mibehirut* ("from clarity," 6)—tell us much about the nature of the process as it is perceived by the speaker. This self-liberation from that which is spiritually degrading is gradual and careful, yet capable of unexpectedly speeding up. It is not to be undertaken lightly or without full devotion. It is also one that clarifies for all who apprehend it the possibility of transcending despair and celebrating what life has to offer.

Addressing God Directly

מַשֶּׁהוּ מַכְאִיב

מַשֶּׁהוּ מַכְאִיב לִי כָּאן, בַּצַּד, אַתָּה רוֹאֶה, קוֹנִי?
מַשֶּׁהוּ תָּפַח לִי, וְיָצָא לִי, וּבָלַט
לַחוּץ, מִתּוֹךְ הַהִרְהוּרִים, כְּמוֹ אֶצְבַּע
שֶׁנָּקְעָה, נַפְשִׁי הִצְמִיחָה
קֶרֶן אֲרֻכָּה שֶׁל יִסּוּרִים.   5

מַשֶּׁהוּ מַכְאִיב לִי כָּאן, בַּצַּד, אַתָּה רוֹאֶה, קוֹנִי?
הַבְּדִידוּת הִצְמִיחָה לִי זָוִית, בְּלִיטָה חַדָּה, עֲוִית,
כְּמוֹ נָחָשׁ־כַּפְתּוֹר אָרֹךְ, צוֹמַחַת וְיוֹצֵאת לִי
מִן הַגַּב אֶל פַּס־הָאוֹר, וּמִתְפַּתֶּלֶת עַל הֶחָזִיק
כְּמוֹ זָנָב שֶׁיֵּשׁ לִכְרֹת, מַהֵר, קוֹנִי, עַכְשָׁו,   10
כָּעֵת. לִגְזֹם וּלְסַלֵּק.

מַשֶּׁהוּ מַכְאִיב לִי כָּאן, בַּצַּד, אַתָּה רוֹאֶה, קוֹנִי?
הַבֶּגֶד לֹא מַסְתִּיר אֶת זֶה. וְהַתְּנוּעוֹת הַמְגֻשָּׁמוֹת שֶׁלִּי
רַק מוֹסִיפוֹת גְּחוּךְ. מַשֶּׁהוּ מַכְאִיב לִי. בָּרְחוֹבוֹת
בַּחוּץ הַחוֹגְגִים יוֹצְאִים בְּרִקּוּדִים וּבִשְׂדוֹת אָבִיב   15
נִפְלָא. פְּרָחִים. נָשִׁים. מַשֶּׁהוּ מַכְאִיב לִי כָּאן, בַּצַּד,
קוֹנִי, הַאִם אֵינְךָ מַקְשִׁיב?

SOMETHING HURTS

Something hurts me here, on my side, do You see, Creator?
Something swelled, protruded, and stuck
out, from my thoughts, like a finger
that's sprained, my soul has grown
5   a long horn of suffering.

Something hurts me here, on my side, do You see, Creator?
Loneliness grew a sharp-cornered protrusion, a spasm,
like a long ornamental serpent, growing out
from my back to the ray of light and twisting around my chest
10   like a tail to be cut, quickly, Creator, now
this time. To clip and to dispose.

Something hurts me here, on my side, do You see, Creator?
My clothing doesn't hide it. And my clumsy movements
only make it more ridiculous. Something hurts me. In the streets

15 outside people celebrate in dance and in the fields is a spring
  so wonderful. Flowers. Women. Something hurts me here, on my
   side,
  Creator, aren't You listening?[31]

It is significant that the speaker continually addresses God with the term *qoni* ("my Creator," or, as it could also be translated, "my Master"). In traditional terms, since God is the petitioner's Creator or Master, He is responsible for protecting him from harm. There is nothing here of the flattering praise that typically accompanies prayers of petition in the Jewish tradition. Furthermore, unlike the style of traditional prayers, the speaker here is not sure what is bothering him. "Something hurts me" (1, 6, 12), he repeatedly declares to God, without being able to define exactly what it is. The repetition of this expression at the beginning of every stanza adds to the sense of urgency and emphasizes how confused and desperate the speaker is. In his calling out to God, he resembles a medical patient who presents the symptoms of his disease to a doctor with the hope that the doctor will know how to diagnose the disease and prescribe a remedy.

The inner emotional turmoil of the speaker is manifest in external distortions of his body. His thoughts give rise to swelling (2–4), his soul grows "a long horn of suffering" (4–5), and his loneliness sends forth a "protrusion," which resembles a serpent that twists around his chest (7–9). When the speaker reaches the climax of the description with the image of the serpent, he urges God to quickly cut it off, as if somehow the solution to his existential anxiety can be as simple as the physical removal of an unwanted growth on one's body (10–11).

In the third stanza, there is a shift to a point of view that is directed outward. The speaker is preoccupied with being distant from others, both because his inner sufferings will be evident to them and because he cannot find joy in life in the way they can. He fears that his "clothing doesn't hide" his inner pain (13) and his "clumsy movements" will make clear to others how awkwardly he relates to life (13–14). Others can celebrate the glorious spring ("In the streets / outside people celebrate in dance and in the fields is a spring / so wonderful. Flowers. Women" 14–16), but he remains inside in a state of inner torment. Unlike many biblical psalms that conclude with the confidence that God will hear the psalmist's prayer and, unlike many rabbinically composed prayers that end with the affirmative praising of God as one who answers human needs, the poem finishes with the speaker wondering whether God is even interested in hearing his prayer: "Creator," he calls out, "aren't You listening?" (17).

הוֹ, הַשֵּׂכֶל הַפּוֹעֵל, הַסִּבָּה הָרִאשׁוֹנָה

הוֹ, הַשֵּׂכֶל הַפּוֹעֵל, הַסִּבָּה הָרִאשׁוֹנָה,
עִלַּת כָּל הָעִלּוֹת, תַּעֲשֶׂה אוֹתִי בְּבַקָּשָׁה צָלוּל.
צָלוּל כְּמוֹ מַיִם מוּל סְדְרַת הַשְּׁאֵלוֹת.
תּוֹרִיד אוֹתִי בְּבַקָּשָׁה לְמַטָּה,
וְתַעֲשֶׂה אוֹתִי לְרֶגַע קָט צָלוּל וְרַךְ לַכֹּל כְּמוֹ מַיִם.   5

הוֹ, עִלַּת כָּל הָעִלּוֹת, אָיֹם, נוֹרָא, רַב-עֲלִילָה,
תּוֹרִיד אוֹתִי בְּבַקָּשָׁה אֶל תּוֹךְ הַיָּם.
שְׁנִיָּה אַחַת לִפְנֵי עֲלוֹת, כְּמוֹ דָג טוֹרֵף, שִׁנֵּי-הַשְּׁאֵלָה.

אִם לֹא אִכְפַּת לְךָ, בְּבַקָּשָׁה לְרֶגַע, לְגֲלוֹת,
אֶשְׂמַח מְאֹד, אַתָּה הֲרֵי הַשֵּׂכֶל הַפּוֹעֵל, אַתָּה אֲדוֹן כָּל הַנְּשָׁמוֹת,   10
הוֹרֵד אוֹתִי בְּבַקָּשָׁה לְרֶגַע קָט אֶל תּוֹךְ הַיָּם הָעַז וְהָעֲמֹק-כָּחֹל שֶׁלְּךָ,
הַמְמַלֵּא רַכּוּת וַעֲדִינוּת אֵין-קֵץ אֶת הַיְרִיעָה שֶׁל הַשָּׁמַיִם.

אִם תַּעֲמִיד אוֹתִי, קוֹנֵה הַכֹּל, אוּלַי
אֲפִלּוּ רֶגַע, מֵרָחוֹק,
בִּמְקוֹם מִי שֶׁשּׁוֹאֵל-   15
כְּלוֹמַר, הַשֵּׂכֶל הַצּוֹלֵל-

אֶהְיֶה מַמָּשׁ צָלוּל-רִבּוֹן שֶׁלִּי, מָתוֹק-
אֶהְיֶה עָדִין וְרַךְ לַכֹּל כְּמוֹ מַיִם.

OH, THE ACTIVE INTELLECT, THE FIRST CAUSE

Oh, the Active Intellect, the First Cause,
the Prime Mover, please make me clear.
Clear as water before that list of questions.
Lower me down please,
and make me for a brief moment clear and soft to all like water.   5

Oh, Prime Mover, dreadful, awesome, doer of great deeds,
lower me down please into the sea.
A second before, like a fish of prey, the teeth of questions arise.

If You don't mind, please for a moment be revealed,
I'll be very happy, You are truly the Active Intellect, You are Lord of   10
    all souls,

lower me down please for a brief moment into Your strong and deep
    blue sea,
that fills the expanse of the sky with softness and delicacy.

If You'll place me, Creator of all, perhaps
if only for a moment, at a distance,
15   so I'm not the one who questions—
Immersed Intellect—

I really will be clear—my Master who is sweet—
I will be delicate and soft to all like water.[32]

This poem is a prayer to God to release the speaker from the "list of ques-
tions" (3) within him that challenge traditional religious faith. Below the poem,
Kosman provides an explanation for the terms referring to God that he uses:

הסיבה הראשונה, עילת כל העילות, השכל הפועל: כינויים שונים לאל בכתבי פילוסופים
יהודיים בימי הביניים בעקבות הפילוסופיה האריסטוטלית. הכינוי האחרון יוחד לישות
שׂכלית הממונה מטעם האל על הנעשה בארץ, אך בשיר זה לא נשמרה משמעותו
הפילוסופית המדויקת. (א.ק.)

The First Cause, the Prime Mover, the Active Intellect: various terms for
God in the writings of Jewish philosophers in the Middle Ages drawing on
Aristotelian philosophy. The last term referred to an entity of intellect as-
signed by God to be in charge of all that occurs on earth, but in this poem
its exact philosophical meaning is not preserved. (A.K.)[33]

Medieval Jewish philosophical terms are appropriate in the context of this poem,
because, like modern intellectuals, medieval Jewish philosophers were troubled
by traditional formulations of faith. However, whereas medieval Jewish philoso-
phers were able to develop a rationalistic theology based on Neo-Aristotelian
concepts that were more in keeping with the intellectual trends of the time, the
speaker, a product of modern skepticism, is not able to take these terms seriously.
The terms reflect an abstractly conceived God, not one who actively intervenes
in the affairs of people, and certainly not one to whom you would turn with such
a pressing personal request. To turn to an "Active Intellect" would appear to be
as efficacious as turning to any impersonal power that is so transcendent as to be
unable to hear any prayers. It is as if in addressing God with these terms the
speaker is making fun of them by suggesting how absurd it was for the medieval
philosophers to think they could pray to an abstract concept such as "the First
Cause." Furthermore, the very fact that the poet feels compelled to offer below
the poem an explanation for these terms suggests that he assumes that contem-

porary readers do not know what they mean, and therefore they will not function well as terminology that will address issues of faith in the present.

Throughout the poem, the speaker requests not that he be granted an intellectual answer to his doubts, but rather that he be transformed into pure water or be immersed in water as if being purified in a ritual bath (*miqvah*). In the first stanza, his request to be turned into water reflects a desire to be purified of doubt and relieved of the tension of his internal intellectual struggles (1–5). In the second stanza, he asks to be immersed in the sea in such a way as to just miss being devoured by questions of religious doubt, metaphorically represented as a shark-like fish of prey (6–8). In the third stanza, he seeks immersion in God's "strong and deep blue sea, / that fills the expanse of the sky with softness and delicacy" (9–12).

In the fourth stanza, the speaker takes a different approach and asks to be distanced from his doubts, so that he will no longer be "the one who questions" (13–15). Following this request, he calls to God with a newly invented term, "the Immersed Intellect" (16). God's intellect is immersed in the same sense that the poet asked earlier in the poem to be immersed in the waters of faith, for God is not subject to intellectual doubts the way people are. If God were to appear this way, He would be transformed for the speaker into a "Master who is sweet" (17), and the speaker's mind would figuratively adopt the qualities of water, which is "clear" (*tsalul*, 17)—a play on *tsolel* ("immersed," 16)—and "delicate and soft" (18). In this state, he will finally find spiritual peace, having achieved the level of religious faith for which he has yearned.

פִּיּוּט (לְאוֹמְרוֹ בַּיָּמִים נוֹרָאִים, מְיֻסָּד עַל מַעֲשֵׂה נוֹרָא
שֶׁאֵרַע לַמְחַבֵּר וּלְזוּגָתוֹ תִּחְיֶ' בְּט' כְּתַמּוּז תשמ"ה)

אֶשְׁלַח לְךָ בְּפַקְס וַאֲקַצֵּר מְאֹד
לֹא לְהַטְרִיד בָּרוּךְ בּוֹרֵא הַזְּמַן
בּוֹרֵא עָבַר בּוֹרֵא עָתִיד בּוֹרֵא
הַכֹּל בּוֹרֵא מִינֵי פֵּרוֹת
בּוֹרֵא פְּרִי־אֲדָמָה בָּרוּךְ בּוֹרֵא   5
צוּרוֹת בּוֹרֵא הַכֹּל יָפֶה וּבְעִתּוֹ

בָּרוּךְ בּוֹרֵא נוֹרָא רַב עֲלִילָה
בּוֹרֵא מִינֵי הַצְּעָקָה וְהַיְלָלָה
בּוֹרֵא מַמְצִיא גָּאוֹן וּמְחַדֵּשׁ
זַנִּים דַּקִּים וַעֲדִינִים שֶׁל הַשְׁפֵּלָה   10
בָּעֶלְיוֹנִים בַּתַּחְתּוֹנִים בְּכָל הַיֵּשׁ
בּוֹרֵא הָעֵץ בּוֹרֵא בַּרְזֶל בּוֹרֵא נְיָר
בּוֹרֵא יָפֶה וּמְקַפֵּל
מַדְבִּיק אֶת כָּל הַחֲבִילָה

בּוֹרֵא פְּרִי הַדִּבּוּר הָאַהֲבָה   15
וְהַחִבּוּר בּוֹרֵא עִוְרִים
בּוֹרֵא חֵרְשִׁים בּוֹרֵא זַנִּים
נָאִים שֶׁל אֲלִימוּת בַּשּׁוּק
גְּדוֹלִים בְּרִיאִים וַחֲדָשִׁים
בּוֹרֵא מִינֵי הַמִּין הַמְשֻׁגָּלִים   20
הַמִּשְׁכָּבִים בּוֹרֵא מִינֵי תְּנוּחוֹת
בּוֹרֵא גּוֹנֵי הָאֲנָחוֹת הַנְּשָׁבוֹת בְּפָנִים
בִּיצִרִיּוּת עַזָּה כְּמוֹ רוּחוֹת הַכֹּל יָפֶה וּבְעִתּוֹ

בָּרוּךְ בּוֹרֵא נוֹרָא רַב עֲלִילָה
בּוֹרֵא מִינֵי הַצְּעָקָה וְהַיְלָלָה   25
בּוֹרֵא מַמְצִיא גָּאוֹן וּמְחַדֵּשׁ
זַנִּים דַּקִּים וַעֲדִינִים שֶׁל הַשְׁפֵּלָה
בָּעֶלְיוֹנִים בַּתַּחְתּוֹנִים בְּכָל הַיֵּשׁ
בּוֹרֵא הָעֵץ בּוֹרֵא בַּרְזֶל בּוֹרֵא נְיָר
בּוֹרֵא יָפֶה וּמְקַפֵּל   30
מַדְבִּיק אֶת כָּל הַחֲבִילָה

בּוֹרֵא שֵׁדִים וּמַלְאָכִים וּמְשָׁרְתִים כֻּלָּם קְצוּבִים לִזְמַנֵּיהֶם
לְגוֹנֵיהֶם לְיוֹם לְלַיְלָה וּלְאוֹפַנֵּי הַתְּרוּחוּתָם עַל הַמַּרְאֶה

עַל הַמִּטָּה עַל הָאָרוֹן עַל הַשָּׂדֶה בָּרוּךְ בָּרוּךְ בָּרוּךְ אַתָּה בָּרוּךְ

בּוֹרֵא פְּרִי הַשְּׁתִיקָה בָּרוּךְ בּוֹרֵא מִינֵי הַפַּחַד הָאֵימָה הַחַלְחָלָה מִינֵי זָדוֹן   35

וְרַע עֲדִינֵי־לְבוּשׁ־וּכְסוּת כְּמַלְמָלָה עַרְמוּמִיּוֹת דַּקָּה וְכַוָּנָה זַכָּה

עֲגַלְגַּלָּה וּפְתַלְתָּלָה נְאַת גִּזְרָה דַּקַּת שִׂמְלָה

לְעֵירָמָּה שֶׁל בְּתוּלַת הַנֶּפֶשׁ בָּרוּךְ בָּרוּךְ בָּרוּךְ

אַתָּה בָּרוּךְ בּוֹרֵא הַבִּץ בִּפְנִים בָּרוּךְ בּוֹרֵא הָרֶפֶשׁ

בָּרוּךְ בּוֹרֵא נוֹרָא רַב עֲלִילָה   40

בּוֹרֵא מִינֵי הַצְּעָקָה וְהַיְלָלָה

בּוֹרֵא מַמְצִיא גָאוֹן וּמְחַדֵּשׁ

זַנִּים דַּקִּים וַעֲדִינִים שֶׁל הַשְּׁפָלָה

בָּעֶלְיוֹנִים בַּתַּחְתּוֹנִים בְּכָל הַיֵּשׁ

בּוֹרֵא הָעֵץ בּוֹרֵא בַּרְזֶל בּוֹרֵא נְיָר   45

בּוֹרֵא יָפֶה וּמְקַפֵּל

מַדְבִּיק אֶת כָּל הַחֲבִילָה

PIYYUT (TO BE SAID ON THE DAYS OF AWE. BASED ON AN
AWESOME EVENT THAT OCCURRED TO THE AUTHOR AND HIS
WIFE, MAY SHE LIVE, ON 9 TAMMUZ 5745)

I'll send You a fax and be very brief
not to disturb the Creator of time
Creator of past Creator of future Creator of
all Creator of all kinds of fruits
5   Creator of the fruit of the earth blessed is the Creator of
troubles Creator of all that's beautiful and in its proper time.

Blessed is the awesome Creator master of events
Creator of all kinds of cries and wails
Creator ingenious inventor and renewer of
10   small and delicate species of humiliation
on high and down below in all there is
Creator of trees Creator of iron Creator of paper
creating beautifully and folding
and gluing together the whole package.

15   Creator of the fruit of speech and love
and connection Creator of the blind
Creator of the deaf and Creator of fitting
species of violence in the market
big healthy and new
20   Creator of all kinds of sexual
intimacies Creator of all kinds of positions

Creator of varieties of sighs expressed within
with great passion like winds all that's beautiful and in its proper
   time.

Blessed is the awesome Creator master of events
25   Creator of all kinds of cries and wails
Creator ingenious inventor and renewer of
small and delicate species of humiliation
on high and down below in all there is
Creator of trees Creator of iron Creator of paper
30   creating beautifully and folding
and gluing together the whole package.

Creator of demons and angels and servants all categorized by their
   times
their hues by day by night and by the ways they stretch out on the
   mirror
on the bed on the closet on the bureau, blessed blessed blessed are
   You blessed
35   Creator of the fruit of silence blessed Creator of all kinds of fear and
   terror and trembling and all kinds of malice
and evil delicately dressed and covered in finest cloth subtle
   deception with pure intention
roundish and twisting fine of figure and dressed lightly
over the nakedness of a virgin soul blessed blessed blessed
are You blessed Creator of mire within blessed Creator of trash.

40   Blessed is the awesome Creator master of events
Creator of all kinds of cries and wails
Creator ingenious inventor and renewer of
small and delicate species of humiliation
on high and down below in all there is
45   Creator of trees Creator of iron Creator of paper
creating beautifully and folding
and gluing together the whole package.[34]

The title and subtitle of this poem place the reader in the world of traditional
Jewish piety. The word *piyyut* associates the poem with traditional synagogue
poetry. The subtitle appears in the original Hebrew in Rashi script, which, as
was noted in the analysis of "Psalm of the Day," is traditionally used for com-
mentaries to the Bible and Talmud, as well as for instructions to the worshipper
in older traditional Jewish prayer books. In the subtitle, the speaker declares that

this is a *piyyut* for the Days of Awe and that it is based on an event of awesome religious significance. His reference to himself and his wife in the third person, his use of the Hebrew date (which corresponds to June 29, 1985), and his reference to "his wife, may she live" (*zugato tiḥyeh*) all add to the creation of a formal pious atmosphere at the beginning of the poem.

The declaration in the first line that, rather than recite the lengthy traditional prayer service in synagogue, the poet will send his prayer by fax to God clashes sharply with the pious atmosphere of the title and subtitle. It may refer, in parodic fashion, to the service set up in recent years at the Western Wall in Jerusalem, to which one can fax a prayer to God to be placed in one of the cracks of the wall. It also suggests that the speaker may have difficulty interacting with God. As a product of contemporary Western culture, he has come to expect the kind of instant communication that a fax provides, but when one engages in traditional prayer, one cannot be sure one's words have reached God.

In the remainder of the poem, the speaker blesses God for being the creator of a variety of aspects of human experience. These aspects include such positive elements as nature ("trees," 12, 29, 45), the food we eat ("all kinds of fruits," 4), raw material ("iron," 12, 29, 45), human made material ("paper," 12, 29, 45), "love" (15), and "all kinds of sexual / intimacies" (20–21), an element not normally mentioned so explicitly in prayer. Many of the elements, however, reflect human suffering, for example, "cries and wails" (8, 25, 41), "humiliation" (10, 27, 43), "the blind / . . . the deaf," (16–17), "violence" (18), "sighs" (22), "fear and terror and trembling and all kinds of malice" (35), and "deception" (36). As iconoclastic as the speaker's approach to prayer is, however, he still links the good and evil of human existence to the traditional supernatural forces of angels and demons (32).

The intensity of the speaker's gratefulness to God for creating the world is reinforced by the frequent repetition throughout the poem of the word "blessed" (*barukh*). The second, fourth, and sixth stanzas are identical and thus serve as a repeated refrain which gives the poem the form of a traditional liturgical work. In this refrain, the speaker declares that this mixture of good and evil is purposefully put together by God and presented as a gift to humanity, who should, presumably, accept it in a grateful manner ("creating beautifully and folding / and gluing together the whole package," 13–14; 30–31; 46–47). In one sense, the poem is very much in the spirit of the Jewish tradition that teaches us to bless the evil that comes upon us as well as the good (Berakhot 48b).[35] One must take into account, however, the strong possibility that the speaker's blessing of God for so much that causes human pain is, to a certain extent, ironic. This irony is saved from bitter nihilism by the playful, almost whimsical nature of the voluminous list of things for which God is to be blessed and by the inclusion of so many positive elements of existence for which one should bless God.

פֶּתֶק בַּכֹּתֶל

אֲנַחְנוּ כָּכָה, בְּהִתְלַבְּטֻיּוֹת.
הַשֶּׁמֶשׁ לֹא רוֹצָה לִשְׁקֹעַ
וְהַשַּׁחַר לַעֲלוֹת. אֲנַחְנוּ
נַאֲמִין לְךָ בַּבֹּקֶר.

תֵּרָאֶה, תֵּרָאֶה בְּבַקָּשָׁה, זֶה   5
לֹא הֶסְכֵּם חָתוּם. בְּלֵית
בְּרֵרָה, אֲנַחְנוּ כָּכָה, זֶה, הַטֹּפֶס,

כָּל הַחֵלֶק שֶׁלְמַעְלָה רֵיק. מָה אַתָּה רוֹצֶה?
הַכֹּל נוֹשֵׁר וּמִתְפָּרֵק. בַּחֵלֶק הָרָדוּם.
נוֹפֵל. כְּמוֹ שְׁנַיִם רְקוּבוֹת. וְלֹא עָשִׂינוּ   10
כְּלוּם.

כִּמְעַט נָפַל לָנוּ לְמַטָּה, בַּדְּהִירָה
הַגּוּמִי, הַמַּחֲזִיק אֶת הַמּוֹשְׁכוֹת
הַחֲזָקוֹת שֶׁל הַגְּבוּרָה. נִשְׁאַרְנוּ כָּכָה.
בְּלִי תְּנוּעָה. כְּמוֹ פַּרְעֹה.   15
עַל הַסּוּסִים בְּתוֹךְ הַמַּיִם. גֵּד.

לְלֹא בְּחִירָה. אֲבָל אַתָּה רָאִיתָ. סוֹף הַפֶּתֶק
עַד. הַפֶּתֶק הַמְקֻמָּט וְהֶעָלוּב.
הֲלֹא כָּתַבְתָּ בַּתּוֹרָה, מִן הַשָּׁמַיִם,
בַּלְּבָנָה עַל הַשְּׁחֹרָה. אַתָּה רָשַׁמְתָּ. בַּפְּסוּקִים   20
שֶׁלְּךָ כָּתוּב.

אֲבָל פִּתְאֹם בִּקַּשְׁתָּ
מֵאָה חֲתִימוֹת! כְּאִלּוּ! מַה קָּרָה לְךָ?! זֶה לֹא מַסְפִּיק?!
תִּשְׁמַע, תִּשְׁמַע, בִּבְהִילוּ, הָיוּ לְךָ בַּפֶּתֶק שֶׁבַּקִּיר כָּל הַבָּנִים,
כָּל הַשֵּׁמוֹת, יָכֹלְתָּ לְהָצִיץ!! אֲנַחְנוּ, כָּכָה, אֱלֹהִים, תִּשְׁמַע.   25
עֲזֹב אוֹתָנוּ רֶגַע מִמַּלְאָךְ אֶחָד, מֵלִיץ! מֵאֵיפֹה לָנוּ? תִּשְׁמַע,
תִּשְׁמַע בְּבַקָּשָׁה אֶת זֶה, תִּשְׁמַע הֵיטֵב. עֲזֹב אוֹתָנוּ רֶגַע
מִזְכֻיּוֹת. אָבוֹת. מֵאֵיפֹה לָנוּ.

רֵד לְמַטָּה רֶגַע.
כִּמְעַט נָטוּי לָנוּ הַכֹּל,   30
בִּשְׂאוֹל, הַצִּדָּה, אֵיזֶה עֶשֶׂר מַעֲלוֹת,
וְגַם הַקִּיר שֶׁלְּךָ בְּהַרְעָשָׁה.
תַּחֲזִיק חָזָק. תִּשְׁמַע,
תִּשְׁמַע אוֹתִי, בְּבַקָּשָׁה.
הֲרֵי הַכֹּל הוֹלֵךְ לִפֹּל.   35

A NOTE IN THE WESTERN WALL

We're like this, struggling.
The sun won't set
nor will it rise. We'll
believe You in the morning.

5   Look, look, please, this
isn't an agreement signed and sealed. With no
alternative, we're like this, this form,

in which the whole top part is empty. What do You want?
It's all coming apart. In the dormant part.
10   Falling. Like rotten teeth. And we didn't do
a thing.

While galloping we almost lost
the rubber band holding the strong reins
of heroism. We're left like this.
15   Without movement. Like Pharaoh.
On horses in the water piled up to the side.

With no choice. But You saw. The note's end
is a witness. The wrinkled, forlorn note.
For You wrote in the Torah, from heaven,
20   White on black. You recorded. In Your verses
it's written.

But suddenly You requested
a hundred signatures! As if! What happened to You? It's not
    enough?!
Listen, listen, this is urgent, You had all the sons on the note on the
    wall,
25   all the names, You could've looked!! We are, like this, God, listen.
Leave us alone with this supportive angel business! Where will we
    get one? Listen,
listen please to this, listen carefully. Leave us alone with this
merits business. Forefathers. Where will we get them?

Come down for a minute.
30   Almost everything is leaning,
in Sheol, to the side, some ten degrees,
and Your wall too is being stormed.
Hold on fast. Listen,
listen to me, please.
35   Everything's about to fall.[36]

Unlike the previous poem, *"Piyyut,"* in which it is suggested that the speaker has faxed his message to the Western Wall in Jerusalem, this poem takes the form of a note to God, which the speaker has himself placed in a crack in the Western Wall. The essential message of the author of the note is that the situation in which he and his fellow Jewish Israelis find themselves is dangerously intolerable, and he desperately wants God to do something about it. The speaker's language runs the gamut from the literary to the colloquial. The mixture of expressions from rabbinic literature and everyday speech is particularly striking, such as, on the one hand, the Aramaic expressions *beleit / bererah* ("with no / alternative," 6–7) and *bivehilu* ("this is urgent," literally: with haste, 24) and the Hebrew expressions *batorah, min hashamayim* ("in the Torah, from heaven," 19), *malakh . . . melits* ("supportive angel," 26), and on the other hand, such everyday expressions as *kakhah* ("like this," 1), *mah attah rotseh?* ("What do You want?" 8), and *mah qarah lekha? zeh lo maspiq?!* ("What happened to You? It's not enough?!" 23). This use of such extremely opposite speech styles makes clear the degree to which the fabric of tradition, represented by rabbinic expressions, is being torn apart by the realities of contemporary suffering. The problems of the present are too urgent to be addressed only in terms of traditional concepts; we must speak to God, the poem suggests, with our most honest contemporary understanding of what is at stake in our existence.

The poem is permeated with expressions that portray a world that is falling apart. The people are plagued by internal struggles (1). The most reliable aspect of nature, the setting and rising of the sun, has ceased (2–3). In general, the author declares, "It's all coming apart" (9) and "Everything's about to fall" (35). The fourth stanza compares the situation to a rider who has lost control of his horse ("While galloping we almost lost / the rubber band holding the strong reins," 12–13) and to the related image of "Pharaoh. / On horses in the water piled up to the side" as a wall (*ned*, 15–16), which is about to come crashing down to drown him (Exodus 14–15).

Of particular significance are references in the poem to written documents: the note being placed in the Western Wall, an "agreement signed and sealed" (6), a "form" (7), a "wrinkled, forlorn note" (18), "the Torah . . . / White on black" (19–20), "a hundred signatures" (23), and "the note on the wall" (24). These written documents confirm the covenant between God and the Jewish people, serve as reminders of that covenant, or allow for the possibility of the breaking of that covenant. The speaker is convinced that God has not honored His side of the covenant that He made with Israel when He gave them the Torah at Mount Sinai, for He has allowed the Jews to suffer too much. This covenant is highly vulnerable. It "isn't an agreement signed and sealed" (6). Furthermore, its terms are most confusing. "[T]he whole top part [in the agreement form to be filled out] is empty," (8), which is a problem, because how will the people know how to fill out the rest of the form and sign it if they do not know what the divine authority has written in the top part of the form? To sign it would be like giving God a blank check.

The angry tone of the poem intensifies when the speaker cries out, "But suddenly You requested / a hundred signatures!" (22–23). This refers to the requirement in Jewish law that, if a man wishes to abrogate the medieval injunction of Rabbi Gershom against taking more than one wife, he needs to receive the agreement of one hundred rabbis in three distinct geographic districts.[37] God appears here as a man who wishes to push his first wife aside and take an additional wife, as if His love for the Jewish people has faded and He is prepared to do all that is necessary to divest Himself of His commitment to the Jews so He can choose a new people to favor. The speaker declares to God that, rather than turn away from the Jews by means of signatures from a hundred rabbis, He should look at the lists of Israel's sons on the wall of each war memorial (known in Israel as *yad labanim*). If God only took the time to even glance at those names of young Israelis who have died in war, unprotected by God ("You had all the sons on the note on the wall, / all the names, You could've looked!!" 24–25), He might realize the dire consequences of his desire to abrogate His original covenant with Israel and abandon His chosen people.

By now the speaker has lost all patience with the traditional avenues for finding favor in God's eyes. One concept he rejects is that of a "supportive angel" (26), or messenger, who argues before God that we are worthy of His acceptance. This concept has its origins in the expression *malakh melits* in Job 33:23 and the expression *melits yosher* in the *piyyut* for the Days of Awe that begins "Have mercy on your works" (*Ḥamol al ma'asekha*). The other concept for which the speaker has no use is that of the merit of the forefathers (*zekhut avot*) ("Leave us alone with this / merits business. Forefathers." 27–28), whereby God continues to care for the people of Israel because of his close relationship with their ancestors, Abraham, Isaac, and Jacob.[38] These have not worked to save Israel from suffering, and the speaker has no idea how to draw on either means of restoring the relationship of the Jewish people with God. The speaker concludes with a call to God to come down and help the Jews, for not only are the people near destruction ("Almost everything is leaning, / in Sheol," 30–31), but even God's "wall" (referred to here not with the term used for the Western Wall, *qotel*, but rather with the less impressive word *qir*, which signifies the inner wall of a house) is under attack ("Your wall too is being stormed," 32). And once God's wall is destroyed, there will be no hope for humanity.

מִזְמוֹר

אָמֵן, שֶׁתַּעֲשֶׂה אוֹתָנוּ קְטַנְטַנִּים כָּאֵלֶּה. קְטַנְטַנִּים
מְאֹד, בְּבַקָּשָׁה, מִתַּחַת לַגָּלַקְסִיּוֹת הַגְּדוֹלוֹת שֶׁלְּךָ.
אָמֵן, שֶׁתַּעֲשֶׂה אוֹתָנוּ קְטַנְטַנִּים מְאֹד, בְּגֹדֶל זֶרֶת, מִתַּחַת
לַגָּלַקְסִיּוֹת, לַשְּׁמָשׁוֹת, וְלַשְּׁבִילִים שֶׁל הֶחָלָב, הַמַּיִם, וְהָאוֹר הָעַז שֶׁלְּךָ.

אָמֵן, שֶׁתַּעֲשֶׂה אוֹתָנוּ בְּמִדָּה אַחֶרֶת, קְטַנְטַנִּים כָּאֵלֶּה, לֹא נִרְאִים, לֹא מְבִינִים   5
וְלֹא רוֹאִים בִּכְלָל מַה יֵּשׁ לְךָ מַה אֵין. מָה אִכְפַּת לְךָ? תַּעֲשֶׂה אוֹתָנוּ
פְּצַפוֹנִים, בְּגֹדֶל זֶרֶת, וּנְהַלֶּלְךָ עַל כָּךְ, אָמֵן.

A PSALM

Amen, make us so small. Very small,
please, under Your enormous galaxies.
Amen, make us very small, the size of a pinky, under
the galaxies, the suns, the milky ways, the waters, and Your strong
   light.

5   Amen, make us another size, so small, unseen, not understanding
   and not seeing at all what You have, what You don't. What do You
      care? Make us
   tiny, the size of a pinky, and we'll praise You for that, Amen.[39]

Presented as a contemporary psalm, this poem has the curious feature that it
begins as well as ends with the word "Amen," which traditionally comes only at
the end of a prayer. The word, in fact, appears at the beginning of each new set
of requests (1, 3, 5). With its original meaning as an affirmation of the truth and
trustworthiness of a statement (the Hebrew word *amen* has the same root as the
Hebrew word for "truth," *emet*, and the Hebrew word for "trust" or "faith," *emu-
nah*), it serves to call the reader's attention to the sincerity of the speaker's re-
quest. In addition, in its location at the beginning of each request of God, it
takes the place of God's name as the entity that is addressed, as if, rather than
directly speak to the traditional God of Israel, the speaker seeks to confront the
truth and trustworthiness of existence on a more abstract level.

   The speaker wants God to grant human beings such a measure of humility
that it will be as if they were as small as a pinky finger before the vast expanses
of space, the oceans, and light (1–4). In this ideal state of humility, we will have
no need to be noticed, and we will make peace with the fact that we cannot

understand everything (5), including the nature of God Himself ("and not see-
ing at all what You have, what You don't," 6). Toward the end of the poem, the
speaker makes use of the informal expression "What do You care?" (*mah ikhpat
lekha*, 6), which is a bit jarring in the context of the more formal language of
this contemporary psalm. Why would it bother You, God, the speaker wonders,
to grant us this humility? After all, once You do, we will be in a position to truly
praise You (6–7).

Israeli Poetry and the Possibility of Religious Discourse in a Secular Age*

T HE NEED TO EXPLORE the religious dimension of human existence is as central to the poetry of an author such as Zelda Mishkovsky, who maintained Orthodox Jewish practice throughout her life, as it is to the works of the less conventionally religious poets Rivka Miriam, Admiel Kosman, and Hava Pinhas-Cohen, and even to those of Yehuda Amichai and Asher Reich, who so radically broke from the Orthodox upbringing of their youth. These poets' shared set of concerns about the presence and absence of God transcends the many differences in identity among them. They seek to situate themselves in relationship to the language of faith they have inherited from the Bible and from traditional Jewish liturgy, while at the same time they feel the impetus to devise new linguistic formulations that speak more directly to a secular age about the divine as an ultimate source of meaning.

Biblical Imagery

Often, biblical imagery is presented in these poems in forms that are similar to those found in the Bible. In such cases, however, the poet calls attention to what is problematic about this imagery by having it function differently from the way it does in the Bible or by eliminating some of the larger context in which it appears. These changes frequently raise serious questions about the nature of God's relationship to humanity. In Zelda's poem "The shadow of the white mountain . . . ," when the speaker utters a prayer that provides her with a sense of reassurance, it gives rise to the same kind of "gourd plant" in which Jonah sought refuge after God forgave the people of Nineveh whose destruction he had prophesied. In the original biblical story, God produced the gourd plant and then sent a worm to destroy it overnight in order to teach Jonah a lesson about divine compassion. In the poem, however, the image of the short-lived gourd plant does not play the role of divine pedagogical device. Instead, it raises questions about the effectiveness of prayer: while the green leaves of the plant represent the comforting reassurance experienced by the speaker as a result of her prayer, the fact that they may be as vulnerable as those of Jonah's gourd plant suggests how fleeting that experience of reassurance may be. In Reich's poem "Ne'ilah," anticipation of the new year at the final prayer service of Yom Kippur is metaphorically presented by means of the image of Moses on the mountain overlooking the Promised Land which God will not allow him to enter. By singling out Moses' divine punishment and eliminating any reference to the more hopeful image of the eventual entrance of the Israelites into Canaan, the poet presents a worrisome view of how assured people can be that God will provide them with a good life in the coming new year. In Kosman's poem "A Note in the Western Wall," he portrays the spiritual plight of humanity by comparing it to the fate of Pharaoh and his forces drowned in the Sea of Reeds, rather than to the more hopeful image of the Israelites being saved when the waters parted for them. In Amichai's poem "I Am the Last of Them," the speaker begs God not to bet against him with Satan because, unlike the original story, in which God triumphs over Satan when Job remains faithful to Him, this time both God and Satan have won. The speaker in Rivka Miriam's poem "Booths" declares herself to be the descendant of the "ever-turning sword" that guards the way to Eden, rather than being the descendant of Adam and Eve. Her association with a weapon of violence makes her sense of expulsion from innocence in a post-Holocaust world even harsher than the expulsion of Adam and Eve from Eden.

At times, biblical imagery in this poetry reflects a more positive view that God's caring extends to our time. In Reich's poem "Instead of a Prayer," the image of the burning bush from which God appeared to Moses is expanded by association with what the speaker refers to as "anything that burns but is not consumed," thereby suggesting that there could be many occasions for divine revelation. Reich extends the range of possible ways to encounter God in his poem "Take My Thoughts," where the pillars of cloud and fire which were the concrete manifestation of God's presence in the wilderness following the Exodus from Egypt are part of a nature scene that could appear anywhere. In Rivka Miriam's poem "My God breathes next to me . . .," the water that flowed for the Israelites in the wilderness after Moses hit the rock has continued to flow ever since then. The miracle by means of which God responded to the needs of the Israelites for a relatively brief period of time in the wilderness is thereby transformed into a more lasting expression of God's concern for humanity throughout the generations. In Pinhas-Cohen's poem "What Is His Intention," the image of God providing nourishment to Elijah is used to convey the hope that God will answer the speaker's concerns about the nature of divine justice, even in her time.

In some cases, changes made in the original imagery of the Bible serve to present the poet's assertion of an individual spiritual direction that differs from the more conventional religious path found in the Bible. In Zelda's poem "At This Thought-filled Hour," the speaker insists that her experience of God is much less intense and more subtle than Abraham's when a dread darkness descended on him. In Pinhas-Cohen's poem "Plea," the speaker is a mother who, in contrast to Abraham, is not prepared to sacrifice her child. In "A Manifest Name," Pinhas-Cohen presents a woman at Sinai who stays home from the revelation in order to tend to household duties and eventually experiences her own personal revelation.

Such changes in biblical imagery sometimes involve reversing the original roles of God and humanity in the biblical story. This may serve as a means for the poet to criticize God. Both Amichai ("And For This You Merit Praise") and Pinhas-Cohen ("Plea") turn God's call "Where are you?" to Adam in the Garden of Eden back to God, in protest of His absence in the face of evil. In Reich's poem "Ne'ilah," it is not Moses who "turns here and there" as he did after he killed the Egyptian taskmaster, but rather God, who is being forced to realize how distant humanity is from Him. In other poems, the poet expresses the aspiration of humanity to divest itself of its subservient relationship to God and become more equivalent to Him in status and ability. In Reich's "If There Are," the words of divine revelation to Moses at the burning bush, "I will be who I will be," refer to the human speaker. In Rivka Miriam's "My God the soul You placed in me . . . ," the frequently used biblical expression of a human being invoking the name of God refers both to how humanity relates to God and to how God relates to humanity. In Kosman's "A Poem," the writings of a poet are in active competition with God's Ten Commandments.

Liturgical Language

These poets frequently allude to post-biblical liturgical expressions in ways that ironically undermine the meaning of the original expression in order to protest some flaw in God's relationship to the world. Such an ironic stance need not necessarily be seen as anti-religious, but rather as a necessary step in the assertion of intellectual honesty in light of legitimate questions about religious faith. In "God Full of Mercy," Amichai plays on the opening words of the traditional Jewish memorial prayer in a way which suggests that God mainly withholds His mercy from us. The speaker in Amichai's "After Auschwitz there's no theology . . ." uses the expression that God has no form, which appears in the "Yigdal" poem based on Maimonides' principles of faith, to compare Him ironically to the Holocaust victims who lost their physical form due to His inaction. In Reich's "*Piyyut* for Days of Awe," the description of God as "great, mighty, and awesome" found in the "Amidah" prayer is presented as the slogan of a "prayer ad" which greatly exaggerates the true nature of God. Rivka Miriam's "Shut" reverses the expression "Open the gate" from the Yom Kippur "Ne'ilah" prayer to "Don't open the gate," pointing to the fact that, given how distant God can be from people, they often experience unfulfilled expectations that are more painful than not having any hope at all. Kosman's "A Note in the Western Wall" challenges the notion that either an angelic advocate or the merit of the biblical patriarchs and matriarchs will help people to find divine favor. In "A Woman's Mourner's Kaddish," Pinhas-Cohen weaves the words of the Kaddish into a poem in which she expresses her anger and disappointment in response to the death of her husband.

Changes in liturgical expression, however, do not only serve as a means for ironic protest. They also convey a more contemporary version of religious experience than that found in the traditional prayers. In "Take My Thoughts," Reich transforms the opening words of the traditional Jewish memorial prayer to suggest that it is the experience of night (*leil*) and not God (*El*) that will comfort the speaker. Kosman presents redefined views of prayer in "When That Man Was Killed," "And As One Prays," and "I Don't Move When I Pray." In "Communion" and "This Is the Time," Pinhas-Cohen explores the possibility of a feminine transcendence of the more limited forms of traditional prayer composed by men.

There are, however, instances in which the speakers make use of liturgical expressions in a more positively straightforward manner. Generally, when poets do this, the expressions are short, take up relatively little space in the poem, and appear in contexts different from their original ones. In "The Delicate Light of My Peace," Zelda uses the term *davaq*, which connotes human cleaving to God, in reference to a butterfly clinging to a flower; and the butterfly comes originally from paradise (*gan eden*). In Zelda's "There was something alarming . . . ," the liturgical expression "[God's] mercies never cease" emerges from the experience of contemplating a garden. In Zelda's "All Night I Wept," the speaker addresses God with the rabbinic formulation "Master of the universe" (*ribbono shel olam*). When Amichai's speakers call out, "Our Father our King" (*avinu malkenu*), or, "My Father, my King" (*avi, malki*), they may display a degree of skepticism about traditional faith, but they are still expressing a yearning for contact with God that resembles that of traditional believers during the Days of Awe.

Reich's speakers, in particular, come across as sincerely seeking God. In poems in which the speaker yearns for forgiveness for his sins ("If There Are" and "How Shall I Come"), although he is uncertain of how acceptable he is to God, he really hopes for God's compassion. In Reich's "*Piyyut* for Nights of

Awe," the speaker expresses a "prayer [*tefillah*] to purify the blood / in every vein within me," and with some degree of doubt hopes for a response from the divine ("perhaps He'll answer me this time"). In "Travel Prayer," the speaker expresses a need for divine guidance. In "A voice . . . ," Reich weaves references to the divine voice in biblical and liturgical contexts to present a sense of God's presence. The speaker in a poem by Rivka Miriam, "I'll Go to Submit My Plea," sincerely yearns to present a plea (*tehinnah*) before God. The speaker in Kosman's poem "A Psalm" declares to God, "[W]e'll praise You," albeit for fulfilling the rather unconventional desire to be made very small. In Pinhas-Cohen's "A Mother's Prayer Before Dawn," the speaker wholeheartedly prays to God to grant her the qualities of a loving mother. In Pinhas-Cohen's "Photosynthesis" and "What Is His Intention," the speaker declares her desire to turn to God for answers to theological questions. When Kosman's speaker in "Something Hurts" cries out to God, he really wants God to take away the pain, even as he suggests that God may not be listening. In Kosman's "*Piyyut*," God is the Creator from the Genesis story, although He is blessed for creating a variety of elements to which the traditional liturgy does not typically refer.

A Contemporary Language of Faith

In addition to adopting a whole range of approaches toward the traditional imagery and language of faith, these poems also present numerous new and original linguistic formulations that convey the experience of divinity in ways that might more directly appeal to contemporary readers than those found in the Bible or traditional liturgy. In a number of cases, this involves the use of anthropomorphic imagery. In Amichai's "God's Hand in the World," the image of divine involvement in the world is associated with the speaker's memory of his mother cleaning out "the guts of a slaughtered chicken / on Sabbath's eve," whereas in his poem "And For This You Merit Praise," God's relationship to the world is analogous to a mechanic who keeps trying to fix a broken car. In another poem by Amichai, "Our Father our King . . . ," God's apparent loss of authority in the modern era is portrayed as "a king . . . / in the republic of pain," and in "After Auschwitz there's no theology . . . ," the numbers on the arms of the concentration camp survivors are "the phone numbers of God." In Reich's "Instead of a Prayer," God moves around "uttering incantations," whereas in his "Black Holes," the black holes of the cosmos are God's footprints. In some poems by Rivka Miriam, God is rather explicitly anthropomorphized as a male figure, in one poem breathing next to the speaker ("My God breathes next to me . . ."), and in another poem very much in need of comfort ("Who Will Take Us"). In Kosman's "We've Reached God," God is a tall, thin male figure who is desperately searching for humanity. In Rivka Miriam's "My God the soul You placed in me . . . ," the divine is analogous to the male seed coursing through her.

Three poets, Rivka Miriam ("In the beginning God created . . ."), Kosman ("When That Man Was Killed"), and Pinhas-Cohen ("A Woman's Mourner's Kaddish"), write of thread or strings that somehow connect humanity on earth with God in heaven.

In some poems, nature imagery represents God's presence in the world. In Zelda's "The Delicate Light of My Peace," the patterns on a butterfly's wings are signs from God. In another poem by Zelda, "At This Thought-filled Hour," God's presence is experienced as "a very faint tremor / passing among the leaves as they meet / the morning light." In Zelda's "Island," the rediscovery of God's presence in the midst of an experience of anxiety is portrayed as "an island in the vortex." In Amichai's "Footprints of birds in the sand by the sea . . . ," the footprints of birds in the sand are analogous to signs of God's presence in the world. Rivka Miriam explores the relationship of God's spirituality to our materialism by means of the image of a pear and its peel ("The God of Pears"). In Rivka Miriam's "Booths," God is the ephemeral branches of the sukkah top. Pinhas-Cohen writes in "Photosynthesis" of the way that God's inspiration of human beings may be analogous to the effect of light on plants.

In their poetry on God and prayer, these writers struggle with the question of whether we can discern in our largely secular existence an ultimate source for meaning, self-worth, or assistance in times of need, as well as guidance in how to conduct our lives. They are clearly not satisfied seeking enlightenment only in the usual secular sources, such as rational thought, science, social convention, or human fellowship. But, at the same time, they are all too aware of the limitations of the traditional language of faith to fully convey their own contemporary exploration of religiosity. As they reshape the language of tradition and invent new language, they write openly about how often they feel abandoned by God and also affirm the occasional glimpses of God's presence that they experience. Underlying all of this poetic expression is a desperate desire for a contemporary equivalent of faith in the traditional God of Israel as the guarantor of meaning and security in this world.

Some might argue that, precisely because each of the six poets covered in this study has had some involvement with the world of traditional Judaism, my choice to focus on them has had the effect of "stacking the deck" in order to support the underlying thesis of this book that matters of religious concern are a central element in Israeli poetry. I admit that it is easier to demonstrate the significant role that God and prayer play in the works of such poets. It is because of that fact that it made sense to me to choose them. I do believe, however, that future studies of many other Israeli poets less directly connected to the Jewish tradition in upbringing or education will reveal that they too cannot escape the universal human drive to find some form of transcendent meaning that is analogous to the spiritual insights of the Bible and all subsequent Jewish religious literature.

NOTES

Introduction

1. In recent discussions of the religious nature of Israeli poetry, the literary scholar Dror Eydar has dismissed most modern Hebrew poems on religious themes as not truly religious. In an article in the literary supplement of *Haaretz*, Eydar acknowledges that modern Hebrew poetry is replete with references to God, yet he dismisses these as not referring to actual religious experience. "Modern Hebrew poetry," he writes, "was born at the time of the death of God . . . . The Jewish God . . . was replaced by new value concepts . . . . The name of God, and even His image, which continued to appear in literary works . . . became from then on not more than a hollow idea, resembling references to the names of Zeus and the other gods of Olympus, a kind of interesting cultural folklore phenomenon that assumed, way back at the beginning of history, the existence of a supreme power that guided world history, and in particular His chosen people, and judged humanity for its merits and failings." He then goes on to assert that even these references to God, so empty of vital content, became rarer over time: "But these references became fewer as the years passed, the more that modern Hebrew literature became distanced from its starting point. The God of Israel became a marginal, neglected character; other matters, more pressing and compelling, were placed on the agenda and pushed aside concern with Him." See Dror Eydar, "Eloah! gadlu ma'ayenot levavi—va'emas beferurei shirah: Elohim bashirah ha'ivrit (A)," *Haaretz*, 21 May 2004. See also Dror Eydar, "Lamah tishqa, aleh, kashemesh, aleh od: Elohim bashirah ha'ivrit (B)," *Haaretz*, 28 May 2004. In an article that appeared later that year, Eydar presents the definition of religious poetry with which he is most comfortable, as poetry "written by a poet (1) obligated in his private life, in some way or another, to the accepted halakhic [Jewish religious legal] norms; (2) belonging, in some way or another, to the religious populace, including all of its different shades and trends (including the Ultra-Orthodox and the semi-Ultra-Orthodox); (3) who is accepted as such by various external circles, literary critics, the various communications media, and the general public." Dror Eydar, "Hashirah ha'ivrit hadatit: qriteryonim, hagdarot vehatsa'ot qeri'ah," *Aqdamot* 15 (2004): 40. At one point in this article, however, Eydar indicates some openness to the existence of "religious poetry written by poets who are not observant of the Torah and the commandments." Ibid., 34. For an analysis by Eydar of the poetry of the religiously observant Hebrew poet Yosef Zvi Rimon (1889–1958), see Dror Eydar, "'Shirat yamim ushehaqim belibbo': Yosef Zvi Rimon bitequfat ha'aliyyah hasheniyyah," *Jewish Studies, An Internet Journal* 4 (2005): 61–107 (http://www.biu.ac.il/JS/JSIJ/4-2005/Eydar.pdf).

2. I am not the first to argue for a proper recognition of the religious dimension of modern Hebrew poetry. In 1950, the poet and scholar Simon Halkin, who himself wrote poetry of a religious nature, declared, "It is commonly assumed that modern Hebrew poetry is almost exclusively secular. Yet nothing could be farther from the truth than this popular notion which even the student of Hebrew literature tends to share with the average reader." Simon Halkin, *Modern Hebrew Literature: From the Englightenment to the Birth of the State of Israel: Trends and Values* (New York: Schocken, 1950), 179. To support his case, Halkin devoted two chapters of this brief history of modern Hebrew literature to a consideration of the religious dimension of modern Hebrew poetry of Europe and the Land of Israel. Halkin's contemporary, the literary critic Barukh Kurzweil, spent much of his career vehemently arguing that the secular, anti-religious spirit of modern Hebrew literature constituted a radical break from the literature of the Jewish tradition. Nevertheless, even he recognized the ongoing importance of religious issues and the persistent presence of notions of divinity in modern Hebrew literature. "When we speak of an anti-religious affect as an important motif in our modern literature, which characterizes its secularism," he wrote, "we do not refer to an anti-deistic or anti-pantheistic position, and we do not intend to argue that atheism is a characteristic of our literature." Barukh Kurzweil, *Sifrutenu haḥadashah: hemshekh o mahpekhah?* (1959; repr., Jerusalem and Tel Aviv: Schocken, 1965), 44. See also James S. Diamond, *Barukh Kurzweil and Modern Hebrew Literature* (Chico, Calif.: Scholars Press, 1983).

3. André Neher, "The Renaissance of Hebrew in the Twentieth Century," *Religion and Literature* 16, no. 1 (1984): 22.

4. Ibid.

5. Ibid., 24.

6. Ibid., 34. In a similar vein, in an essay titled "The Absent God," Harold Fisch notes the degree to which "[m]odern Hebrew poetry moves strangely between the poles of messianic hope and metaphysical despair." Harold Fisch, "The Absent God," *Judaism* 21 (1972): 415.

7. Eli Schweid, "Hapeniyyah lElohim basifrut ha'ivrit hatse'irah," *Molad* 17 (1959): 181.

8. Ibid., 182.

9. Ibid.

10. Ariel Hirschfeld, "Shivat he'elohi: al meqomo shel Elohim bashirah ha'ivrit bador ha'aḥaron," in *Ha'eglah hamele'ah: me'ah ve'esrim shenot tarbut Yisra'el*, ed. Israel Bartel (Jerusalem: Magnes Press, 2002), 169.

11. Hirschfeld was referring to the articles in *Haaretz* by Dror Eydar (see intro., n. 1). Ariel Hirschfeld, "Hashirah ha'ivrit vehayetser hara," *Haaretz*, 4 June 2004.

12. Ibid. One cannot separate the question of how secular or religious Israeli poetry is from the larger cultural context of secular and religious trends within contemporary Israel. Although these two trends have often been polarized, there is also much evidence for the fact that the boundary lines between the secular and the religious in Israel are not as firmly drawn as is often assumed, and that frequently members of each camp venture into the realm of the other. This blurring of the distinction between the secular and the religious finds its expression, in part, in the poetry included in this study. For discussions of the interaction of secularism and religiosity in Israeli culture, see Charles S. Liebman, ed., *Religious and Secular: Conflict and Accommodation between Jews in Israel* (Jerusalem: Keter Publishing House, 1990); Charles S. Liebman and Elihu Katz, eds., *The Jewishness of Israelis: Responses to the Guttman Report* (Albany: State University of New York Press, 1997); and Yair Sheleg, *Hadatiyyim haḥadashim:mabbat akhshavi al haḥevrah hadatit beYisra'el* (Jerusalem: Keter, 2000).

13. Zvi Luz, *Merivah im ha'Elohim: massot peratiyyot* (Tel Aviv: Hakibbutz

Hameuchad, 2002), 120. See also Zvi Luz, *Hayesod hapilosofi bashirah ha'ivrit* (Tel Aviv: Hakibbutz Hameuchad, 2001). For additional discussions of the religious dimension of modern Hebrew poetry, see Glenda Abramson, "A Reasonable Rapture," *CCAR Journal* (Spring 2003): 46–68; Joseph Dan, "The Sweet Voice of the Lord: Four Contemporary Israeli Poets," in *The Heart and the Fountain: An Anthology of Jewish Mystical Experiences*, ed. Joseph Dan (Oxford: Oxford University Press, 2002), 263–275; Rochelle Furstenberg, "Israeli Poetry as Prayer," in *Pray Tell: A Hadassah Guide to Jewish Prayer*, ed. Jules Harlow et al. (Woodstock, Vt.: Jewish Lights Publishing, 2003), chapter 12; and Hana Yaoz, "Tefisot datiyyot basifrut ha'ivrit hatse'irah bishenot hashemonim," *Itton 77* 72–73 (1986): 16–17, 40.

14. Luz, *Merivah im ha'Elohim*, 120.

15. Ibid.

16. Writing in the preface of an anthology of poetry on religious themes that was published in the 1990s, the poet Erez Biton speaks of "a group of poets growing in recent years that is characterized by a clear relationship to Jewish faith either directly or indirectly. Most of these poets are religious [i.e., traditionally observant], but not necessarily. A faith-based religious trend is not new in Hebrew poetry. Fascinating figures like Yosef Zvi Rimmon or Zelda were like shining stars, but were limited, individual cases; however, now we are witness to a phenomenon that has almost become an actual movement." Miron H. Isaacson and Admiel Kosman, eds., *Shirah ḥadashah*, Apirion 44–45 (1996–1997): 1. Dror Eydar more recently referred to this trend as follows: "Toward the end of the twentieth century there emerged, albeit with some hesitation, an extensive wave of religious [i.e., traditionally observant] female and male poets who aspired to integrate into the existing poetic discourse, without sacrificing their spiritual and cultural world, parts of which were essentially different from the prevailing tone of the hegemonic trend in Israeli literature." Dror Eydar, "Hashirah ha'ivrit hadatit," 32. Eydar notes in this article that two journals in particular served as important vehicles for the development of this trend, *Dimui*, edited by one of the poets in this study, Hava Pinhas-Cohen, and *Mashiv haruaḥ*, edited by young religiously observant Israelis. An anthology of selected poems from the first decade of its existence may be found in *Mashiv haruaḥ* 17 (2005). The journal *Pesifas*, edited by the poet Itamar Yaoz-Kest, who became religiously observant as an adult, has also played a role in fostering this trend. For a discussion of Yaoz-Kest's poetry on religious themes, see David C. Jacobson, "'Bless Each Day that Passes': The Search for Religious Faith in the Poetry of Itamar Yaoz-Kest," in *Religious Perspectives in Modern Muslim and Jewish Literatures*, ed. Glenda Abramson and Hilary Kilpatrick (Oxford: Routledge, 2005), 34–54. For a discussion of a comparable phenomenon, in which religiously observant Israelis have played an increasing role in film and television production, see David C. Jacobson, "The Ma'ale School: Catalyst for the Entrance of Religious Zionists into the World of Media Production," *Israel Studies* 9, no. 1 (2004): 31–60.

17. Hamutal Bar-Yosef, "Yesh inyan," *Mashiv haruaḥ* 17 (2005): 170. See also a statement by Bar-Yosef, in which she explains why, although she considers herself to be a secular Jew, she is so drawn to the newly emerging poetry on religious themes. Hamutal Bar-Yosef, "Ha'im ha'adam ma'amin kefi shehatul melaqeq et parvato?" *Dimui* 15 (1998): 4–5.

18. A. M. Habermann, ed., *Beran yaḥad: yalqut shirei tefillah attiqim gam ḥadashim* (Jerusalem: Mosad Harav Kook, 1945), 3.

19. Ibid.

20. The recent appearance of these anthologies would seem to have brought about what Halkin predicted in the middle of the twentieth century: "[T]he historians and critics . . . have developed this view of the nonreligious character of Hebrew literature so suc-

cessfully that it may take decades to correct their error and place the so-called secularism of this literature within its legitimate bounds." Halkin, *Modern Hebrew Literature*, 179.

21. Hillel Weiss, ed., *Va'ani tefillati: shirat hatefillah shel meshorerim benei zemanenu* (Bethel: Sifriat Bethel, 1991), 8.

22. Ibid., 7.

23. Ibid., 8.

24. Amir Or and Irit Sela, eds., *Elohim Elohim*, special issue of *Heliqon: sidrah antologit leshirah akhshavit* 6 (1992): 12.

25. Ibid.

26. Ibid., 13.

27. Isaacson and Kosman, eds., *Shirah ḥadashah*, 3.

28. Ibid., 2.

29. Another recent, mystically oriented anthology, which seeks to expand the definition of religious poetry even to those poems not explicitly on religious themes, is Oded Mizrahi, ed., *Ḥamishim shirei binah: hitbonenut bashirah ha'ivrit haḥadashah al pi penimiyyut hatorah* [Fifty Meditative Poems: Meditations on Modern Hebrew Poetry Based on Jewish Mysticism] (Jerusalem and Tel Aviv: Sifrei Bitzaron, 2000). An example of an attempt to collect poetry only by observant Jews is Pinchas Peli, ed., *Emunim* (Jerusalem: Mosad Harav Kook, 1954). In his brief preface, Peli writes that the themes of the poetry in the anthology are "like the themes of all poetry of our generation, but we believe that the way of life of these poets, the atmosphere of Torah and the observance of commandments in which they are located, is reflected as in a mirror in their poetry." In this preface and in that of an accompanying anthology of prose by religiously observant writers that he later published (Pinchas Peli, *Ḥamishim sippurim* [Jerusalem: Mosad Harav Kook, 1956]), Peli expresses the hope that this body of literature by religiously observant writers will make a significant contribution to the world of Hebrew literature, which has been dominated by non-observant Jewish writers. See also the discussion of religious themes in modern Hebrew poetry from a religiously observant point of view in Avraham Blatt, *Orḥot emunim* (Tel Aviv: Moreshet, 1983).

30. J. Hillis Miller, *The Disappearance of God: Five Nineteenth-Century Writers* (Cambridge, Mass.: Harvard University Press, 1975), 13–14.

31. Haim Nahman Bialik, "Revealment and Concealment in Language" (trans. Jacob Sloan) in *Revealment and Concealment: Five Essays* (Jerusalem: Ibis Editions, 2000), 24. See the discussion of this essay in Arnold J. Band, "Hagaluy bakissuy," *Meḥqerei Yerushalayim Besifrut Ivrit* 10–11 (1989): 189–200; Zvi Luz and Ziva Shamir, eds., *Al "gilluy vekhissuy balashon": iyyumin bemassato shel Bialik* (Ramat Gan: Bar Ilan University, 2001); Natan Rotenstreich, "Gilluy vekhissuy balashon," in *Bialik: yetsirato lesugeha bire'i habiqqoret*, ed. Gershon Shaked (Jerusalem: Mosad Bialik, 1974), 323–333; and Azzan Yadin, "A Web of Chaos: Bialik and Nietzsche on Language, Truth, and the Death of God," *Prooftexts* 21 (2001): 179–203.

32. Bialik, "Revealment and Concealment in Language," 24–25.

33. Yochanan Muffs, "Theology and Poetics," *Conservative Judaism* 51, no. 1 (1998): 4.

34. Ibid.

35. Jakob J. Petuchowski, *Theology and Poetry: Studies in Medieval* Piyyut (London: Routledge and Kegan Paul, 1978), 3.

36. Ibid. Emphasis in the original.

37. Ibid., 4.

38. Ibid., 4–5.

39. Gordon D. Kaufman, *The Theological Imagination: Constructing the Concept of God* (Philadelphia: Westminster, 1981), 22.

40. Ibid.

41. T. R. Wright, *Theology and Literature* (Oxford: Basil Blackwell, 1988), 129.

42. Ibid., 130.

43. Ibid., 132.

44. "A dead metaphor," observes Wright, "loses the tension between its two senses, settling on a single meaning. . . . Literature . . . sets out to defamiliarize, foregrounding its violation of the literal and advertising its difference from ordinary language." Ibid., 133. As George Steiner notes, "religious thought and practice metamorphize, make narrative images of, the rendezvous of the human psyche with absolute otherness, with the strangeness of evil or the deeper strangeness of grace." George Steiner, *Real Presences* (Chicago: University of Chicago Press, 1989), 147. "It takes uncanny strength and abstention from *re*-cognition, from implicit *re*-ference," observes Steiner, "to read the world and not the text of the world as it has been previously encoded for us. . . . The exceptional artist or thinker reads being anew. . . . Because we are language and image animals, and because the inception and transmission of the fictive (the mythical) is organic to language, much, perhaps the major portion, of our personal and social existence is already bespoken. And those who speak us are the poets." Ibid., 195. Emphasis in the original.

45. Robert Schaible, "Literature, Religion, and Science: A Personal and Professional Trajectory," *Zygon* 32, no. 2 (1997): 283. Emphasis in the original.

46. Ibid. As Garrett Green puts it, "Paradigms serve the imagination analogically: by their likeness to the objects they exemplify. In the natural sciences, analogies are frequently embodied in models, which can be articulated in theories. In literature, metaphor is the typical analogical structure, the means by which the poet or novelist creates an imaginative world using the same words ordinarily employed to describe the everyday world." Garrett Green, *Imagining God: Theology and the Religious Imagination* (1989; repr., Grand Rapids, Mich.: William B. Eerdmans Publishing Company, 1998), 69.

47. Schaible, "Literature, Religion, and Science," 285–286. Emphasis in the original. "Few contemporary theorists," writes Frank Burch Brown, "question the thesis that metaphor, far from being a mere ornament, plays a crucial role in language of almost every kind, from the scientific to the aesthetic. Many, following Aristotle's lead, view metaphor as the central figure of speech and thought. . . . [M]any students of metaphor are convinced, as I am, that its unique semantic properties are correlated with equally unique epistemic and pragmatic potentials. From such a perspective, metaphor is seen as having the capacity to provide highly significant transformations of language, thought, and experience—transformations of a kind not duplicated by other linguistic strategies." Frank Burch Brown, *Transfiguration: Poetic Metaphor and the Languages of Religious Belief* (Chapel Hill: University of North Carolina Press, 1983), 4–5.

48. An articulate formulation of the crisis of religion in our time has been presented by David Tracy: "We are those Westerners shaped by the seventeenth-century scientific revolution, the eighteenth-century Enlightenment, and the nineteenth-century industrial revolution and explosion of historical consciousness. We late-twentieth-century Westerners find ourselves in a century where human-made mass death has been practiced, where yet another technological revolution is occurring, where global catastrophe or even extinction could occur. We find ourselves unable to proceed as if all that had not happened, is not happening, or could not happen. We find ourselves historically distanced from the classics of our traditions . . . . We find ourselves distanced even from ourselves, suspicious of all our former ways of understanding, interpreting, and acting." David Tracy, *Plurality and Ambiguity: Hermeneutics, Religion, Hope* (1987; repr., Chicago: University of Chicago Press, 1994), 8.

49. As J. Hillis Miller puts it, "Man the murderer of God . . . wanders through the infinite nothingness of his own ego. Nothing now has any worth except the arbitrary value he sets on things as he assimilates them into his consciousness. Nietzsche's transvaluation of values is the expunging of God as the absolute value and source of the valuation of

everything else. In the emptiness left after the death of God, man becomes the sovereign valuer, the measure of all things. . . . The world no longer offers any resistance to man's limitless hunger for conquest." J. Hillis Miller, *Poets of Reality: Six Twentieth-Century Writers* (Cambridge, Mass.: Harvard University Press, 1966), 3–4.

50. Derek Stanford, "God in Modern Poetry," in *Mansions of the Spirit: Essays in Literature and Religion*, ed. George A. Panichas (New York: Hawthorn Books, 1967), 290.

51. Ibid., 293.

52. Ibid., 295. For additional discussions of approaches to God and prayer in poetry, see Henri Bremond, *Prayer and Poetry: A Contribution to Poetical Theory*, trans. Algar Thorold (London: Burns Oates and Washbourne, 1927); David Daiches, *God and the Poets* (Oxford: Clarendon, 1984); Helen Gardner, *Religion and Literature* (Oxford: Oxford University Press, 1971); Charles I. Glicksberg, *Literature and Religion: A Study in Conflict* (Dallas: Southern Methodist University Press, 1960); Giles Gunn, "Literature and Religion," in *Interrelations of Literature*, ed. Jean-Pierre Barricelli and Joseph Gibaldi (New York: Modern Language Association of America, 1982), 47–66; Friedrich Heiler, *Prayer: A Study in the History and Psychology of Religion* (Oxford: Oxford University Press, 1932); Stanley Romaine Hopper, *The Way of Transfiguration: Religious Imagination as Theopoiesis* (Louisville, Ky.: Westminster/John Knox, 1992); William James, *The Varieties of Religious Experience* (1902; repr., Cambridge, Mass.: Harvard University Press, 1985); William T. Noon, *Poetry and Prayer* (New Brunswick, N.J.: Rutgers University Press, 1967); Paul Ricoeur, *Figuring the Sacred: Religion, Narrative, and Imagination*, trans. David Pellauer (Minneapolis, Minn.: Fortress, 1995); George Santayana, *Interpretations of Poetry and Religion* (New York: Charles Scribner's Sons, 1900); Nathan A. Scott, Jr., "Poetry and Prayer" in *Literature and Religion*, ed. Giles B. Gunn (New York: Harper and Row, 1971), 191–210; Helen C. White, *Prayer and Poetry* (Latrobe, Pa.: Archabbey, 1960).

53. Nathan A. Scott, Jr., *The Wild Prayer of Longing: Poetry and the Sacred* (New Haven, Conn.: Yale University Press, 1971), 48.

54. Ibid., 56.

55. Langdon Gilkey, *Naming the Whirlwind: The Renewal of God-Language* (Indianapolis and New York: Bobbs Merrill Co., 1969), 310–311. David Tracy suggests an explanation for the intricate connection between despair and hope, doubt and faith, by declaring that "[t]he religious dimension is most clearly recognized in such limit experiences as (negatively) anxiety or (positively) fundamental trust in the very worthwhileness of our existence." David Tracy, "Metaphor and Religion: The Test Case of Christian Texts," in *On Metaphor*, ed. Sheldon Sacks (Chicago: University of Chicago Press, 1979), 93. The intricate connection between despair and hope in the human psyche may account, to some extent, for the sudden shift from lament to praise in so many biblical psalms.

56. Steiner, *Real Presences*, 221.

57. Ibid.

58. Colin Falck, *Myth, Truth and Literature: Towards a True Post-modernism* (Cambridge: Cambridge University Press, 1989), 139.

59. Ibid., 118.

60. Ibid., 121.

61. Ibid., 134. Emphasis in the original.

1. Zelda Mishkovsky

1. This biographical background is based on information found in Hamutal Bar-Yosef, *Al shirat Zelda* (Tel Aviv: Hakibbutz Hameuchad, 1988), 7–19; Marcia Falk,

"Strange Plant: Nature and Spirituality in the Poetry of Zelda, A Translator's Reading," *Religion and Literature* 23, no. 3 (1991): 97–108; the Introduction by Marcia Falk to Zelda Mishkovsky, *The Spectacular Difference: Selected Poems* (Cincinnati, Ohio: Hebrew Union College Press, 2004), 1–23; the biographical sketch by Zerubavel Gilad in Zelda Mishkovsky, *Shirei Zelda* (Tel Aviv: Hakibbutz Hameuchad, 1985), 231–236; and Rachel Hollander-Steingart, "Zelda—shirah—pegishah," *Zehut* 3 (1983): 232–236. The notes by Marcia Falk in the back of Zelda Mishkovsky, *The Spectacular Difference* helped me to identify some references to classical texts in Zelda's poetry.

2. Bar-Yosef, *Al shirat Zelda*, 14.
3. Mishkovsky, *Shirei Zelda*, 234–235.
4. Ibid.
5. Hollander-Steingart, "Zelda—shirah—pegishah," 232.
6. Bar-Yosef, *Al shirat Zelda*, 24.
7. Mishkovsky, *Shirei Zelda*, 235.
8. Bar-Yosef, *Al shirat Zelda*, 142.
9. Ibid., 143.
10. Falk, "Strange Plant," 106.
11. Bar-Yosef, *Al shirat Zelda*, 76.
12. Ibid., 43–45.
13. Ibid., 136.
14. Ibid., 140.
15. Ibid.
16. Ibid., 135.
17. Hollander-Steingart, "Zelda—shirah—pegishah," 235.

18. See Bar-Yosef, *Al shirat Zelda*, 133–135, 148: "The possibility [in Zelda's poetry] to discover in every situation and every experience—even the most trivial—'signs of God'…and to understand them as part of the dynamics of the contact between the upper and lower worlds," as noted by Bar Yosef (135), can certainly be seen to be in the spirit of Hasidic teachings. See also Dov Sadan, *Bein she'ilah leqinyan* (Tel Aviv: Mifal-Hashichpul, Tel Aviv University, 1968), 155–157; Tsevi Tsameret, "'Sovev halev binetivo ha'afel—vehozer el ha'Elohim' o: optimiyyut ufesimiyyut besifrah shel Zelda *Hashoni hamarhiv*," *Petahim* 57–58 (1982): 87–90; Aryeh Wineman, "Hedim shel hasidut Bratslav beshirat Zelda," *Shdemot* 65 (1978): 57–61; Ora Yaniv, "Hahavayyah hadatit beshirat Zelda: motivim, dimmuyyim, utemunot kiyesod po'eti le'itsuv hayahas ani-olam" (Master's thesis, Bar Ilan University, 1990).

19. For a discussion of the theme of mortality in Zelda's poetry, see Aryeh Wineman, "Death, Redeeming Moments, and God in Zelda's Later Poems," *Conservative Judaism* 56, no. 2 (2004): 60–69.

20. Mishkovsky, *Shirei Zelda*, 170. The poem was published in the collection *Hashoni hamarhiv* (Tel Aviv: Hakibbutz Hameuchad, 1981). An alternative translation of this poem, by Marcia Falk, "The Fine Light of My Peace," may be found in Mishkovsky, *The Spectacular Difference*, 189.

21. Marcia Falk suggests that the expression "letters from on high" (*otiyyot shel malah*) alludes to the kabbalistic notion of "the supernal letters, ideal forms of the letters of the alphabet through which God is believed to have created the universe." Mishkovsky, *The Spectacular Difference*, 264.

22. Mishkovsky, *Shirei Zelda*, 192. The poem was published in the collection *Hashoni hamarhiv* (1981). An alternative translation of this poem, by Marcia Falk, "Island," may be found in Mishkovsky, *The Spectacular Difference*, 213.

23. Marcia Falk suggests that the poet is alluding here to a story told in the Talmud

(Bava Batra 73b) about Rabbah bar Bar Hana. Mishkovsky, *The Spectacular Difference*, 266. The text of the story reads: "Rabbah bar Bar Hana further stated: Once we were travelling on board a ship and saw a fish whose back was covered with sand out of which grew grass. Thinking it was dry land we went up and baked and cooked upon its back. When, however, its back was heated it turned, and had not the ship been nearby we should have been drowned." This translation, by Israel W. Slotki, is from *Baba Bathra* vol. 1 (London: Soncino, 1935), 291.

24. This interpretation follows a note to Isaiah 27:1 in *JPS Hebrew-English Tanakh*, 2nd ed. (Philadelphia: The Jewish Publication Society, 1999), 902.

25. Bar-Yosef writes: "The 'here and now' revealed to the eye is perceived as a deceptive appearance, lacking stable actuality. The things that are revealed are a chorus of voices recounting that which is hidden behind them . . . . There is no possibility of grabbing onto the passing concrete existence and finding in it existential redemption." Bar-Yosef, *Al shirat Zelda*, 90–91. Ora Yaniv suggests that the hidden realm beneath the earth can be understood as the hidden dimension of divinity of which mysticism teaches. Yaniv, "Haḥavayyah hadatit beshirat Zelda," 53.

26. Mishkovsky, *Shirei Zelda*, 189. The poem was published in the collection *Hashoni hamarhiv* (1981). An alternative translation of this poem, by Marcia Falk, "There was something startling . . . ," may be found in Mishkovsky, *The Spectacular Difference*, 205.

27. As Marcia Falk notes, the expression "that His mercies never cease," as it appears in the poem, may be found in Lamentations 3:22. Mishkovsky, *The Spectacular Difference*, 265.

28. Mishkovsky, *Shirei Zelda*, 202. The poem was published in the collection *Hashoni hamarhiv* (1981).

29. Bar-Yosef notes that Zelda tends to use images of kingship (*malkhut*) to signify an "ideal internal state" in which one has overcome despair. Bar-Yosef, *Al shirat Zelda*, 32.

30. Bar-Yosef writes: "Material things are revealed here as uncovered, lacking all meaning, bereft of a metaphorical or symbolic dimension, and so they are like a cruel sketch, bereft of color and bereft of life. 'The universe's skeleton' is uncovered in all of its cruelty. This is a world in which it is impossible to live; it is only possible to die of fear. In order to continue to exist it is necessary to arrive, on the basis of examining those very facts, at 'a new perception of the Creator.' Precisely the light, the shining (*nogah*) of the sunset, is what reveals the attribute of judgment in the universe, for it is *nogah* of *qelippat nogah* (a Kabbalistic-Habad concept that describes an intermediate realm between holiness and impurity), while the attribute of grace is revealed out of 'a new perception,' which comes into being when 'the soul soars' above concrete things." Bar-Yosef, *Al shirat Zelda*, 42.

31. Mishkovsky, *Shirei Zelda*, 33. The poem was published in the collection *Penay* (Tel Aviv: Hakibbutz Hameuchad, 1967). An alternative translation of this poem, by Marcia Falk, "I Am a Dead Bird," may be found in Mishkovsky, *The Spectacular Difference*, 37.

32. Bar-Yosef, *Al shirat Zelda*, 54.

33. Ibid., 48.

34. Ibid., 32.

35. Ibid., 121.

36. Bar-Yosef notes that this epithet for God appears at the end of the blessing "Borei nefashot rabbot," traditionally recited by Jews after consuming certain foods and drinks. Bar-Yosef, *Al shirat Zelda*, 54.

37. Ibid., 37.

38. Ibid., 54.

39. Mishkovsky, *Shirei Zelda*, 89. The poem was published in the collection *Hakarmel ha'iy-nireh* (Tel Aviv: Hakibbutz Hameuchad, 1971). An alternative translation

of this poem, by Marcia Falk, "Be Not Far," may be found in Mishkovsky, *The Spectacular Difference*, 107.

40. Mishkovsky, *The Spectacular Difference*, 258. The expression "be not far" without "from me" following it appears in Psalms 22:20.

41. In Avraham Even-Shoshan, *Hamillon hehadash* (Jerusalem: Kiryat Sefer, 1985), 1101, the *parsah* is said to be approximately four and one-half kilometers.

42. Yaniv writes: "This is expressed in the picture of the comforters stopping by the gate, restricted and withdrawn before the burden of terror; and this is the absolute truth: no one can narrow the distance that separates one from one who is wounded by a tragedy." Yaniv, "Hahavayyah hadatit beshirat Zelda," 93.

43. Yaniv writes: "Zelda sees in Job's religious stance an approach with which it is worthy to identify. This stance sees nothing wrong in the protest of humanity against divinity for the lack of justice in life from the human point of view." Yaniv, "Hahavayyah hadatit beshirat Zelda," 114.

44. Ibid., 95.

45. Mishkovsky, *Shirat Zelda*, 141. The poem was published in the collection *Halo har halo esh* (Tel Aviv: Hakibbutz Hameuchad, 1977). An alternative translation of this poem, by Marcia Falk, "The shadow of the white mountain . . . ," may be found in Mishkovsky, *The Spectacular Difference*, 161, 163.

46. Bar-Yosef, *Al shirat Zelda*, 158.

47. Mishkovsky, *The Spectacular Difference*, 262.

48. Yaniv, "Hahavayyah hadatit beshirat Zelda," 125.

49. Bar-Yosef, *Al shirat Zelda*, 55.

50. Mishkovsky, *Shirat Zelda*, 122. The poem was published in the collection *Al tirhaq* (Tel Aviv: Hakibbutz Hameuchad, 1974). An alternative translation of this poem, by Marcia Falk, "All Night I Wept," may be found in Mishkovsky, *The Spectacular Difference*, 145.

51. Mishkovsky, *Shirat Zelda*, 140. The poem was published in the collection *Halo har halo esh* (1977).

52. Mishkovsky, *Shirat Zelda*, 199. The poem was published in the collection *Hashoni hamarhiv* (1981). An alternative translation of this poem, by Marcia Falk, "Heavy Silence," may be found in Mishkovsky, *The Spectacular Difference*, 221.

2. Yehuda Amichai

1. This biographical background is based on Glenda Abramson, *The Writing of Yehuda Amichai: A Thematic Approach* (Albany: State University of New York Press, 1989), 13–16; Joseph Cohen, *Voices of Israel* (Albany: State University of New York Press, 1990), 9–43; Dan Omer, "Ba'arets halohetet hazot, millim tserikhot lihyot tsel . . . ," *Prozah* 25 (1978): 4–11; and Yehudit Tsvik, ed., *Yehuda Amichai: mivhar ma'amarei biqqoret al yetsirato* (Tel Aviv: Hakibbutz Hameuchad, 1988), 237–239.

2. Yehuda Amichai, *Baruah hanora'ah hazot* (1961; repr., Jerusalem and Tel Aviv: Schocken, 1985), 133.

3. Ortsion Bartana, "Mahpkhan simpati: Yehuda Amichai—sikkum beinayim," *Nativ* 13, no. 6 (2000): 109.

4. Ibid.

5. Ibid., 108.

6. Eliezer Cohen, "'Zavit hare'iyah hi Elohei hasdi': Yehuda Amichai meshorer al Elohim," *De'ot* 10 (2001): 31.

7. Bartana, "Mahpkhan simpati," 111.

8. Boaz Arpaly, "On the Political Significance of Amichai's Poetry," in *The Experienced Soul: Studies in Amichai*, ed. Glenda Abramson (Boulder, Colo.: Westview, 1997), 41.

9. Shlomo Sadeh, "Hatsad hasheni shel haqodesh vehaḥol beshirat Amichai," *Itton* 77 290 (2004): 18.

10. Ibid.

11. Ibid., 19.

12. Eliezer Cohen, "'Zavit hare'iyah hi Elohei ḥasdi,'" 31.

13. Rafi Weichert, "Baginnah hatsibborit shel Elohim: qeri'ah beshirei Yehuda Amichai hamuqdamim vehame'uḥarim," *Itton* 77 248 (2000): 26.

14. Ibid.

15. Dan Miron, "Reshito shel Yehuda Amichai," *Hadoar* 79, no. 22 (2000): 19.

16. Ibid.

17. Admiel Kosman, "Mayim einam yekholim laḥazor biteshuvah: he'arah al megillat Amichai," *Haaretz*, 20 October 2000.

18. Esther Fuchs, *Encounters With Israeli Authors* (Marblehead, Mass.: Micah Publications, 1982), 90–91.

19. Cohen, *Voices of Israel*, 35.

20. Ibid.

21. David Montenegro, "Yehuda Amichai: An Interview," *American Poetry Review* 16, no. 6 (1987): 20.

22. Yehuda Amichai, "Yoman," *Moznayim* 29, no. 1 (1969): 22.

23. Boaz Arpaly, "Millim 'shelo mikan velo me'akhshav': al ma'amadam shel arakhim beshirat Yehuda Amichai," *Hasifrut* 29 (1979): 50. This article later appeared in a revised version as chapter nine of Boaz Arpaly, *Haperakhim veha'agartal: shirat Amichai, 1948–1968: mivneh, mashma'ut, po'etiqah* (Tel Aviv: Hakibbutz Hameuchad, 1986).

24. Barukh Kurzweil, "Shirah otobiyyografit bamidbar hagadol: he'arot le*Shirim, 1948–1962*," in Tsvik, ed., *Yehuda Amichai*, 83.

25. Ibid., 89.

26. Ibid.

27. Ibid., 84.

28. Ibid. Kurzweil does not find Amichai's ironic use of biblical and liturgical texts to be completely acceptable. He considers some of Amichai's treatment of biblical texts to be "a mere associative game [whose] purpose was not to establish a new reality, but [it was] rather a game whose purpose was grotesque effect" (90).

29. Abramson, *The Writing of Yehuda Amichai*, 56.

30. "Eikh attah maggia leshir?" (Interview with Yehuda Amichai), *Ḥadarim* 6 (1987): 132.

31. Ibid.

32. Arpaly, "Millim 'shelo mikan velo me'akhshav,'" 50.

33. Abramson, *The Writing of Yehuda Amichai*, 59.

34. Ibid., 63

35. Ibid.

36. Arpaly, "Millim 'shelo mikan velo me'akhshav,'" 50.

37. Abramson, *The Writing of Yehuda Amichai*, 59.

38. Ibid., 60–61.

39. Chana Kronfeld, "'The Wisdom of Camouflage': Between Rhetoric and Philosophy in Amichai's Poetic System," *Prooftexts* 10 (1990): 472.

40. Weichert, "Baginnah hatsibborit shel Elohim," 28.

41. See discussions of references to God in Amichai's poetry in Nili Scharf Gold, *Lo*

kaberosh: gilgulei imazhim vetavniyyot beshirat Yehuda Amichai (Jerusalem and Tel Aviv: Schocken, 1994).

42. Yehuda Amichai, *Shirim 1948–1962*, 1962 reprint (Jerusalem and Tel Aviv: Schocken, 1977), 65–66. The poem was published in Amichai's collection *Bemerḥaq shetei tiqvot* (Tel Aviv: Hakibbutz Hameuchad, 1958). An alternative translation, by Benjamin and Barbara Harshav, "God's Hand in the World," may be found in Yehuda Amichai, *Yehuda Amichai: A Life of Poetry, 1948–1994*, trans. Benjamin and Barbara Harshav (New York: HarperCollins, 1994), 29. Another alternative translation, by Chana Bloch and Stephen Mitchell, "God's Hand in the World," may be found in Yehuda Amichai, *The Selected Poetry of Yehuda Amichai*, trans. Chana Bloch and Stephen Mitchell (Berkeley and Los Angeles: University of California Press, 1996), 10.

43. The positive cultural connotation of the *shikkunim* during the early years of the State of Israel was captured most effectively in the Israeli film *Salaḥ Shabbati* (1964), in which North African Jewish immigrants engage in acts of desperation in order to force the authorities to give them an apartment in such a housing development to replace the substandard living conditions of their transit camp.

44. Amichai, *Shirim 1948–1962*, 69–70. The poem was published in Amichai's collection *Bemerḥaq shetei tiqvot* (1958). My analysis draws in part on interpretive points in Naomi B. Sokoloff, "On Amichai's *El male raḥamim*," *Prooftexts* 4 (1984): 127–140. An alternative translation, by Glenda Abramson, "O Lord Full of Mercy," may be found in Abramson, *The Writing of Yehuda Amichai*, 56–57. Another alternative translation, by Benjamin and Barbara Harashav, "God Full of Mercy," may be found in Amichai, *Yehuda Amichai: A Life of Poetry*, 31.

45. Abramson writes: "The recurring mannerism of the repeated 'I, who' and other examples of word play (*geviyyot min hageva'ot, melekh hamelah*) add a rhetorical stance to the analysis in the poem of some of the personal reasons for the speaker's bitterness. 'I, who counted angels' footsteps' is a similar rhetorical flourish, pointing to angels who are not seen but who represent a vanished world of religious or aesthetic unity." Abramson, *The Writing of Yehuda Amichai*, 57.

46. Amichai, *Shirim 1948–1962*, 71–72. The poem was published in Amichai's collection *Bemerḥaq shetei tiqvot* (1958). My analysis draws in part on interpretive points in Abramson, *The Writing of Yehuda Amichai*, 39–42. A literal translation of the Hebrew title of the poem, "Vehi tehillatekha" would be: "And It Is Your Praise." This translation, however, does not convey the full meaning of the expression in Hebrew, which is that the various attributes and actions of God give people reason to praise Him. An alternative translation, by Glenda Abramson, "And This Is Your Praise," may be found in Abramson, *The Writing of Yehuda Amichai*, 39–40. Another alternative translation, by Benjamin and Barbara Harshav, "And This Is Your Glory," may be found in Amichai, *Yehuda Amichai: A Life of Poetry*, 32. Another alternative translation, by Chana Bloch and Stephen Mitchell, "And That Is Your Glory" may be found in Amichai, *The Selected Poetry of Yehuda Amichai*, 11.

47. As Glenda Abramson observes: "This poem, which through its refrain suggests a parody of the liturgical doxology, is built on the strong contrasts which are the purpose of the original [*piyyut* on which it is based]: 'faithful and mighty angels' are compared in the prayer with 'dust-made men,' 'roaring camps of angelic hosts' with 'men whose glory fades away.' These juxtapositions, maintained throughout the prayer, multiply the praise of God, verse by hyperbolic verse, each of which then concludes with the refrain 'And this is your praise.' Amichai's contrasts are less exalted, occurring not among the heavenly host but solely within the confines of the experience of his lyric 'I.'" Abramson, *The Writing of Yehuda Amichai*, 39.

48. Ibid., 40–41.

49. Ibid., 55.

50. Ibid., 41.

51. Ibid., 42.

52. Yehuda Amichai, *Patuaḥ sagur patuaḥ* (Jerusalem and Tel Aviv: Schocken, 1998), 8. An alternative translation, by Chana Bloch and Chana Kronfeld, identified as poem number 7 of "Gods Change, Prayers Are Here to Stay," may be found in Yehuda Amichai, *Open Closed Open*, trans. Chana Bloch and Chana Kronfeld (New York: Harcourt, 2000), 41.

53. Amichai, *Patuaḥ sagur patuaḥ*, 18–19. An alternative translation, by Chana Bloch and Chana Kronfeld, identified as poem number 23 of "Gods Change, Prayers Are Here to Stay," may be found in Amichai, *Open Closed Open*, 47–48.

54. See Weichert, "Baginnah hatsibborit shel Elohim," 29. In "Edut," by Pagis, the speaker describes himself as a Holocaust victim rising to God as "smoke to omnipotent smoke / that has no body or form." Dan Pagis, *Gilgul* (Ramat Gan: Massada, 1970), 24. For a translation of this poem, by Stephen Mitchell, "Testimony," see Dan Pagis, *Points of Departure*, trans. Stephen Mitchell (Philadelphia: Jewish Publication Society, 1981), 25.

55. Yehuda Amichai, *Akhshav bara'ash* (Jerusalem and Tel Aviv: Schocken, 1968), 36. An alternative translation, by Assia Gutmann, "God's Fate," may be found in Yehuda Amichai, *Poems*, trans. Assia Gutmann (New York and Evanston, Ill.: Harper and Row, 1969), 26.

56. Hillel Barzel, *Shirah umorashah* (Tel Aviv: Eked, 1971), 66.

57. Amichai, *Patuaḥ sagur patuaḥ*, 6–7. An alternative translation, by Chana Bloch and Chana Kronfeld, identified as poem number 3 of "Gods Change, Prayers Are Here to Stay," may be found in Amichai, *Open Closed Open*, 40.

58. Amichai, *Patuaḥ sagur patuaḥ*, 7. An alternative translation, by Chana Bloch and Chana Kronfeld, identified as poem number 4 of "Gods Change, Prayers Are Here to Stay," may be found in Amichai, *Open Closed Open*, 40.

59. Amichai, *Patuaḥ sagur patuaḥ*, 8. An alternative translation, by Chana Bloch and Chana Kronfeld, identified as poem number 6 of "Gods Change, Prayers Are Here to Stay," may be found in Amichai, *Open Closed Open*, 41.

60. Amichai, *Akhshav bara'ash*, 29–30.

61. Ibid., 49–50.

62. Abramson writes: "The spokesman begs God for a rest from disaster, even for the brief time between the two statements, each of which heralds some new catastrophe and each of which is brought with breathless speed, pointing to the multitude of problems, the rapidity of their occurrence, one following on the heels of the other, in modern life." Abramson, *The Writing of Yehuda Amichai*, 37.

63. Amichai, *Patuaḥ sagur patuaḥ*, 10–11. Alternative translations of these poems, by Chana Bloch and Chana Kronfeld, identified as poems 10, 11, and 12, respectively, of "Gods Change, Prayers Are Here to Stay," may be found in Amichai, *Open Closed Open*, 42.

3. Asher Reich

1. This biographical background is based on Asher Reich, "Al habiyyopo'etiqah shelli: hayaldut kegalut," in *Me'ayin naḥalti et shiri: sofrim umeshorerim medabberim al meqorot hashra'ah*, ed. Ruth Kartun-Blum (Tel Aviv: Yedioth Ahronoth, 2002), 269–285; Gershon Shaked, ed., *Hebrew Writers: A General Dictionary* (Ramat Gan: The Institute for the Translation of Hebrew Literature, 1993), 98; Hana Yaoz and Itamar Yaoz-Kest,

"Im hameshorer Asher Reich," *Pesifas* 33 (1996): 4–5; Itamar Yaoz-Kest, "Re'ayon im Asher Reich," *Pesifas* 44 (2000): 4–7; and "Shireshet" Web site (http://www.snunit.k12.il). An introduction to the poetry of Asher Reich, accompanied by selected translations into English of some of his poems, may be found in Yair Mazor, *Asher Reich: Portrait of a Hebrew Poet* (Madison: University of Wisconsin Press, 2003).

2. Reich, "Al habiyyopo'etiqah shelli," 269.

3. Ibid., 273.

4. Ibid., 270.

5. Ibid., 271.

6. Yaoz and Yaoz-Kest, "Im hameshorer Asher Reich," 4.

7. Ibid.

8. Ibid.

9. Reich, "Al habiyyopo'etiqah shelli," 276.

10. Yaoz-Kest, "Re'ayon im Asher Reich," 5.

11. Ibid.

12. Ibid., 6.

13. Reich, "Al habiyyopo'etiqah shelli," 270.

14. Asher Reich, *Zerikhat halaylah* (Tel Aviv: Eked, 1972), 32.

15. Ibid., 33.

16. Asher Reich, *Temunat matsav* (Tel Aviv: Hakibbutz Hameuchad, 1975), 73.

17. See Avraham Even-Shoshan, *Hamillon hehadash* (Jerusalem: Kiryat Sefer, 1985), 661.

18. Asher Reich, *Mareh maqom* (Ramat Gan: Massada, 1978), 82.

19. Asher Reich, *Seder hashirim* (Tel Aviv: Sifriat Poalim, 1986), 53.

20. Asher Reich, *Atid domem* (Tel Aviv: Keshev Publishing House, 2002), 9.

21. Marcus Jastrow, *A Dictionary of the Targumim, the Talmud Babli and Yerushalmi, and the Midrashic Literature* (New York: Pardes Publishing House, 1950), 1071; Even-Shoshan, *Hamillon hehadash*, 735.

22. Reich, *Atid domem*, 26.

23. "Black Hole," *Encyclopaedia Britannica*, 2004, Encyclopaedia Britannica Online, 30 June 2004 (http://search.eb.com./eb/article?eu=15686).

24. *Merriam-Webster's Collegiate Dictionary*, 10th ed. (Springfield, Mass., 1997), 119.

25. Asher Reich, *Bashanah hashevi'it lineduday* (Tel Aviv: Eked, 1963), 35.

26. Ibid., 42.

27. Reich, *Temunat matsav*, 60.

28. Ibid., 78.

29. See, for example, the translation in *JPS Hebrew-English Tanakh*, 2nd ed. (Philadelphia: Jewish Publication Society, 1999).

4. Rivka Miriam

1. This biographical background is based on Haim Chertok, *We Are All Close: Conversations with Israeli Writers* (New York: Fordham University Press, 1989), 133–147; Anat Hadar, "Sihah im hameshoreret hayerushalmit Rivka Miriam," *Alei Siah* 27–28 (1990, recorded in 1988): 233–238; Rivka Miriam, "Ribbono shel olam, mah hasheqet hazeh? mah hester hapanim hazeh?" in *Massa el tokh atsmenu: benei nitsolei hasho'ah medabberim*, ed. Shoshana Tsingel (Tel Aviv: Elisar, 1985), 157–165; Rivka Miriam, "Et hahafradah," *Apirion* 15 (1989): 48–49; Yehudit Rotem, "Re'ayon: Rivka Miriam," *Moznayim* 69, no. 5 (1995): 35; Itamar Yaoz-Kest and Hana Yaoz, "Im Rivka Miriam," *Pesifas* 35 (1997): 1–3;

Dorit Yisrael, "Halikhah liqrat: re'ayon im Rivka Miriam," *Dimui* 17 (1999): 30–32; "Rivka Miriam—meshoreret vetsayyeret: ani basar mibesaram," *Apirion* 2 (1983/1984): 50–51; and interviews of the poet that I conducted at her home in Jerusalem in the summer of 1995 and in the summer of 2002.

2. Yaoz-Kest and Yaoz, "Im Rivka Miriam," 3.

3. Miriam, "Ribbono shel olam," 163.

4. Ibid.

5. Yisrael, "Halikhah liqrat," 30.

6. Miriam, "Ribbono shel olam," 157.

7. Yisrael, "Halikhah liqrat," 30.

8. Miriam, "Ribbono shel olam," 157.

9. Yaoz-Kest and Yaoz, "Im Rivka Miriam," 2.

10. Miriam, "Ribbono shel olam," 161.

11. Ibid.

12. Yisrael, "Halikhah liqrat," 30.

13. Ibid., 31.

14. Miriam, "Ribbono shel olam," 165.

15. Ibid.

16. Miriam, "Et hahafradah," 49.

17. Ibid.

18. Ibid.

19. Ibid.

20. Yaoz Kest and Yaoz, "Im Rivka Miriam," 3.

21. Ibid., 1.

22. Hadar, "Siḥah im hameshoreret," 238.

23. Ibid.

24. Chertok, *We Are All Close*, 136.

25. Rivka Miriam, *Haqolot liqratam* (Jerusalem and Tel Aviv: Dvir, 1982), 44.

26. Rivka Miriam, *Mishirei immot ha'even* (Tel Aviv: Sifriat Poalim, 1988), 30.

27. Rivka Miriam, *Maqom namer* (Jerusalem: Carmel, 1994), 61.

28. Miriam, *Haqolot liqratam*, 35.

29. Ibid., 48.

30. Ibid., 59.

31. Miriam, *Mishirei immot ha'even*, 44.

32. Ibid., 50.

33. Rivka Miriam, *Miqarov hayah hamizraḥ* (Jerusalem: Carmel, 1996), 76.

34. Ibid., 77.

5. Hava Pinhas-Cohen

1. This biographical background is based on Vered Levy-Barzilai, "Bo'etet lekhol hakivvunim," *Haaretz*, 18 January 2006; Hava Pinhas-Cohen, "Em, ahuvah, moledet," *Panim* 7 (1998): 102–110; Leah Snir, "Me'ever lashorashim haḥatukhim," Alei Siaḥ 41 (1998): 59–72; "Siḥah im Hava Pinhas-Cohen," *Pesifas* 29 (1995): 14–16; the Web site of the Institute for the Translation of Hebrew Literature (http://www.ithl.org.il); and an interview of the poet which I conducted in Jerusalem in June 2002.

2. Pinhas-Cohen, "Em, ahuvah, moledet," 105.

3. "Siḥah im Hava Pinhas-Cohen," 15.

4. Snir, "Me'ever lashorashim haḥatukhim," 69–70.

5. Levy-Barzilai, "Bo'etet lekhol hakivvunim."

6. "Siḥah im Hava Pinhas-Cohen," 70.

7. Ibid.

8. Ibid., 60.

9. Pinhas-Cohen, "Em, ahuvah, moledet," 104.

10. Snir, "Me'ever lashorashim haḥatukhim," 67.

11. "Siḥah im Hava Pinhas-Cohen," 15.

12. "Datiyyut veḥiloniyyut: arba'ah monologim," *Moznayim* 65, no. 6 (1991): 24.

13. For more information on Beit Morasha of Jerusalem, see their Web site (http://www.bmj.org.il/).

14. "Datiyyut veḥiloniyyut," 24.

15. Ibid.

16. Pinhas-Cohen, "Em, ahuvah, moledet," 109.

17. Hava Pinhas-Cohen, *Hatseva be'iqqar* (Tel Aviv: Am Oved, 1990), 52. The poet has dated the poem 4 Ḥeshvan 5750.

18. See the examples in Avraham Even-Shoshan, *Hamillon heḥadash* (Jerusalem: Kiryan Sefer, 1985), 488.

19. Pinhas-Cohen, *Hatseva be'iqqar*, 55. The poet has dated the poem 4 Ḥeshvan 5750.

20. Hava Pinhas-Cohen, *Massa ayyalah* (Tel Aviv: Hakibbutz Hameuchad, 1994), 7. An alternative translation, by Miryam Glazer, "The Ineffable Name," may be found in *Dreaming the Actual: Contemporary Fiction and Poetry by Israeli Women Writers*, ed. Miryam Glazer (Albany: State University of New York Press, 2000), 317–318.

21. Pinhas-Cohen, *Massa ayyalah*, 63.

22. Hava Pinhas-Cohen, *Nehar veshikheḥah* (Tel Aviv: Hakibbutz Hameuchad, 1998), 34.

23. Pinhas-Cohen, *Massa ayyalah*, 30. An alternative translation of the poem, by Ruth Kartun-Blum and Sonya Grubber, "Entreaty," along with an analysis of the poem, by Ruth Kartun Blum, in the context of other poems on the Binding of Isaac theme by contemporary Israeli women poets may be found in Ruth Kartun-Blum, "Political Mothers: Women's Voice and the Binding of Isaac in Israeli Poetry," in *History and Literature: New Readings of Jewish Texts in Honor of Arnold J. Band*, ed. William Cutter and David C. Jacobson (Providence, R.I.: Brown Judaic Studies, 2002), 419–438.

24. Pinhas-Cohen, *Massa ayyalah*, 33. In a recent interview that she conducted with Pinhas-Cohen, Vered Levy-Barzilai conveys what the poet told her about the genesis of this poem: "Hava Pinhas-Cohen wrote this poem when her daughter, Kineret, was a baby. . . . She remembers herself then as a young, frightened mother, in great distress. She got up early in the morning before all the other members of the household 'so that I would have an hour to myself before I nursed,' agitated, full of worries, unable to find relief for her soul. 'My panic became increasingly intense,' she relates. 'My need to be a perfect mother, free of pressures and concerns, along with my need to write and to create. And all this created in me terrible tension, anger, fear, obligation, responsibility, fright, guilt feelings, all on my shoulders. . . .' She took up the prayer book that was lying on the kitchen table and came across a prayer for before the morning service. But then she felt that something was bubbling up from within her, 'the words burst out of me, undermining the solidity and the security that the canonical prayer book grants,' she says, 'security, as it were, almost against every human anxiety, out of unequivocal faith. But within me, a young mother, faith was cracked by fears.' She allowed the words to come out and discovered how 'only from between the cracks are words likely to come out that have the power to teach that the partner of fear is love, and that faith is a prayer for the ability of the two to live together.'" Levy-Barzilai, "Bo'etet lekhol hakivvunim."

25. Pinhas-Cohen, *Nehar veshikhehah*, 74.

26. Hava Pinhas-Cohen, *Shirei Orfe'ah* (Tel Aviv: Hakibbutz Hameuchad, 2000), 77.

6. Admiel Kosman

1. This biographical background is based on Neri Livneh, "Manoa hippus," *Haaretz*, 3 May 2002. All quotations are from passages in the abridged version of the article in the English edition of *Haaretz*, titled "Member of the Tribe," except for one passage found only in the original Hebrew version, which I translated. The background is also based on Itamar Yaoz-Kest, "Sihah im hameshorer Admiel Kosman," *Pesifas* 25 (1994): 6–11; an interview of Kosman that I conducted in his office at Bar Ilan University in June 2002; and a communication from him to me in February 2005.

2. Yaoz-Kest, "Sihah im hameshorer Admiel Kosman," 8.

3. Ibid., 9.

4. Admiel Kosman, "Forget the Jews, But Judaism Is Wonderful," *Haaretz* (English edition), 14 June 2002. The Hebrew version of the review appeared in *Haaretz*, 5 June 2002.

5. Livneh, "Member of the Tribe."

6. Yaoz-Kest, "Sihah im hameshorer Admiel Kosman," 8.

7. Ibid.

8. Ibid., 9.

9. Livneh, "Member of the Tribe."

10. Ibid.

11. Ibid.

12. Ibid.

13. Yaoz-Kest, "Sihah im hameshorer Admiel Kosman," 8.

14. Livneh, "Member of the Tribe."

15. Ibid.

16. Livneh, "Manoa hippus."

17. Ibid.

18. Admiel Kosman, "Ha'omanut, hahalakhah vehadat," *Mahanayim* 10 (1995): 68.

19. Ibid., 63.

20. Ibid., 64.

21. Admiel Kosman, *Massekhet gevarim: rav vehaqatsav ve'od sippurim al gavriyyut, ahavah ve'otentiyyut besippur ha'aggadah uvasippur hahasidi* (Jerusalem: Keter, 2002), 8.

22. Admiel Kosman, *Ve'aharei morot ma'aseh hashir* (Givatayim: Massada, 1980), 7.

23. Amiel Kosman, *Bigdei nasikh* (Jerusalem: Keter, 1988), 54.

24. Ibid., 57. An alternative translation, "I Don't Sway When I Pray," may be found in *No Sign of Ceasefire: An Anthology of Contemporary Israeli Poetry*, ed. and trans. Warren Bargad and Stanley F. Chyet (Los Angeles: Skirball Cultural Center, 2002), 158.

25. Admiel Kosman, *Higanu lElohim* (Tel Aviv: Hakibbutz Hameuchad, 1998), 5–6. An alternative translation, "We Reached God," may be found in Bargad and Chyet, *No Sign of Ceasefire*, 169–170.

26. Nitza Gurevitch, "Hezyonot mehasug hashelishi," *Itton 77* 232 (1999): 7. Gurevtich identifies some of the biblical references I consider, but I have expanded her analysis to include others as well.

27. Dror Eydar, "Lamah tishqa, aleh, kashemesh, aleh od: Elohim bashirah ha'ivrit (B)," *Haaretz*, 28 May 2004.

28. Dror Eydar cites this imagery to condemn Kosman's approach to the writing of

poetry on religious themes: "Kosman thereby leads his readers from illusion to illusion while in the process of breaking up faith in God into word games and in effect emptying it of content. This way faith becomes a relative and dialectal matter and a game in which at times it [faith] is liable to be revealed as nothing less than a trick presented by the evil inclination." Eydar, "Lamah tishqa."

29. Kosman, *Higanu lElohim*, 43. See the comments on this poem in Hannah Yaoz, "Shirah, dat umeha'ah: Admiel Kosman," *Pesifas* 41 (1999): 27. An alternative translation, "Poem," may be found in Bargad and Chyet, *No Sign of Ceasefire*, 177.

30. Admiel Kosman, *Perush hadash bsd* (Tel Aviv: Hakibbutz Hameuchad, 2000), 10. See the analysis of this poem and other comments on the nature of Israeli poetry on religious themes in Dorit Lemberger, "Al gevulot mishtanim bashirah: datiyyut, hatrasah umah shebeineihen," *Aqdamot* 14 (2004): 131–154.

31. Admiel Kosman, *Mah ani yakhol* (Tel Aviv: Hakibbutz Hameuchad, 1995), 11. An alternative translation, "Something Hurts," by Lisa Katz, may be found in *The 5th International Poets' Festival: The Poems*, ed. Nissim Calderon and Anna Orgel (Jerusalem: Babel, 1999), 362, 364.

32. Kosman, *Higanu lElohim*, 25.

33. Ibid.

34. Ibid., 26–27. See the comments on this poem in Yaoz, "Shirah, dat umeha'ah," 28–29. An alternative translation, "Hymn," by Lisa Katz, may be found in *The 5th International Poets' Festival*, 364, 366. Another alternative translation, "*Piyyut*," may be found in Bargad and Chyet, *No Sign of Ceasefire*, 174–175.

35. Yaoz, "Shirah, dat umeha'ah," 28.

36. Admiel Kosman, *Higanu lElohim*, 36–37. I thank Admiel Kosman for insights about this poem.

37. See *Encylopaedia Judaica*, vol. 4 (Jerusalem: Keter, 1971), 986.

38. One rabbinic text traces this concept of the merit of the forefathers to Moses' attempt to convince God not to destroy the Israelites after the golden calf incident in the wilderness: "Remember Your oath in Your own name to Your servants, Abraham, Isaac, and Jacob, saying to them I will make your seed as numerous as the stars of the heaven, and I will give all of this land that I said I would give to your seed, and they will possess it forever" (Exodus 32:13). According to the rabbinic interpretation, Moses evoked not only God's oath to the patriarchs, but also the principle that since the patriarchs were righteous, their descendents should get special consideration: "Moses said, 'Master of the universe, were the forefathers righteous or wicked? Distinguish one from the other. If they were wicked it is appropriate for You to do this [destroy the Israelites], because the forefathers have not stored with You any [good] deeds. But, if they [the forefathers] were righteous, give them [the Israelites] credit for the [good] deeds of their forefathers" (Exodus Rabbah 44:9).

39. Admiel Kosman, *Higanu lElohim*, 44.

Conclusion

*The title of the conclusion is borrowed from the chapter "The Possibility of Religious Discourse in a Secular Age" in Langdon Gilkey, *Naming the Whirlwind: The Renewal of God-Language* (Indianapolis and New York: Bobbs-Merrill Co., 1969).

BIBLIOGRAPHY

Abramson, Glenda. "A Reasonable Rapture." *CCAR Journal* (Spring 2003): 49–68.

———. *The Writing of Yehuda Amichai: A Thematic Approach.* Albany: State University of New York Press, 1989.

Amichai, Yehuda. *Akhshav bara'ash.* Jerusalem and Tel Aviv: Schocken, 1968.

———. *Baruaḥ hanora'ah hazot.* 1961. Reprint, Jerusalem and Tel Aviv: Schocken, 1985.

———. *Bemerḥaq shetei tiqvot.* Tel Aviv: Hakibbutz Hameuchad, 1958.

———. *Open Closed Open.* Trans. Chana Bloch and Chana Kronfeld. New York: Harcourt, 2000.

———. *Patuaḥ sagur patuaḥ.* Jerusalem and Tel Aviv: Schocken, 1998.

———. *Poems.* Trans. Assia Gutmann. New York and Evanston, Ill.: Harper and Row, 1969.

———. *The Selected Poetry of Yehuda Amichai.* Trans. Chana Bloch and Stephen Mitchell. Berkeley and Los Angeles: University of California Press, 1996.

———. *Shirim 1948–1962.* 1962. Reprint, Jerusalem and Tel Aviv: Schocken, 1977.

———. *Yehuda Amichai: A Life of Poetry, 1948–1994.* Trans. Benjamin and Barbara Harshav. New York: HarperCollins, 1994.

———. "Yoman." *Moznayim* 29, no. 1 (1969): 18–23.

Arpaly, Boaz. *Haperakhim veha'agartal: shirat Amichai, 1948–1968: mivneh, mashma'ut, po'etiqah.* Tel Aviv: Hakibbutz Hameuchad, 1986.

———. "Millim 'shelo mikan velo me'akhshav': al ma'amadam shel arakhim beshirat Yehuda Amichai." *Hasifrut* 29 (1979): 44–57.

———. "On the Political Significance of Amichai's Poetry." In *The Experienced Soul: Studies in Amichai,* ed. Glenda Abramson, 27–50. Boulder, Colo.: Westview, 1997.

Band, Arnold J. "Hagaluy bakissuy." *Meḥqerei Yerushalayim Besifrut Ivrit* 10–11 (1989): 189–200.

Bargad, Warren, and Stanley F. Chyet, ed. and trans. *No Sign of Ceasefire: An Anthology of Contemporary Israeli Poetry.* Los Angeles: Skirball Cultural Center, 2002.

Bartana, Ortsion. "Mahpkhan simpati: Yehuda Amichai—sikkum beinayim." *Nativ* 13, no. 6 (2000): 107–111.

Bar-Yosef, Hamutal. *Al shirat Zelda.* Tel Aviv: Hakibbutz Hameuchad, 1988.

———. "Ha'im ha'adam ma'amin kefi sheḥatul melaqeq et parvato?" *Dimui* 15: 4–5.

———. "Yesh inyan." *Mashiv haruaḥ* 17 (2005): 170–172.

Barzel, Hillel. *Shirah umorashah.* Tel Aviv: Eked, 1971.

Bialik, Haim Nahman. "Revealment and Concealment in Language," trans. Jacob Sloan. In *Revealment and Concealment: Five Essays,* 11–26. Jerusalem: Ibis Editions, 2000.

Blatt, Avraham. *Orḥot emunim.* Tel Aviv: Moreshet, 1983.

Bremond, Henri. *Prayer and Poetry: A Contribution to Poetical Theory.* Trans. Algar Thorold. London: Burns Oates and Washbourne, 1927.

Brown, Frank Burch. *Transfiguration: Poetic Metaphor and the Languages of Religious Belief.* Chapel Hill: University of North Carolina Press, 1983.

Calderon, Nissim, and Anna Orgel, eds. *The 5th International Poets' Festival: The Poems.* Jerusalem: Babel, 1999.

Chertok, Haim. *We Are All Close: Conversations with Israeli Writers.* New York: Fordham University Press, 1989.

Cohen, Eliezer. "'Zavit hare'iyah hi Elohei ḥasdi': Yehuda Amichai meshorer al Elohim." *De'ot* 10 (2001): 31–33.

Cohen, Joseph. *Voices of Israel.* Albany: State University of New York Press, 1990.

Daiches, David. *God and the Poets.* Oxford: Clarendon Press, 1984.

Dan, Joseph. "The Sweet Voice of the Lord: Four Contemporary Israeli Poets." In *The Heart and the Fountain: An Anthology of Jewish Mystical Experiences,* 263–275. Oxford: Oxford University Press, 2002.

"Datiyyut veḥiloniyyut: arba'ah monologim." *Moznayim* 65, no. 6 (1991): 24–27.

Diamond, James S. *Barukh Kurzweil and Modern Hebrew Literature.* Chico, Calif.: Scholars Press, 1983.

"Eikh attah maggia leshir?" *Ḥadarim* 6 (1987): 129–134.

Eydar, Dror. "Eloah! gadlu ma'ayenot levavi—va'emas beferurei shirah: Elohim bashirah ha'ivrit (A)." *Haaretz,* 21 May 2004.

———. "Hashirah ha'ivrit hadatit: qriteryonim, hagdarot vehatsa'ot qeri'ah. *Aqdamot* 15 (2004): 31–51.

———. "Lamah tishqa, aleh, kashemesh, aleh od: Elohim bashirah ha'ivrit (B)." *Haaretz,* 28 May 2004.

———. "'Shirat yamim usheḥaqim belibbo:' Yosef Zvi Rimon bitequfat ha'aliyyah hasheniyyah." *Jewish Studies, An Internet Journal* 4 (2005): 61–107. http://www.biu.ac.il/JS/JSIJ/4-2005/Eydar.pdf.

Falck, Colin. *Myth, Truth and Literature: Towards a True Post-modernism.* Cambridge: Cambridge University Press, 1989.

Falk, Marcia. "Strange Plant: Nature and Spirituality in the Poetry of Zelda: A Translator's Reading." *Religion and Literature* 23, no. 3 (1991): 97–108.

Fisch, Harold. "The Absent God." *Judaism* 21 (1972): 415–427.

Fuchs, Esther. *Encounters with Israeli Authors.* Marblehead, Mass: Micah, 1982.

Furstenberg, Rochelle. "Israeli Poetry as Prayer." In *Pray Tell: A Hadassah Guide to Jewish Prayer,* ed. Jules Harlow et al., chapter 12. Woodstock, Vt.: Jewish Lights, 2003.

Gardner, Helen. *Religion and Literature.* Oxford: Oxford University Press, 1971.

Gilkey, Langdon. *Naming the Whirlwind: The Renewal of God-Language.* Indianapolis: Bobbs Merrill Co., 1969.

Glazer, Miryam, ed. *Dreaming the Actual: Contemporary Fiction and Poetry by Israeli Women Writers.* Albany: State University of New York Press, 2000.

Glicksberg, Charles I. *Literature and Religion: A Study in Conflict.* Dallas: Southern Methodist University Press, 1960.

Gold, Nili Scharf. *Lo kaberosh: gilgulei imazhim vetavniyyot beshirat Yehuda Amichai.* Jerusalem and Tel Aviv: Schocken, 1994.

Green, Garret. *Imagining God: Theology and the Religious Imagination.* 1989. Reprint, Grand Rapids, Mich.: William B. Eerdmans, 1998.

Gunn, Giles. "Literature and Religion." In *Interrelations of Literature,* ed. Jean-Pierre Barricelli and Joseph Gibaldi, 47–66. New York: Modern Language Association of America, 1982.

Gurevitch, Nitza. "Ḥezyonot mehasug hashelishi," *Itton 77* 232 (1999): 7.

Habermann, A. M., ed. *Beran yaḥad: yalqut shirei tefillah attiqim gam ḥadashim.* Jerusalem: Mosad Harav Kook, 1945.

Hadar, Anat. "Siḥah im hameshoreret hayerushalmit Rivka Miriam." *Alei Siaḥ* 27–28 (1990): 233–238.

Halkin, Simon. *Modern Hebrew Literature: From the Englightenment to the Birth of the State of Israel: Trends and Values.* New York: Schocken, 1950.

Heiler, Friedrich. *Prayer: A Study in the History and Psychology of Religion.* Oxford: Oxford University Press, 1932.

Hirschfeld, Ariel. "Hashirah ha'ivrit vehayetser hara," *Haaretz,* 4 June 2004.

———. "Shivat ha'elohi: al meqomo shel Elohim bashirah ha'ivrit bador ha'aharon." In *Ha'eglah hamele'ah: me'ah ve'esrim shenot tarbut Yisra'el,* ed. Israel Bartel, 165–176. Jerusalem: Magnes, 2002.

Hollander-Steingart, Rachel. "Zelda—shirah—pegishah." *Zehut* 3 (1983): 232–236.

Hopper, Stanley Romaine. *The Way of Transfiguration: Religious Imagination as Theopoiesis.* Louisville, Ky.: Westminster/John Knox, 1992.

Isaacson, Miron H., and Admiel Kosman, eds. *Shirah ḥadashah. Apirion* 44–45 (1996–1997).

Jacobson, David C. "'Bless Each Day That Passes': The Search for Religious Faith in the Poetry of Itamar Yaoz-Kest." In *Religious Perspectives in Modern Muslim and Jewish Literatures,* ed. Glenda Abramson and Hilary Kilpatrick, 34–54. Oxford: Routledge, 2005.

———. "The Ma'ale School: Catalyst for the Entrance of Religious Zionists into the World of Media Production." *Israel Studies* 9, no. 1 (2004): 31–60.

James, William. *The Varieties of Religious Experience.* 1902. Reprint, Cambridge, Mass.: Harvard University Press, 1985.

Kartun-Blum, Ruth. "Political Mothers: Women's Voice and the Binding of Isaac in Israeli Poetry." In *History and Literature: New Readings of Jewish Texts in Honor of Arnold J. Band,* ed. William Cutter and David C. Jacobson, 419–438. Providence, R.I.: Brown Judaic Studies, 2002.

Kaufman, Gordon D. *The Theological Imagination: Constructing the Concept of God.* Philadelphia: Westminster, 1981.

Kosman, Admiel. *Bigdei nasikh.* Jerusalem: Keter, 1988.

———. "Forget the Jews, But Judaism Is Wonderful." *Haaretz,* English Edition, 14 June 2002.

———. "Ha'omanut, hahalakhah vehadat." *Maḥanayim* 10 (1995): 58–69.

———. *Higanu lElohim.* Tel Aviv: Hakibbutz Hameuchad, 1998.

———. *Mah ani yakhol.* Tel Aviv: Hakibbutz Hameuchad, 1995.

———. *Massekhet gevarim: rav vehaqatsav ve'od sippurim al gavriyyut, ahavah ve'otentiyyut besippur ha'agaddah uvasippur haḥasidi.* Jerusalem: Keter, 2002.

———. "Mayim einam yekholim laḥazor biteshuvah: he'arah al megillat Amichai." *Haaretz,* 20 October 2000.

———. *Perush ḥadash bsd.* Tel Aviv: Hakibbutz Hameuchad, 2000.

———. *Ve'aḥarei morot ma'aseh hashir.* Givatayim: Massada, 1980.

Kronfeld, Chana. "'The Wisdom of Camouflage': Between Rhetoric and Philosophy in Amichai's Poetic System." *Prooftexts* 10 (1990): 469–491.

Kurzweil, Barukh. "Shirah otobiyyografit 'badmibar hagadol': he'arot le*Shirim, 1948–1962.* In *Yehuda Amichai: mivḥar ma'amarei biqqoret al yetsirato,* ed. Yehudit Tsvik, 79–94. Tel Aviv: Hakibbutz Hameuchad, 1988.

———. *Sifrutenu haḥadashah: hemshekh o mahpekhah?* 1959. Reprint, Jerusalem and Tel Aviv: Schocken, 1965.

Lemberger, Dorit. "Al gevulot mishtanim bashirah: datiyyut, hatrasah umah shebei-
    neihen." *Aqdamot* 14 (2004): 131–154.
Levi-Barzilai, Vered. "Bo'etet lekhol hakivvunim." *Haaretz*, 18 January 2006.
Liebman, Charles S., ed. *Religious and Secular: Conflict and Accommodation between
    Jews in Israel.* Jerusalem: Keter Publishing House, 1990.
Liebman, Charles S. and Elihu Katz, eds. *The Jewishness of Israelis: Responses to the
    Guttman Report.* Albany: State University of New York Press, 1997.
Livneh, Neri. "Manoa ḥippus," *Haaretz*, 3 May 2002.
Luz, Zvi. *Hayesod hapilosofi bashirah ha'ivrit.* Tel Aviv: Hakibbutz Hameuchad, 2001.
———. *Merivah im Elohim: massot peratiyyot.* Tel Aviv: Hakibbutz Hameuchad, 2002.
Luz, Zvi and Ziva Shamir, eds. *Al "gilluy vekhissuy balashon": iyyunim bemassato shel
    Bialik.* Ramat Gan: Bar Ilan University, 2001.
Mazor, Yair. *Asher Reich: Portrait of a Hebrew Poet.* Madison: University of Wisconsin
    Press, 2003.
Miller, J. Hillis. *The Disappearance of God: Five Nineteenth-Century Writers.* Cam-
    bridge, Mass.: Harvard University Press, 1975.
———. *Poets of Reality: Six Twentieth-Century Writers.* Cambridge, Mass.: Harvard Uni-
    versity Press, 1966.
Miriam, Rivka. "Et hahafradah." *Apirion* 15 (1989): 48–49.
———. *Haqolot liqratam.* Jerusalem: Dvir, 1982.
———. *Maqom namer.* Jerusalem: Carmel, 1994.
———. *Miqarov hayah hamizraḥ.* Jerusalem: Carmel, 1996.
———. *Mishirei immot ha'even.* Tel Aviv: Sifriat Poalim, 1988.
———. "Ribbono shel olam, mah hasheqet hazeh? mah hester hapanim hazeh?" In
    Massa el tokh atsmenu: benei nitsolei hasho'ah medabberim, ed. Shoshana Tsingel,
    157–165. Tel Aviv: Elisar, 1985.
Miron, Dan, "Reshito shel Yehuda Amichai." *Hadoar* 79, no. 22 (2000): 17–19.
Mishkovsky, Zelda. *Al tirhaq.* Tel Aviv: Hakibbutz Hameuchad, 1974.
———. *Hakarmel ha'iy-nireh,* Tel Aviv: Hakibbutz Hameuchad, 1971.
———. *Halo har halo esh.* Tel Aviv: Hakibbutz Hameuchad, 1977.
———. *Hashoni hamarhiv.* Tel Aviv: Hakibbutz Hameuchad, 1981.
———. *Penay.* Tel Aviv: Hakibbutz Hameuchad, 1967.
———. *Shirei Zelda.* Tel Aviv: Hakibbutz Hameuchad, 1985.
———. *The Spectacular Difference: Selected Poems.* Ed. and trans. Marcia Falk. Cincin-
    nati, Ohio: Hebrew Union College Press, 2004.
Mizrahi, Oded, ed., *Ḥamishim shirei binah: hitbonenut bashirah ha'ivrit haḥadashah
    al pi penimiyyut hatorah.* Jerusalm and Tel Aviv: Sifrei Bitzaron, 2000.
Montenegro, David. "Yehuda Amichai: An Interview." *American Poetry Review* 16, no.
    6 (1987): 15–20.
Muffs, Yochanan. "Theology and Poetics." *Conservative Judaism* 51, no. 1 (1998): 3–9.
Neher, André. "The Renaissance of Hebrew in the Twentieth Century." *Religion and
    Literature* 16, no. 1 (1984): 21–35.
Noon, William T. *Poetry and Prayer.* New Brunswick, N.J.: Rutgers University Press,
    1967.
Omer, Dan. "Ba'arets halohetet hazot, millim tserikhot lihyot tsel . . . ." *Prozah* 25
    (1978): 4–11.
Or, Amir and Irit Sela, eds. *Elohim Elohim. Heliqon: sidrah antologit leshirah akh-
    shavit* 6 (1992).
Pagis, Dan. *Gilgul.* Ramat Gan: Massada, 1970.

———. *Points of Departure*. Trans. Stephen Mitchell. Philadelphia: Jewish Publication Society, 1981.

Peli, Pinchas, ed. *Emunim*. Jerusalem: Mosad Harav Kook, 1954.

———, ed. *Ḥamishim sippurim*. Jerusalem: Mosad Harav Kook, 1956.

Petuchowski, Jakob J. *Theology and Poetry: Studies in Medieval Piyyut*. London: Routledge and Kegan Paul, 1978.

Pinhas-Cohen, Hava. "Em, ahuvah, moledet." *Panim* 7 (1998): 102–110.

———. *Hatseva be'iqqar*. Tel Aviv: Am Oved, 1990.

———. *Massa ayyalah*. Tel Aviv: Hakibbutz Hameuchad, 1994.

———. *Nehar veshikheḥah*. Tel Aviv: Hakibbutz Hameuchad, 1998.

———. *Shirei Orfe'ah*. Tel Aviv: Hakibbutz Hameuchad, 2000.

Reich, Asher. "Al habiyyopo'etiqah shelli: hayaldut kegalut." In *Me'ayin naḥalti et shiri: sofrim umeshorerim medabberim al meqorot hashra'ah*, ed. Ruth Kartun-Blum, 269–285. Tel Aviv: Yedioth Ahronoth, 2002.

———. *Atid domem*. Tel Aviv: Keshev Publishing House, 2002.

———. *Bashanah hashevi'it lineduday*. Tel Aviv: Eked, 1963.

———. *Mareh maqom*. Ramat Gan: Massada, 1978.

———. *Seder hashirim*. Tel Aviv: Sifriat Poalim, 1986.

———. *Temunat matsav*. Tel Aviv: Hakibbutz Hameuchad, 1975.

———. *Zerikhat halaylah*. Tel Aviv: Eked, 1972.

Ricoeur, Paul. *Figuring the Sacred: Religion, Narrative, and Imagination*. Trans. David Pellauer. Minneapolis, Minn.: Fortress, 1995.

"Rivka Miriam—meshoreret vetsayyeret: ani basar mibesaram." *Apirion* 2 (1983/1984): 50–51.

Rotem, Yehudit. "Re'ayon: Rivka Miriam." *Moznayim* 69, no. 5 (1995): 35.

Rotenstreich, Nathan. "Gilluy vekhissuy balashon." In *Bialik: yetsirato lesugeha bire'i habiqqoret*, ed. Gershon Shaked, 323–333. Jerusalem: Mosad Bialik, 1974.

Sadan, Dov. *Bein she'ilah leqinyan*. Tel Aviv: Mifal-Hashichpul, Tel Aviv University, 1968.

Sadeh, Shlomo. "Hatsad hasheni shel haqodesh vehaḥol beshirat Amichai." *Itton* 77 290 (2004):18–22.

Santayana, George. *Interpretations of Poetry and Religion*. New York: Charles Scribner's Sons, 1900.

Schaible, Robert. "Literature, Religion, and Science: A Personal and Professional Trajectory." *Zygon* 32, no. 2 (1997): 277–288.

Schweid, Eli. "Hapeniyyah lElohim basifrut ha'ivrit hatse'irah." *Molad* 17 (1959): 181–186.

Scott, Nathan A., Jr. "Poetry and Prayer." In *Literature and Religion*, ed. Giles B. Gunn, 191–210. New York: Harper and Row, 1971.

———. *The Wild Prayer of Longing: Poetry and the Sacred*. New Haven, Conn.: Yale University Press, 1971.

Shaked, Gershon, ed. *Hebrew Writers: A General Directory*. Ramat Gan: The Institute for the Translation of Hebrew Literature, 1993.

Sheleg, Yair. *Hadatiyyim haḥadashim: mabbat akhshavi al haḥevrah hadatit beYisra'el*. Jerusalem: Keter, 2000.

"Siḥah im Hava Pinhas-Cohen." *Pesifas* 29 (1995): 14–16.

Snir, Leah. "Me'ever lashorashim haḥatukhim." *Alei Siaḥ* 41 (1998): 59–72.

Sokoloff, Naomi B. "On Amichai's *El male raḥamim*." *Prooftexts* 4 (1984): 127–140.

Stanford, Derek. "God in Modern Poetry." In *Mansions of the Spirit: Essays in Literature and Religion*, ed. George A. Panichas, 289–312. New York: Hawthorn Books, 1967.

Steiner, George. *Real Presences*. Chicago: University of Chicago Press, 1989.

Tracy, David. "Metaphor and Religion: The Test Case of Christian Texts." In *On Metaphor*, ed. Sheldon Sacks, 89–104. Chicago: University of Chicago Press, 1979.

———. *Plurality and Ambiguity: Hermeneutics, Religion, Hope*. 1987. Reprint, Chicago: University of Chicago Press, 1994.

Tsameret, Tsevi, "'Sovev halev binetivo ha'afel—vehozer el ha'Elohim' o: optimiyyut ufesimiyyut besifrah shel Zelda *Hashoni hamarhiv*." *Petahim* 57/58 (1982): 87–90.

Tsvik, Yehudit, ed. *Yehuda Amichai: mivhar ma'amarei biqqoret al yetsirato*. Tel Aviv: Hakibbutz Hameuchad, 1988.

Weichert, Rafi. "Baginnah hatsibborit shel Elohim: qeri'ah beshirei Yehuda Amichai hamuqdamim vehame'uharim." *Itton* 77 248 (2000): 26–29.

Weiss, Hillel, ed. *Va'ani tefillati: shirat hatefillah shel meshorerim benei zemanenu*. Bethel: Sifriat Bethel, 1991.

White, Helen C. *Prayer and Poetry*. Latrobe, Penn.: The Archabbey Press, 1960.

Wineman, Aryeh. "Death, Redeeming Moments, and God in Zelda's Later Poems." *Conservative Judaism* 56, no. 2 (2004): 60–69.

———. "Hedim shel hasidut Bratslav beshirat Zelda." *Shdemot* 65 (1978): 57–61.

Wright, T. R. *Theology and Literature*. Oxford: Basil Blackwell, 1988.

Yadin, Azzan. "A Web of Chaos: Bialik and Nietzsche on Language, Truth, and the Death of God." *Prooftexts* 21 (2001): 179–203.

Yaniv, Ora. "Hahavayyah hadatit beshirat Zelda: motivim, dimmuyyim, utemunot kiyesod po'eti le'itsuv hayahas ani-olam." Master's thesis, Bar Ilan University, 1990.

Yaoz, Hana. "Shirah, dat umeha'ah: Admiel Kosman." *Pesifas* 41 (1999): 26–29.

———. "Tefisot datiyyot basifrut ha'ivrit hatse'irah bishenot hashemonim. *Itton* 77 72–73 (1986): 16–17, 40.

Yaoz, Hana, and Itamar Yaoz-Kest. "Im hameshorer Asher Reich." *Pesifas* 33 (1996): 4–5.

Yaoz-Kest, Itamar. "Re'ayon im Asher Reich." *Pesifas* 44 (2000): 4–7.

———. "Sihah im hameshorer Admiel Kosman." *Pesifas* 25 (1994): 6–11.

Yaoz-Kest, Itamar, and Hana Yaoz. "Im Rivka Miriam." *Pesifas* 35 (1997): 1–3.

Yisrael, Dorit. "Halikhah liqrat: re'ayon im Rivka Miriam." *Dimui* 17 (1999): 30–32.

INDEX OF HEBREW POEMS

239

INDEX

ABOUT THE AUTHOR

David C. Jacobson is Professor of Judaic Studies at Brown University. His previous books are *Modern Midrash: The Retelling of Traditional Jewish Narratives by Twentieth-Century Hebrew Writers; Does David Still Play for You?: Israeli Poetry and the Bible; Israeli and Palestinian Identities in History and Literature* (co-edited with Kamal Abdel-Malek); and *History and Literature: New Readings of Jewish Texts in Honor of Arnold J. Band* (co-edited with William Cutter).